ARKANSAS NATIONAL GUARD

AFRICAN AMERICAN PIONEERS

UNTOLD STORIES

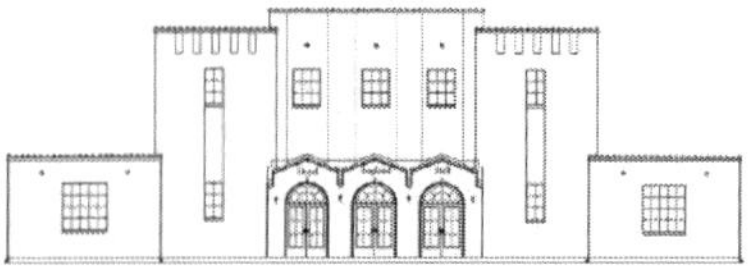

www.arngmuseum.com

This project was a collaborative effort from the Black History Committee chaired by BG Leland Tony Shepherd and facilitated by CW3 Darrell Daniels. The committee consisted of retired servicemembers, active servicemembers and the Arkansas National Guard Museum Staff.

ISBN 979-8987527221– Paperback
ISBN 979-8987527238 – Hardcover

For information about custom editions, special sales, and premium and corporate purchases, please contact the Arkansas National Guard Museum at 501-435-2400 or *arngmuseum@gmail.com.*

This project was funded by the Arkansas National Guard Foundation, which funds programs to preserve the military heritage of the Arkansas National Guard, its units, and its militia predecessors.

Table of Contents

ARK
SAS

Preface: Changing the Narrative African American Contributions to the Arkansas National Guard

African Americans have served in the Arkansas National Guard for many decades without a full recognition of their service, being told in a complimentary way. They were dedicated men and women who committed to the ideals of service to our community and our country. In many instances of the past, their fight for equality and inclusion was not welcomed by all and many were marginalized in opportunity and greater areas of responsibility. This book was created to help share the historical narrative and present-day actions and contributions of African Americans in the Arkansas National Guard. The intended purpose is to highlight both the struggles of inequality and celebrate the triumphs of success of those who served and continue to serve.

MG Kendall Penn, a strong advocate of diversity and personal mentor of mine, is dedicated to the diversity of our organization and has aptly demonstrated so with his priority agenda for the Arkansas National Guard. He is acutely focused on promoting a sense of culture and excellence by ensuring that we value service members for what they bring to the table not by the color of their skin, but the merits of their works. I am certainly a direct result of this type of action which speaks to his "walk the talk" disposition.

I hope you are enriched and enjoy the stories dedicated in this book, which will also be featured in an electronic format as well. I will encourage each of you to share this book and the stories, with as many within our community, so the narrative of the African American pioneers is well told and understood. It is with a sense of high personal duty that I commissioned the development of this book and I dedicate it to many of the trailblazers you will read about. May their courage and tenacity continue to live.

To the members of the panel, it is with a deep sense of gratitude that I express to you a big thank you. CW3 Darrell Daniels thanks for saying yes to this project and being the champion in leading the team. CW4 (Ret) Settles and COL (Ret) Damon Cluck thanks for your historical context and stories you contributed to the project. Dr. Raymond Screws and Erica McGraw your significant contributions to this project are fully acknowledge, thank you very much. CMSgt. (Ret) Normal Gilcrest, CW3 Patrick Jacob, MAJ Krystle Browning, CW4 Cornelius Charles and LTC Will Phillips thank you for being panelists. The work you all have contributed made this work possible.

To another mentor of mine, BG (Ret) William Johnson – a special thank you to you Sir. You were the lifeline of this book. You conducted the interviews and shaped the narratives, so the story was properly written and told. This project took on a new meaning with your contributions. We really appreciate you being the handrail for us.

BG Leland Tony Shepherd
Arkansas National Guard

Black Participation in the Arkansas State Militia

Black participation as members in the Arkansas State Militia came about because of the Civil War. Prior to the Civil War it is probably safe to say that Black Americans were prohibited from militia membership, because of the white fears that to arm Blacks would suggest that they were citizens and probably promote slave revolts. However, as the Civil War dragged on the North suffered heavy battle losses and increased numbers of deserting White troops. President Lincoln was forced to make the uncomfortable decision to enlist Blacks in the Union Army. In 1863, Black Militia units were formed to serve in the Union Army. During the Civil War, over 209,000 African Americans served in Union regiments, 5,526 of whom came from Arkansas. Black units formed in Arkansas were as follows:

- First Arkansas Colored Infantry formed 1 May 1863
- Third Arkansas Colored Infantry formed 12 Aug 1863
- Second Arkansas Colored Infantry formed 4 Sep 1863
- Fourth Arkansas Colored Infantry formed 2 Dec 1863
- Fifth Arkansas Colored Infantry formed 8 Nov 1864
- Sixth Arkansas Colored Infantry formed 25 Jun 1864
- Fourth Arkansas U.S. Infantry formed Jan 1864

As with all colored Civil War units, the Arkansas Colored units were led by White officers and their units were frequently known by an alternate designation derived from the Unit Commander's name. For example, the Fourth Arkansas (U.S.) Infantry was unofficially referred to as the Edward L. Brook's Infantry and later the Elisha Baxter's Infantry.

The First Arkansas Colored Infantry contained 663 officers and enlisted men and served in Louisiana and Mississippi. The regiment's designation was later changed to the Forty-Sixth U.S. Colored Infantry and the unit was finally disbanded on January 30, 1866. The marching song of the First became a widely popular song for all Black soldiers during the war, which was sung to the tune of "John Brown's Body." The first stanza and chorus are as follows:

> *Oh, we're the bully soldiers of the First of Arkansas, we are fighting for the union, we are fighting for the law, we can hit a rebel further than a white man ever saw, as we go marching on.*
>
> Chorus
>
> *Glory, glory hallelujah. Glory, glory, hallelujah, Glory, glory hallelujah, as we go marching on ...*

The Second Arkansas Colored Infantry was composed of Blacks mostly from the counties bordering the Mississippi River south of Helena. The regiment spent most of its career on post duty at Helena and Little Rock. The unit's designation was later changed to the Fifty-Fourth U.S. Colored Infantry, which was disbanded between August 8, and December 31, 1866.

The Third Arkansas Colored Infantry was composed of 783 officers and men. The unit served at Helena and Little Rock and participated in two active military campaigns. The unit's designation was changed to the Fifty-Sixth U.S. Colored Infantry on March 11, 1864, in which it saw action in five engagements. The unit was disbanded from federal service at Helena in mid-September 1866.

The Fourth Arkansas Colored Infantry was organized at Devall's Bluff, Little Rock, and Helena. The unit designation was changed to the Fifty-Seventh U.S. Colored Infantry on March 11, 1864. The regiment served on garrison and fatigue duty in eastern Arkansas and served as engineers and bridge train guards during Steele's expedition to Camden, Arkansas. The unit was disbanded between October 18, and December 31, 1866.

The Fifth Colored Infantry which was later designated the One Hundred Twelfth U.S. Colored Infantry was mustered at Little Rock and served at Little Rock for its entire career. The unit was later combined with the Sixth, which later became the One Hundred Thirteenth U. S. Colored Infantry. The unit performed post and garrison duty and most of the time was quartered directly northeast of the Little Rock penitentiary. On April 1, 1865, the unit was combined with the Eleventh U.S. Colored Infantry (members mostly from Kansas) to form a new organization known as the Second One Hundred Thirteenth U.S. Colored Infantry. After the Civil War, the unit continued to serve at Little Rock until it was finally disbanded on April 9,1866.

Photo Caption: *Recruiting poster for U.S Colored Troops During the Civil War*

The Fourth Arkansas U.S. Infantry was formed at Batesville and Fort Smith, Arkansas in January 1864. The unit participated in three Arkansas skirmishes and at various times was located at Batesville,

Clarksville, Fort Smith, and Little Rock. The unit was later consolidated into the Second Arkansas Infantry and disbanded between August 8, and December 31, 1866.

After the Civil War

As the Civil War in Arkansas ended, a new era of lawlessness threatened to consume the state. Former Confederates returning to their homes began organizing to oppose the Reconstruction policies of the Republican Administration. White groups, sometimes in the name of the local militia, and later under the umbrella of the newly organized and rapidly spreading Ku Klux Klan began disarming and intimidating newly freed African American and returning Union soldier, black and white. The Federal Government responded with laws that disenfranchised former Confederates from voting, holding office, and serving in the militia.

Governor Powell Clayton, a former union officer, was elected Governor of the state in 1868, and set about organizing a new state militia to oppose the Klan and other organized bands of former Confederates. Known as "Clayton's Negro Militia," these African American troops, under the command of white, former Union officers, participated in several pitched battles across the state against Klan forces. Governor Clayton declared Martial Law in Ashley, Bradley, Columbian, Craighead, Green, Lafayette, Little River, Mississippi, Sevier, Woodruff, Conway, Crittenden, Drew, and Fulton counties. The newly organized state militia moved into these counties and began operations against the Klan. In November, a battle occurred against armed citizens at Center Point in Howard County.

Militia operations in arrest and executions in Sevier and Drew Counties.

Some of the most pitch battles occurred in northeast Arkansas with skirmishes in Batesville and Augusta and movements into Fulton, Crittenden, and St. Francis Counties.

The Militia occupied and fortified the Crittenden County seat and withstood repeated attacks from Klan forces including groups from nearby Memphis, Tennessee. While there were accusations from local Democrats that the Militia themselves committed acts of looting, rape and even murder, the operations of Governor Clayton's militia were ultimately successful in restoring order across the state and breaking up larger formations of Klansmen who directly opposed Republican Reconstruction in the state.

Pope County in west-central Arkansas had been the scene of several politically motivated assassinations following the Civil War. In 1872, it appeared that another round of assassinations of county officials was imminent and local officials convinced Governor Ozra A. Hadley, who had been installed by Governor Powell, who was now a senator, to allow the raising of a militia company to deal with the troubles. This militia company arrested the suspected assassins but was then accused itself of murdering its prisoners. As the situation continued to spiral out of control and more killings followed Adjutant General Daniel Phillips Upham was sent to investigate. Following a round of shootouts and killings in Dover and threats to burn the town, martial law was declared, and a regiment of the mostly black state militia was sent in to maintain the peace. Captain George R. Herriot, in command of the black troops in Pope County, was subsequently murdered in the county courthouse, but his killer was never brought to trial.

In the state election of 1872, Joseph Brooks represented the Liberal Republicans and Elisha Baxter represented the old Radical Republicans. In a contested election, the legislature reviewed the returns and declared Baxter the winner, but on April 12, 1874, over a year after Baxter took office, a judge declared Brooks to be the winner. Brooks and an armed group of supporters forcibly evicted Governor Baxter from the statehouse. In the confusion that followed, both "governors" called on the militia for support, and both received it. Former Confederate General Robert C. Newton led the pro-Baxter militia forces. Former Union General Robert Francis Catterson and former Confederate General James Fleming Fagan led pro-Brooks militia forces. Brooks maintained control of the statehouse, and Baxter established a headquarters nearby in the Anthony House. One man was killed in fighting that erupted along Markham Street on April 16, 1874. Baxter managed to raise over 1,300 troops, while Brooks secured more than 2000 rifles for his supporters. With orders from Washington, DC to prevent a clash, Colonel Thomas E. Rose, commander at the Little Rock Arsenal, deployed U.S. regulars from the Sixteenth Infantry, plus two pieces of artillery on Markham Street, between the parties. As violence continued, Federal Troops erected a barricade along Markham Street between the warring factions to prevent further encounters.

Hostilities quickly spread to other parts of the state. Nine Brooks supporters were killed and thirty wounded in an ambush set by Baxter forces at New Gascony in Jefferson County, south of Pine Bluff. Engagements between the two sides also occurred on May 1, in Lincoln and Arkansas counties, and two days later, they fought another battle near Arkansas Post (Arkansas County), killing five more men.

On May 8, Brooks men ambushed a steamboat, the *Hallie*, and a company of pro-Baxter militia near Palarm Creek, south of present-day Mayflower, on the Arkansas River. The boat was captured by Brooks forces but was eventually sunk by Baxter supporters.

Baxter forces occupied Argenta (present-day North Little Rock) across the river from the statehouse and kept up a steady stream of sniper fire on Brooks forces at the statehouse. Brooks forces eventually declared that unless the sniping was stopped, they would shell the city of Argenta with the two six pounder cannons present at the statehouse.

On May 13, 1874, a four-hour skirmish was fought near the site of the present state capital. Pro-Baxter militia arrived by steamboat from Fort Smith, and pro-Brooks forces intercepted them. The number of casualties from this engagement is unknown.

Both sides appealed to President Ulysses S. Grant for aid and on May 15, 1874, Grant recognized Baxter as the governor and ordered all "turbulent and disorderly persons to disperse and return to their homes." By May 16, Brooks supporters disbanded and began returning home. The total number of casualties in this political war is estimated at above 200.

Armed conflict between warring factions broke out in Waldron, Scott County, in West Central Arkansas in the Summer of 1875. Governor Garland and eventually Governor Miller used the state militia forces to maintain peace, with up to seven companies of militia stationed in the county in 1877 and 1878. Eventually, tensions between local militias rose to the point that Adjutant General James Pomeroy "took up his residence at Waldron," directing the militias and ensuring an orderly term of the circuit court in the spring of 1878. By then, the political pendulum had swung. Reconstruction was over, and the new state legislature, now back firmly in the control of the previously disenfranchised Democrats, objected to the governor's use of the militia in what the legislature saw as a local issue. The reaction was so severe that in March 1879, the legislature, over the Governor's veto, enacted a law abolishing the office of adjutant general.

In addition to abolishing the office of adjutant general, the legislature also cut all funding for the militia. Despite the efforts of each succeeding governor, this situation continued for over twenty-eight years, until 1907, when the legislature finally reauthorized the office of adjutant general.

Interest in the state militia waned following Reconstruction. Officially the state militia consisted of two regiments of infantry, one battery of artillery, one troop cavalry, and one signal unit. The Regimental headquarters of the 1st Infantry, Arkansas State Guards was in Little Rock, but with little or no state funding, the militia units that existed were supported with private funds. Local militia companies participated in drill and ceremony competitions, with all the funding for travel, uniforms and equipment coming from private sources.

The Cherokee Guards were an African American company organized in Little Rock in 1881. The Garland Greys were a militia company organized in Jefferson County and commanded by Captain Sam Helzheim. In 1881, Helzheim was ordered to muster black troops into a new company to be called the Neel Guards. However, Helzheim refused to enroll black troops and Governor Churchill had him court-martialed. Helzheim was convicted and sentenced to be suspended from his rank for six months. Governor Churchill revoked the suspension when Captain Helzheim agreed to obey his orders. The Neel Guards were then mustered into state service in June 1881. The Garland Grey's disbanded following Helzheim's conviction.

In 1891, Captain E. D. Thomas, a captain of the 5th Cavalry was ordered to inspect Arkansas State Guard on behalf of the Inspector General of the Army. Upon reaching Little Rock, Captain Thomas found that the only military organizations in existence at that time in the state were at the local level. Captain Thomas indicated that regimental and brigade level organizations had not been maintained in several years. Thomas indicated that the existing local companies were supported through "benevolence." He also indicated that the state had not used funds that Congress has recently passed to support the state militia. Captain Thomas' visit apparently spurred the state into action because he indicated that an order had been issued prior to his departure from Little Rock, which organized the First Regiment, Arkansas State Guard. No mention of African American troops was made in this reorganization, nor is there evidence of their existence again before the official integration of the Arkansas National Guard in the 1960s.

AFRICAN AMERICAN PIONEERS

It is essential to consider the history of African Americans in the armed forces to understand the attitude of today's Black military members. Their attitude toward the military is based in no small part on the awareness that racial discrimination existed for many years in the military as a matter of official policy. African Americans are also acutely aware that, while discrimination is officially proscribed, they may encounter vestiges of yesterday's unequal treatment in the military service. Black members of today's military insist that they be treated with the same respect and dignity as White counterparts receive as a matter of course.

In the twentieth century, one - unless Black- is apt to forget the impact that slavery had on American life. It encompassed nearly all aspects of human degradation through racial discrimination and denials of the protection of the law. It rested upon and sanctioned prejudice. It made race and color the sole basis for accord or denial of human rights. It touched every phase of life and human contact. Slaves, by reason of race, could be kept in bondage for their natural lives. Slaves, by reason of race, could be denied citizenship, the right to contract, or the right to hire out for a wage.

By Executive Order dated July 26, 1948, President Truman abolished segregation as a matter of official policy in the armed forces. But discrimination and prejudice remained. Another fifteen years passed before the issue of discrimination was officially addressed at the departmental level. In 1963, Secretary of Defense Robert McNamara issued Department of Defense Directive 5120.36, entitled "Equal Opportunity in the Armed Forces." It stated that the Department of Defense was to conduct all its activities free from racial discrimination and that it was to provide equal opportunity for all personnel regardless of their color. The directive placed responsibility upon all members of the Department of Defense to oppose discrimination and to foster equal opportunity for servicemen and their families on and off post.

In the 1960s, the Arkansas National Guard changed policy and allowed African Americans to join.

Taylor v. Jones, Untold History...Then & Now

The United States has a long and unfortunate history of racial discrimination in different aspects of life such as public accommodation, workplace, employment, and education among other things. Staff Sergeant Corenna Taylor in the *Taylor v. Jones* case was yet another workplace discrimination case where SSG Taylor an African American woman was treated unfavorably because of her race. SSG Taylor had to work in uncomfortable and dangerous work environments for more than 5 years before she filed her lawsuit in 1974. SSG Taylor served as a brave advocate in this case, not only for self-interest, but taking a stance to protect the rights of African Americans in the Arkansas National Guard against workplace discrimination. SSG Taylor fought for racial justice through various measures. The measures that brought significant change were 1) escalating her complaint outside of the organization and, 2) endorsing legal representation for corrective action. She stood steadfast in her principles of fairness and lived by her favorite quote "It doesn't cost me anything to be kind" (SSG Corenna Taylor, 1992). She was a trailblazer, an extraordinary African American and a Soldier.

SSG Taylor grew up in North Little Rock, Arkansas approximately nine miles from Camp Joseph T. Robinson. She joined the Arkansas

Army National Guard, Company B (Med) (-), 39th Support Battalion in Lonoke, Arkansas at the age of 24. She served in several 39th Support Battalion Detachments before transitioning to the 739th Ordnance Detachment in April of 1976. SSG Taylor held numerous military occupational specialties, General Clerk (71B), Post Clerk (71F), Card Punch Operator (74B) and Unit Clerk (75B) to name a few. She enlisted as Private (PV1/E-1) and with excellent performance she was promoted to the rank of Staff Sergeant (SSG/E6) in a 12-year timeframe. SSG Taylor was professional, competent, and consistently worked above her pay grade. She demonstrated high, ethical standards adroitly in the way she managed her career and served as an example of the NCO creed. It was a teaching point for her NCOs to emulate. Her story is one of persistence, a continued fight for balance of race and gender inequalities.

There are several discrimination cases over the course of 100 years in the United States. The Rosa Parks case, for example, was a key landmark case of *Browder v. Gayle* (1956). Rosa Park refused to give up her seat in the designated "colored" passenger section, spurred the Montgomery Bus Boycott, the largest and most successful mass protest against racial segregation in history. Many people wonder if the Rosa Parks case was premeditated. On December 1, 1955, after a long day's work she was truly frustrated and decided not to comply with the bus driver's demand for her to stand and give up her seat to a white passenger.

Rosa Park's refusal was not due to physical exhaustion but because she was tired of giving in to unfair prejudicial practices of race and blatant demonstration of discriminatory actions. She made a historic stance to claim space for future generations of African Americans in the U.S. Rosa Park took her case of discrimination to court to challenge the abuse of power by authorities and Alabama's segregation laws to seek justice for herself and to set precedence of correct and moral behaviors for the future. On December 20, 1956, when the federal ruling *Browder v. Gayle* took effect, and led to a

United States Supreme Court decision that declared the Alabama and Montgomery laws that segregated buses were unconstitutional.

Similarly, the role of Daisy Bates in the story of the Little Rock Nine bears resemblance to that of Rosa Parks (Edelman, Luca, & Svirsky, 2017). In this case, the nine students were not just any random school students that were selected to integrate Central High. There was a great deal of work devoted to The Blossom Plan generated by Superintendent Virgil Blossom. The Blossom Plan was created to desegregate schools in Little Rock. The plan was finalized September of 1957, to integrate one school, Central High.

Eighty students expressed interest in attending Little Rock's Central High and were interviewed by the Little Rock School Board. Eighty interested students quickly decreased to nine, and the Little Rock Nine fearlessly battled their way into Central High School. The nine students were admitted to Little Rock Central High under the protection of the 101st Airborne Division (and later the Arkansas National Guard), but they were still exposed to a year of physical and verbal abuse (being spat on and called names) by many of the white students. Their enrollment caused the Little Rock Crisis of 1957. On September 12, 1958, a unanimous Supreme Court declined a Little Rock School District request to delay desegregation mandated by the Court's *Brown v. Board* ruling by more than two years.

SSG Taylor's case emulates both the Rosa Park's discrimination and the Little Rock Nine desegregation cases. These individuals played a critical role in shaping the State of Arkansas and the United States for years to come.

Arkansas Army National Guard *"Then"*

On the 12th of March 1974, Corenna Taylor filed a lawsuit against her employer, the Arkansas Army National Guard for alleged discrimination in two segments: first, on behalf of African American members as well as employees and, secondly, on behalf of the African Americans eligible for high-ranking positions (Justia U.S. Law, 1980). SSG Taylor was an employee with the Arkansas National Guard for less than one year, a period between the 1st of March 1974 and the 2nd of October 1974 (Open Jurist, 1980). From the first day of her employment, SSG Taylor served as a recruiter until June 30, 1974. She was demoted from her position as a recruiter to a clerk in the mailroom, a position from which she resigned following futile attempts at receiving a promotion or transfer to another Unit (Justia U.S. Law, 1981).

Throughout the period of her employment, SSG Taylor was a member of the National Guard and had been drilling one weekend per month to include a two-week training during summer. In the suit against her employer, SSG Taylor charged the Arkansas National Guard with two counts of discrimination, (1) under classification; and (2) being underpaid during her employment as a mailroom clerk (Dillahunty, Chavis, Loewenburg, & De Mets, 2018). Moreover, she alleged that the company had subjected her to racial epithets and that her employer had denied her both transfer and promotion opportunities in spite of her repeated requests. SSG Taylor also sought for relief at a wide range, with affirmative efforts by the Arkansas National Guard to offer employment opportunities to African American Guard members as well as civilian employees being an inclusion (Williams, 1980).

On February 20, 1980, the proceedings of SSG Taylor's trial were presented before the Honorable Judge Richard Arnold (Justia U.S. Law, 1980). Upon conclusion of the trial, it was found that the defendant, James Jones - the Arkansas Army National Guard Adjutant General, intentionally discriminated against the plaintiff based on her race, violating Title VII of the Civil Rights Act of 1964, as well as 42 United States Code1983 (42 U.S.C. 1983). The court also found that the unauthorized transfer of SSG Taylor from her previous position, as a recruiter to the mailroom clerk was racially motivated. Moreover, the court found that the resignation by SSG

Taylor from her position as a clerk in the mailroom was the result of coercion and racially motivated prejudice.

It is this author's option that Major General Jones failed to construct a safe environment conducive for all persons to work in unity. Furthermore, his lack of disciplinary actions toward any of SSG Taylor's supervisors and other perpetrators encouraged discriminatory behaviors throughout the organization. SSG Taylor's working environment had become extremely difficult for her to work free of worry. She was subjected to repeated and undue discriminatory gestures by fellow services members and leadership. As a result, the court ordered MG Jones to reinstate SSG Taylor with retroactive pay. He was also ordered to place her in her previous recruiter position or a comparable position. The court made an injunction barring the defendant from recruiting any new employees for vacant positions, but later modified it to permit Arkansas National Guard to fill such positions if half of the newly recruited were African Americans (Dillahunty, Chavis, Loewenburg, & De Mets, 2018).

Subsequently, the defendant, MG Jones, filed a motion calling for a new trial claiming that the recruiter position introduced into the case was an unfair surprise to him (Justia U.S. Law, 1981). The court granted the motion; however, the appeal addressed just two issues: whether the nonrenewal of SSG Taylor as a recruiter was within legal means and whether there was racial discrimination and the exact equitable relief that should be granted.

The new trial went before the United States Court of Appeals, Eighth Circuit. By the 8th of August 1980, the district court had not only entered its opinion but also the final judgment (Open Jurist, 1980). There were no disturbances of the earlier findings by the court that the plaintiff had suffered constructive discharge from her position of recruiter to mailroom clerk owing to her race, violating Title VII of the 1964 Civil Rights Act (Justia U.S. Law, 1980). Moreover, the court reiterated the findings of deliberate discrimination by the defendant against the plaintiff based on the account of her race through failure to renew the appointment of SSG Taylor as a recruiter. In addition, the court found the basis of liability for the unlawful act was on 42 U.S.C. 1981 (Justia U.S. Law, 1981). However, there was dissolution of the injunction during litigation, as the court directed the defendant to recruit at least one African American Soldier for every two white employees up to the point where the population of African American employees would be 16% of the total force (Open Jurist, 1980).

MG Jones appealed the orders of the district court on the foundation that neither jurisdictional nor factual basis were present for the findings of the court on liability. Moreover, MG Jones appealed that the relief of the court according to the plaintiff was not proper (Justia U.S. Law, 1981). The United States Court of Appeals, Eighth Circuit, made an appeal in content that the plaintiff had no standing. The United States contended that the court denied the ARNG the adequate opportunity to defend its interests and that the sovereign immunity doctrine prevents the court-ordered reliefs. However, the arguments by the appellants had no merit as the judgment of the district court was affirmed safe for the award of the back pay (Open Jurist, 1980).

In an interview with Command Sergeant Major (Retired) Ira Blueford, when the court ordered the Arkansas Army National Guard to fill positions with African Americans to reach 16%, the organization failed to adhere completely to the order. The interviewee articulated, during the time period of 1975 the majority of African American personnel hired were in lower positions with limited career growth potential. For instance, a minimal number of African Americans were afforded supervisory positions. This action demonstrates there was little improvement on racial discrimination. The court order to improve racial diversity was seemingly ignored by the organization. However, by the time African Americans had a small population of senior officers and enlisted there were subtle challenges (Blueford, 22 March 2018).

This author interviewed COL (Retired) Nathaniel McGee on his experiences being one of the first African Americans hired into the Arkansas Guard. He expressed the racial turmoil and discrimination he experienced during his tenure. When he first joined the organization, he expressed how his commander conducted the Oath of Enlistment with a wall between them. His commander stated that he "did not want to see no Negroes joining his detachment." COL (R) McGee further stated that he had to eat in a separate location from the white Soldiers.

COL (R) McGee articulated that he was not permitted to offer recommendations during staff meetings. He would have to share his recommendations with the Battalion Operations Officer. The staff officer would decide if the information would be shared in the staff meeting. COL (R) McGee expressed that respect alone is very important, not only personally, but also equally important in the workplace. It is in this aspect that most Americans have failed to ensure that racial discrimination ends. Some Caucasians believed they are superior as a race and could never treat other races with their due respect. This mentality is conducive to biased behaviors, racial inequality, and discriminatory practices.

Arkansas National Guard Personnel

The Arkansas National Guard is comprised of both military and civilian personnel. The organization is led by The Adjutant General (TAG) who is an appointee of the Governor of the State of Arkansas. The TAG is responsible for the supervision appointment of all personnel enlisting into the National Guard. This responsibility extends into all categories of employment. The ARNG civilian personnel includes state employees as well as federal military technicians. The military technicians are required to be members of the ARNG and maintain credible attendance to the multiple unit training assemblies (MUTAs) and two-week annual training periods.

There are distinctive challenges for the organization in maintaining these categories of full-time employees. The majority of the organization's full-time duty positions fall into the category of military technicians. At the time of the Taylor lawsuit, there were 986 technician positions in the organization. The greatest number of technician positions were either technical or specialized skilled positions assigned throughout the State.

The state employees, who totaled 115 in 1980, did not require enlistment into the National Guard. The state employment positions were created by the State of Arkansas and funded by both state and federal dollars. The majority of the state employees working with the National Guard were clerical workers or, in most cases, lower-level administrative employees. The placement of the federal funds that is purposed for the payment of state employees came through the State Treasury and disbursement is according to the appropriations bills passed by the General Assembly of the State (Justia U.S. Law, 1981).

SSG Taylor's Claim

Following the proceedings of the first trial, the district court found that the termination of the plaintiff from the recruiting position was influenced through racial bias. It held that her discharge as the mailroom clerk was under the same racial biases. The district court found that SSG Taylor was working as a mailroom clerk under the protection of Title VII, The Civil Rights Act of 1964. It was further held that the constructive discharge of the plaintiff from the mailroom violated the law.

Subsequently in the retrial, the court was of the conclusion that the tenure of the plaintiff as a recruiter was a full-time military duty (Arnold, 1980). Therefore, the intentional racial discrimination that SSG Taylor suffered while working in this capacity was actionable under the provisions of 42 U.S.C., 1981, Equal Rights Under the

Law (Justia U.S. Law, 1980). During the first trial, the district court was under the impression that SSG Taylor was a federal employee, dual status technician, rather than an active military service member. However, the Title VII, Civil Rights Act of 1964, was applicable under either category of employment with the Arkansas National Guard.

It was clear from the evidence presented in the trial that SSG Taylor was neither a federal nor a state employee during her tenure as an Arkansas National Guard recruiter. She was both a military member and employee of the organization. It was determined that SSG Taylor had met all the requirements to maintain her job as a recruiter.

The Arkansas National Guard organization did not have adequate reason to discontinue her employment in the organization as a recruiter. SSG Taylor presented two claims of discrimination. One was their violation of her Fifth Amendment Rights of Due Process. The second, was the violation of the Civil Rights Act of 1964.

The court considered that if a private right of action was valid in addressing racial discrimination in the Fifth Amendment Rights clause, then SSG Taylor was entitled to relief under 42 U.S.C. 1981 for the intentional discrimination she suffered. Additionally, the court found it unnecessary to prove that her failure of re-appointment as a recruiter was due to intentional racial bias by the organization.

The profile of this case gained popularity as the momentum built. The plaintiff was fighting for justice, while the defendant was exerting every effort to block justice being served. There were many people who became involved in the case. One person of interest was Mr. Marcellus Person. He was a full-time employee of the organization, serving as a Military Technician (federal employee) and military service member. Mr. Person agreed to testify on behalf of SSG Taylor. He received many threats and there were attempts to prevent him from testifying in court. After failed attempts to bar him from testifying, he rendered his testimony in court. Following his willingness to testify, he received physical and verbal attacks.

Final Judgment

After the hearing, the Court entered nine judgments. The court first ruled the defendant's failure to renew the appointment of the plaintiff as a recruiter was in direct violation of 42 U.S.C. of 1981. The court found that the plaintiff's constructive discharge from being a mailroom clerk was in violation of Title VII, The Civil Rights Act of the 1964. The court awarded the plaintiff the recovery of $2,470.64 in retribution pay.

The defendant was ordered to pay all legal fees that totaled $19,671.73. Attorney John Walker was the most notable and instrumental figure in the case. Being a renowned man of justice, especially when racial discrimination was rampant in the United States. Attorney Walker held that the defendant would accept responsibility if found guilty of racial discrimination against SSG Taylor.

The court also directed the defendant to reinstate SSG Taylor in her previous recruiter position or into a comparable federal job. The index of comparability would be based on factors such as pay, responsibility, benefit, and status (Justia U.S. Law, 1981). However, the injunction by the previous court suffered dissolution and the defendant was directed to hire at least one African American for every two white employees. This order was to be in place until the population of African American employees comprised 16% of the work force (Open Jurist, 1980).

The defendant would be expected to keep records of all its employees. Additionally, they were directed to maintain employee demographics that were subject to inspections by the plaintiff's lawyers. The court also ordered the defendant to provide demographic reports of all recruits. The duration of the report was to be provided until further notice from the court. However, the jurisdiction for the purpose of the enforcement of the judgment remained with the court (Justia U.S. Law, 1980).

The court denied the plaintiff punitive damages, prejudgment interests, the affirmative-action formulation plan, and the request to have a committee appointed to oversee compliance to the order. Similarly, the court denied the cessation of the funding by the federal government as per the provisions of Title VII of the 1964 Civil Rights Act (Justia U.S. Law, 1981). However, the court also made a judgment that the financial awards of the ruling would bear interest at 10% per year from the date of entry. There was no injunction against the intervenor, the United States; however, the claim against the Adjutant General held.

Arkansas National Guard *"Now"*

Since 1984, service in the Arkansas National Guard has been a community-based and combat-proven force. The military force consists of Soldiers and Airmen (Arkansas National Guard Posture Statement, 2018). The organization's total force is comprised of Active Guard Reserve (AGR), Dual Status and Non-Dual Status Federal Technicians, and State Employees. The Adjutant General (TAG) is the head of the organization. The TAG has a Command Group, as well as Directorates, who govern, develop, and oversee the organization's daily affairs. As of 2018, the Command Group consists of nine Caucasian males. There are seven Directorate positions, two of the seven positions are held by female officers. The force structure today exceeds 8,600 Soldiers and Airmen. Working as a team, the men and women continue to achieve great accomplishments. The challenges of budgetary cuts and constraints, repeated deployments, and State emergencies continue to galvanize the force. Arkansas National Guard members are trained professionals.

Soldiers and Airmen are geographically located across the State of Arkansas and are well-equipped with skills suitable for war fighting, as well as responding to natural disasters. Among the 8,600 members assigned to the organization, over 6,700 are Army National Guard and over 1,800 are Air National Guard (Arkansas National Guard Posture Statement, 2018). The full-time workforce comprises of nearly 1140 Army and 765 Air National Guard members. Among the 6,758 members of the Army National Guard, 76.3% (5,158) are Caucasian while African Americans secure 21% (1,419) of the membership. The male population secures 84% (5,678) and female population secures 16% (1,080).

The Arkansas Army National Guard has made significant strides to ensure racial equality. However, racial discrimination has not completely ended, as much as it has been reduced. Putting it to an imminent end has remained a challenge. Inferences that can be derived by this behavior suggest that racial injustices will persist and pejorative dispositions towards minorities will remain in effect. The 13th Amendment of the U.S Constitution has declared that any form of social and racial injustice is prohibited, and all races and classes of citizens should be treated equally under the law. These actions reflect a sense of division among the members in the organization when comradery should be the principal narrative.

While interviewing COL (Retired) Anita Deason, she reveals that she had to work harder, giving 110%, compared to her male counterparts. This had been a feeling for most African American women who worked in the Arkansas Army National Guard in the earlier years. However, according to COL (R) Deason, the organization changed for the better from her arrival to Camp Robinson in 1978 until her retirement in 2013. She states that there was positive transformation. Although positive change was displayed over a 35-year timeframe, the positive change has not produced a racially equal workforce (Deason, 23 March 2018).

Nonetheless, it is true to say that the case of Corenna Taylor against Jones was pivotal in starting the fight against racial discrimination against African Americans in the Arkansas Army National Guard. It has, over the years, produced positive results. Chief Warrant Officer 4 Celquetta D. Pride states that her experiences in the Guard were an eye opener for her. Before the *Taylor v. Jones* case, the African Americans experienced the cruelty of racial discrimination but most of them sat on their experiences, never complaining. However, with the win for Mrs. Taylor, the discrimination was publicly identified and deemed wrong. The way minorities were treated, while in the Guard, was publicized on the national level (Pride, 20 March 2018).

African Americans have defended their right to serve equally in the National Guard. The Declaration of Independence declares that "All men are created equal." Civil rights activists have labored and suffered to ensure that racial discrimination becomes a thing of the past. As a result, there are African Americans in virtually all positions, both high and low ranking. An African American Officer has served at the Generalship level; BG William Johnson was promoted a decade ago to Brigadier General and is the only Soldier to achieve that status in the Arkansas National Guard [since 2018, BG Tony Shepherd is the second African American to be promoted to that rank]. The U.S. has undergone a significant era of transformation since the 60s and 70s to ensure that an African American could be President. However, it has not reached the full potential of a community free from racial biases and discrimination.

Conclusion

SSG Corenna Taylor, in the case of *Taylor v. Jones*, was an activist for safeguarding the rights of African Americans against discrimination in workplaces. She did not pursue this case with self-interest to protect her job as a recruiter in Arkansas National Guard. During the trial, there were many African American employees who testified that they had suffered extreme racial inequality. They stated that there were several instances in which they were subjected to racial epithets, slurs, and jokes (Open Jurist, 1980). From the day of her employment, SSG Taylor served as a recruiter until June 30, 1974, when she was demoted from the position to work as a clerk in the mailroom. She resigned from the mail clerk position after several attempts to transfer or be promoted.

Throughout the period of her employment, SSG Taylor was a member of the National Guard and drilled one weekend per month to include two weeks annual training during the summer. The court reiterated the findings that there was deliberate discrimination by the defendant against the plaintiff based on the account of her race through failure to renew the appointment of SSG Taylor as a recruiter. In addition, the court also found that the basis of liability for the unlawful act was on 42 U.S.C. 1981 (Justia U.S. Law, 1981).

Moreover, the court found that the resignation by SSG Taylor from her position as a clerk in the mailroom was resultant from the coercion by the noxious and toxic racial environment in the workplace (Dillahunty, Chavis, Loewenburg, & De Mets, 2018). Therefore, the Corenna Taylor case is one of the lawsuits that have protected individuals in the U.S. against racial discrimination. In a sense, SSG Corenna Taylor has become a champion for racial equality in National Guard workplaces nationally. Her courage and tenacity were paramount in making this stand for justice.

Building a Foundation for Change: Changing of the Arkansas National Guard

On March 12, 1976, Corenna Taylor filed a lawsuit alleging that the Arkansas National Guard discriminated against Black service members and who were employees of the Guard, and against Black service members who were/are eligible for such positions. She charged that she was under classified and underpaid when employed by the Guard, subjected to racial epithets and slurs, and that she had been denied transfer or promotion despite repeated requests. She sought wide-ranging relief, including affirmative efforts by the Arkansas National Guard to recruit Black Guard members and civilian employees.

On February 20-21, 1980, the case was tried before the Honorable Richard S. Arnold. At the conclusion of the trial, Judge Arnold ruled in Taylor's favor, labeling the Guard's racial atmosphere in a word; "dismal," and found that discrimination in the Guard was pervasive. Not only was Corenna Taylor entitled to reinstatement, but she was also entitled "to be reinstated in a workplace where all people are treated with decency and respect." The court found that this goal would be materially impeded unless the Arkansas National Guard is required to step up its employment of qualified Black persons. Although Judge Arnold preferred not to order a hiring quota, the proof left him no choice. There was simply no other way to ensure that the law would be complied in the future. The court ordered the Arkansas National Guard to hire one Black employee for each two White employees hired until an employment goal of sixteen percent (16%) was reached. The Court found that this carefully tailored hiring plan was necessary to assure the plaintiff a workplace free of racial discrimination.

How would the Arkansas National Guard respond? First, Major General Jimmie "Red" Jones, the Adjutant General of the Arkansas National Guard, realized that although the Arkansas National Guard was an outstanding military organization, it had some real challenges. In order to change, one must first acknowledge that there are real problems that need to be addressed. Throughout history, there are people who faced systemic racism and discrimination in our country. It was clear that the Arkansas National Guard needed to do more to combat racism and discrimination in its various forms. MG Jones responded by developing a three-pronged strategy to correct the racial discrimination that was prevalent in his ranks.

Building a Foundation for Change: Arkansas National Guard's Anti-Discrimination Strategy

The Anti-Discrimination Strategy consisted of efforts and programs aimed at eliminating inequities by focusing on three guiding principles: Leadership Commitment, Building Awareness and Changing Attitudes, and Community Engagement.

MG Jones recognized that a tremendous amount of work was ahead to eliminate racism and discrimination in the Arkansas National Guard, however, through this strategy, the Arkansas National Guard was taking action by Building a Foundation for Change. By focusing on the three principals, (1) the organization could work towards building a more inclusive and equitable National Guard that has a culture and (2) an environment that is free of racial discrimination and prejudice and (3) an organization that provides opportunities to all its members.

Guiding Principles

Leadership Commitment. The Arkansas National Guard leadership understood that it must take a leading role addressing systemic racism and discrimination when found to exist within its organization's policies, program, and services. Leadership requires taking proactive steps to remove those barriers that impose a limit on one's full potential.

Building Awareness and Changing Attitudes. The Arkansas National Guard leadership needed to increase awareness of the historical roots of racism and discrimination, and their impacts on the Black soldiers in their ranks. Data and evidence were indispensable tools for identifying and addressing inequities and enabling corrective action toward the elimination of racism and discrimination.

Community Engagement. The engagement process confirmed that combatting racism and discrimination must be a priority for military and citizens alike. The leadership engaged the racialized and religious minority communities and meaningfully involved them in decision-making related to proposed actions as it moved forward.

Building a Foundation for Change: Leadership Commitment

MG Jimmie "Red" Jones, in his letter to Lieutenant General La Vern E. Weber, Chief of the National Guard Bureau, and the newspaper article written in the *Arkansas Gazette* on July 13, 1980, outlined his strategies for Change in the Arkansas National Guard. MG Jones discussed immediate actions he and his leadership team was committed to affecting change:

- MG Jones stated that after Governor William "Bill" Clinton appointed him, he announced to his Commanders and Staff, his command policy on non-discrimination in all areas of the Arkansas National Guard. This policy was reinforced by him and his staff on a continuing basis.

- He reissued that his command policy letter on June 16, 1980, requiring that his policy letter be read to every unit, with the unit commander reporting to his Equal Employment Officer (EEO) when the letter was read, where, and to what unit, within 30 days from the date of the letter.

- MG Jones conducted a Supervisors Conference in which he specifically outlined to the Arkansas Army National Guard and Arkansas Air National Guard supervisors his command policy of non-discrimination. The supervisors were warned against making any reference to race in any of their activities and urged them to seek out prospective Black employees. (And Guardsmen?)

- On May 3, 1980, MG Jones held a Senior Commanders Conference in conjunction with the Arkansas National Guard's State Convention wherein he reemphasized his command policy of non-discrimination. Additionally, he spent 90 minutes placing heavy emphasis on finding Black employees and hiring them in positions with the Arkansas National Guard.

- MG Jones instructed his staff to prepare a handbook for distribution to minorities on how to get a job with the Arkansas National Guard. The handbook was sent to all Arkansas National Guard units, State Employee Security offices and minority organizations throughout the State.

- The Major Command Administrative Assistants were counseled to actively seek out Black applicants for jobs under their supervision.

- MG Jones ensured that a process was developed in which records of all persons employed and all persons who applied for employment, by race, were available for inspection and those records were reported to the Court on the first day of each calendar quarter until the court order was suspended.

- On May 1980, MG Jones brought to duty (CFTM) a Black Captain as a member of his full-time EEO Staff. One of the duties was to assist in finding Black employees.

Building a Foundation for Change: Building Awareness and Changing Attitudes

- Education and awareness are essential to effectively work toward the elimination of racial discrimination and inequality. MG Jones instituted the conduct of the Unit Discussion Leaders Course for unit EEO representative during Annual Training. The course was extremely beneficial in assisting with the eradication of prejudices at the unit level. Arkansas was one of the few states in the nation to make this course a part of Annual Training.

- MG Jones sent two (2) Officers to the four-month EEO school. One (1) of the officers sent was black.

- The "Arkansas Guard" newspaper carried an editorial by MG Jones, urging commanders at every level to find and motivate young Black soldiers to attend The Arkansas Military Academy's Officer Candidate School and airmen to be trained on a national level at the Academy of Military Science. Those schools can change the percentage of minority officer shortages but only through command emphasis.

- The Army Guard developed a program called Minority Officer Recruiting Effort (MORE). The Air Guard had a similar program called Minority Officer Recruiting Program (MORP). The programs were efforts to recruit minority officers in the Arkansas National Guard. They were directed primarily toward minority colleges and universities with ROTC programs but were ongoing at all schools.

- MG Jones directed his Recruiting and Retention Manager to contact the United States Army Reserve Components Personnel and Administration Center (RCPAC) in an effort to find Black Officers residing in Arkansas.

Building a Foundation for Change: Community Awareness

- The engagement process confirmed that combatting racism and discrimination must be a priority for the Arkansas National Guard and the citizens of Arkansas alike. Building a Foundation for Change required the Arkansas National Guard to engage racialized and religious minority communities and organizations to meaningfully involve them in their proposed actions and ensure them that they were important partners in the fight against racism and discrimination.

- MG Jones and his staff visited minority organizations in Little Rock and other parts of the State to make presentations on the Arkansas National Guard programs and recruitment initiatives.

- Local minority organizations were asked to submit names of anyone who may be interested in enlisting into the Arkansas National Guard.

- The Arkansas National Guard became a member of the Urban League Guild as a sponsoring organization.

- MG Jones directed his staff to lend equipment and support to minority organizations, especially to youth organizations whenever the opportunity presents.

- MG Jones personally contacted the minority groups and youth organizations offering assistance where needed.

Ultimately, the strategy of Building a Foundation of Change in the Arkansas National Guard through Leadership Commitment, Building Awareness and Changing Attitudes and Community Engagement, was expected to increase equity of access and participation, and ensure that there will be no discrimination of any kind and that all actions would be made without regard to race, color, religion, sex, or national origin.

On October 15, 1986, Judge George Howard Jr., United States District Judge, Eastern District of Arkansas, Western Division, removed the Arkansas National Guard from the Court ordered hiring plan of August 8, 1980. In his order, Judge Howard, Jr. stated that the Arkansas National Guard had exceeded the Court ordered Sixteen (16%) percent and exceeded the overall hiring goal by 19 persons. By attaining and exceeding the Court ordered hiring goal, the Arkansas National Guard demonstrated that it had substantially assured the plaintiff a workplace free of racial discrimination. Lastly, the Court accepted the Arkansas National Guard's representation that it would make further progress as it continued to educate its managers and supervisors concerning equal opportunity. And further progress would continue as Black people are hired for jobs located throughout Arkansas and at all employment grades and positions. The effects of the ruling of the Corenna Taylor's case changed the whole system not only in the Arkansas National Guard, but National Guard systems in other states as well. The one for three hiring ratios resulted in great opportunities and prompted benefits to thousands of Black Soldiers and Airmen in this State. The Arkansas National Guard is now a stunning success because of the court ruling.

Arkansas National Guard
Black Heritage Committee History

History provides a sense of collective identity. Knowing from whence it comes helps a people understand its present situation and how it must proceed into the future.

The Arkansas National Guard Black Heritage Committee was supported by the Adjutant General with the intent that future generations would know and cherish the accomplishments of the Arkansas National Guard Black Soldiers and Airmen. It was a strategic effort to inclusion and the committee didn't function solely on its own.

So, why Black History? Isn't history, history for all? Why do we need special clarifications or additions to history? These questions only seem to bring up others. Who was excluded in "all" when history was recorded? Moreover, who recorded it, and which contributions were seen as significant enough to record?

The significance of contributions changes with social awareness. Blacks have, since the beginning, contributed much to the making of these great United States. Much about Blacks' contributions, dedication, and sacrifices to our country has been omitted from the pages of history. An understanding of these elements to history is essential in helping to develop a better understanding of the current conditions and issues for Blacks in the United States and in the military service today.

Major Wayne Berger was the driving force behind the creation of the Arkansas National Guard Black Heritage Planning Committee in 1987 and served as the committee's First Chairman. On February 1, 1991, Major Berger published the first volume of "A Look at History's Missing Pages" presented by the Black Heritage Commemorative Book Committee. Over a span of ten years the Committee successfully recorded and preserved the contributions and milestones of African Americans in the Arkansas National Guard.

This Arkansas National Guard Black Heritage Committee was created with the intent to help enlighten those who never knew and remind those who may have forgotten the triumphs of some of history's "unsung" makers, past and present, within the Arkansas National Guard. When we are able to recognize all such contributions, irrespective of race and gender, then we can truly say history is history for all.

The work, preservation and history of the Arkansas National Guard's Soldiers and Airmen from the early years is what provided a guide in launching the blueprint for this publication.

We would like to take this time to honor and thank the men and women of The Black Heritage Committee, who preserved the history, contributions and achievements of African Americans in the Arkansas Army and Air National Guard.

Black Heritage Committee Members

PRESIDENTS		
Nathaniel McGee **1991**	Chauncey Sumpter **1994**	Rhonda Dickerson **1997**
Rhonda Dickerson **1992**	Timothy Pighee **1995**	Rhonda Dickerson **1998**
Ples Johnson **1993**	Rhonda Dickerson **1996**	Gregory Settles **1999**

COMMITTEE MEMBERS		
Verlene Alexander	Sheryl Huiett	Bonnie Pettus
Gene Alexander	William Johnson	Emanuel Pierre
Robert Avery	Mildred Johnson	Kathy Roy
Eddie Brown	William Jones	Ernest Scott
Joseph Cooley	Walter Jones	Teresa Shelton
Huey Davis	Myntrobia Jordan	Veronica Sims
Carla Earls	Keitra Kerr	Ernest Slater
Reginald Eskew	Janice Kindall	Minnie Smith
Joanna Gallagher	Barbara Lunon	Leroy Smith
Cleodis Gatson	Robin McNeal	Gloria Topps
Wesley Holt	Virgil Miller	Andre Watson
Sammy Hood	Marian Moore	Heath Welch
Pamela Huff	Thomas North	Danny West
	John Parker	Joan Williams

Introduction to the Pioneer Timeline

The committee realizes this book is a "living document" and is aware that all the accomplishments for the past pioneers may not have been fully inclusive of everyone. The committee was also mindful that as the pioneers moved through the various ranks and positions, that they were often trailblazers for the future servicemembers coming behind them. In many cases, the servicemember's highest rank and/or position is what was documented in this publication with the understanding, that they were also the first in their subsequent ranks and positions.

As more information is discovered it can be added to the digital format of this book that will reside on the Arkansas National Guard Museum's website. This book is a great framework to document a large majority, and as future African American Guard members become firsts, names will be added to the timeline, and biographies will be added.

If you have information you'd like to share with the committee, please scan the QR code below and submit your information. Once the information is verified, we will have it added to the digital and/or print version of this book.

Timeline of African American Pioneers in the Arkansas National Guard

ARMY GUARD		AIR GUARD
	1960s	
1964 (December) **1SG Jeff Hayes** *First African American to Enlist in the Army Guard*		**1964 (July)** **MSgt Willie Tyiska** *First African American to Enlist in the Air Guard*
		1965 **MSgt Robert Bell** *First African American to Enlist in the 188th Tactical Fighter Wing*
	1970s	
1971 **CW4 Marcellus Person** *First African American Full-Time Military Technician Hired in a Supervisory Capacity*		
1971 **SSG John C. Watson** *First African American Male Hired as a Full-Time Employee*		
1972 **SSG John Parker** *First African American Hired Combined Support Maintenance Shop*		
1973 **LTC Alice Taylor** *First African American Nurse*		**1973** **TSgt Julia Green** *First African American female to Enlist in the 189th Tactical Airlift Group and first African American female hired as a full-time employee with the 189th Fighter Group as a supply technician*
1973 **SG Correna Taylor** *First African American Female Recruiter*		
1974 **MAJ Eddie Brown** *First African American to Complete Arkansas Military Academy's (AMA) and Officer Candidate School (OCS)*		**1974** **Lt. Col. Lester Piggee** *First African American Commander, 189th Security Police Squadron*

ARMY GUARD	AIR GUARD
1974 **SSG Lillie M. Carter** *First African American Female Hired Full-Time Employee*	
1974 **SSG John Parker** *First African American to get promoted to the grade of WG-12 and first African American to be hired in the Quality Assurance Section*	
1975 **CW5 Arthur Montgomery** *First African American Warrant Officer*	
1976 **LTC Danny Johnson** *First African American Helicopter Pilot*	**1976** **MSgt Willie Tyiska** *First Hired into the National Guard Technician Program*
1978 **MSG Margarett "Margo" Linton** *First African American Female Assigned to the 172nd Maintenance Battalion*	
1978 **CW4 Paul Williams** *First African American Unit Administrator*	
1980s	
1980 **CW4 Paul Williams** *First African American First Sergeant 39th Infantry Brigade*	**1980** **Lt. Col. Lester Piggee** *First African American Officer to Serve as Flight Commander*
1982 **LTC Danny Johnson** *First African American Instructor Pilot*	
1983 **MSG Margarett "Margo" Linton** *First African American Female Technician Hired Full-Time in the 142nd Field Artillery Brigade*	

ARMY GUARD

1983
SFC Marilyn E. Matthews
First African American Unit Administrator 1122nd Transportation Company

1984
MSG Margarett "Margo" Linton
First African American Female Hired in the Active Guard/Reserve Programs 142nd Field Artillery Brigade

1984
LTC Claudell Woods
First African American Judge Advocate General

1985
CW4 Gregory Settles
First African American First Sergeant, D Company, 212th Signal Battalion and First African American Command Sergeant Major, 212th Signal Battalion

1990s

1990
CPT Oneida D. Battle
First Female Equal Employment Manager

1990
MSG Margarett "Margo" Linton
First Female to Receive the Bronze Star

1990
LTC (CH) J. Dawson Williams
First African American Chaplain in the 212th Signal Battalion

AIR GUARD

1987
Lt. Col. Wayne E. Berger
First African American to Serve as Group Commander 189th Air Wing

1989
Dora J. Williams
First African American Female Civilian Supervisor 189th Security Forces Squadron 189th Airlift Wing

1990
Col. James L. Abernathy
First African American and First Arkansas Air National Guard Commander of the newly formed National Guard Marksmanship Training Unit

ARMY GUARD

1992
CW3 Kenneth R. Franklin
First African American AH-1 Cobra Helicopter Pilot

1992
1SG Eugene Fultz
First African American First Sergeant of Company B, 212th Signal Battalion

1992
COL Burthel Thomas
First African American Battalion Commander

1993
SGM Robert Blue
First African American Sergeant Major

1994
COL Sherman Tate
First African American Battalion Commander 39th Support Battalion, 39th Infantry Brigade

1995
COL Nathaniel McGee
First African American Promoted to Colonel

1995
COL Nathaniel McGee
First African American to Command Installation Site Command

1996
LTC (CH) J. Dawson Williams
First Full-Time African American Chaplain in the National Guard US and First African American Chaplain in the Arkansas National Guard

AIR GUARD

1991
SMSgt Harold Terry
189t^h Air Wing's Minority Affairs Sub-Committee

1992
CCM Normal Gilchrest
First African American Human Resource Advisor

1994
Maj. Magnolia Winkler
First African American Female Officer

1995
MSgt Teresa James
First African American Female 189th Airlift Wing Base Records Manager 189th Airlift Wing Privacy Act Manager 189th Airlift Wing Freedom of Information Act Manager

1996
MSgt Kenneth R. Esaw
First African American Recruiter

ARMY GUARD	AIR GUARD
1999 **LTC David Savage, Sr.** *First African American Battalion Commander 1st Battalion, 153rd Infantry 39th Infantry Brigade (Separate)*	**1999** **CCM Normal Gilchrest** *First African American Command Chief Master Sergeant*
	2000s
2001 **LTC Willie Chapple** *First African American Officer to Serve as Aide-de-Camp For the Assistant Adjutant General-Army*	**2000** **Col. James L. Abernathy** *First African American Colonel*
2001 **SMG Danny J. Fletcher** *First African American First Sergeant for the 106th Army Band*	
2002 **CW4 Celquetta D. Babb-Pride** *First African American Female Property Book Officer and First African American Property Book Officer For the 233rd Regiment Regional Training Institute*	
2002 **CSM Ira Blueford, Jr.** *First African American Command Sergeant Major 35th Aviation Brigade*	
2002 **COL Walter L. Jones** *First African American Commander 2nd Battalion, 233rd Regiment, Regional Training Institute*	
2002 **CW4 Barbara Lunon** *First African American Female Personnel Branch Chief For the Deputy Chief of Staff-Personnel*	

ARMY GUARD	AIR GUARD
2003 **LTC Betty Anderson** *First Female Commander to Deploy to Guantanamo Bay, Cuba In Support of the Global War on Terrorism with the 216th Military Police Guard Company*	
2004 **CW4 Heath A. Welch** *First African American Property Book Officer Headquarters and Headquarters Company 39th Infantry Brigade*	**2004** **CMSgt Alwina "Collette" Freeman** *First Female African American Chief Master Sergeant 188th Fighter Wing*
2004 **LTC Sandra Y. Young** *First United States Army African American Soldier to complete the International Staff Course under the Canada National Defense Training Center*	
2005 **CW5 Veronica Y. Alexander** *First African American GS-11 Systems Analyst in the United States Property and Fiscal Office Supply & Services Division*	
2005 **COL Marcus R. Hatley** *First African American Arkansas National Guard 61st Civil Support Team Commander*	
2005 **CW4 Timothy D. Pighee** *First African American GS-12 Contract Specialist*	
2006 **CW4 Celquetta D. Babb-Pride** *First African American Female Property Book Officer For the 39th Infantry Brigade Combat Team*	

ARMY GUARD	AIR GUARD
2006 **CW4 Timothy D. Pighee** *First African American to receive Level III Certified Acquisition Professional Contracting Division United States Property and Fiscal Office for Arkansas* **2008** **BG William Johnson Jr.** *First African American General and First African American Deputy Adjutant General* **2009** **CW5 Veronica Y. Alexander** *First Female African American Property Book Officer for the National Guard Marksmanship Training Center Arkansas Army National Guard* **2009** **CW5 Cornelius Charles** *First African American S1/XO for the Recruiting Sustainment Program and First African American First Company Commander of B Company, Recruiting and Retention Battalion and First and First African American Warrant Officer to serve as Aide-de-Camp* **2009** **CW3 Cassandra Green** *First African American Female Warrant Officer 39th Infantry Brigade* **2009** **CW3 Courtney E. Wallace** *First African American Surface Maintenance Supervisor Army National Guard Consolidated Maintenance Facility* **2009** **CW4 Heath A. Welch** *First African American Property Book Officer 77th Combat Aviation Brigade*	**2007** **CMSgt Delphine D. Crumpton** *First African American Female Chief Master Sergeant 189th Airlift Wing* **2008** **CMSgt Sandra R. Jackson** *First African American Female Cyber Operations Manager, 189th Airlift Wing* **2009** **Col. Ronald W. McDaniel** *First African American Colonel in the 189th Airlift Wing*

2010s

ARMY GUARD

2010
SFC Stephanie Eddington
First African American Executive Assistant To The Adjutant General

2010
CW5 Pamela Huff
First African American Female Chief Warrant Officer Five

2011
COL Marcus R. Hatley
First African American Arkansas National Guard Counterdrug Coordinator

2012
CSM Ira Blueford, Jr.
First African American Command Sergeant Major 77th Aviation Brigade

2012
LTC Willie Chapple
First African American to Serve as Commander For the Sniper and Small Arms School National Guard Marksmanship Training Center

2012
SGM Ester L. Crockett
First African American Female Sergeant Major

2012
COL Julius M. Johnson
First African American Commander of the Information Technology Training Center at the National Guard Professional Education Center

2014
CW3 Cassandra Green
First African American Female Warrant Officer Equal Opportunity Advisor

2014
COL Erica L. Johnson Ingram
First African American Female Battalion Commander

AIR GUARD

2010
Lt. Col. Bridgette Delaine Scott Griffin
First African American Female Bronze Star Recipient

2011
Lt. Col. Phylinthia Givens
First African American Female Lieutenant Colonel and First African American Female Inspector General of Dispute Resolutions, 189th Airlift Wing

2012
Lt. Col. Anderson Neal, Jr.
First African American Group Commander188th Fighter Wing

2012
Maj. Daryl A. Taylor
First African American Female
Assistant Staff Judge Advocate 189th Airlift Wing

2014
CMSgt Ronald O. Boston
First African American Command Chief Master Sergeant 189th Airlift Wing

ARMY GUARD	AIR GUARD
2015 **CW3 Ife Caldwell** *First African American Female Pilot* **2015** **COL Anthony Sanders** *First African American Legislative Liaison* **2016** **COL Alex Finger** *First African American to Command the 233rd Regiment Regional Training Institute* **2017** **SGM Lorine M. Mosley** *First African American Active Guard/ Reserve Sergeant Major and First African American G1 Sergeant Major Joint Force Headquarters* **2017** **LTC William B. Phillips, II** *First African American Public Affairs Officer* **2017** **SFC Tasheenia L. Wallace** *First African American Female and First Female in the Arkansas Army National Guard to Graduate From the 11B Infantry Transition Course* **2018** **CW5 Kenneth D. Brown** *First African American State Command Chief Warrant Officer* **2018** **LTC Sharetta Glover** *First African American Female Deputy Commander, 61st Civil Support Team* **2018** **COL Erica L. Johnson Ingram** *First African American Female Colonel*	**2017** **Lt. Col. Phylinthia Givens** *First African American Female Inspector General Officer* *188th Air* Wing

ARMY GUARD		AIR GUARD
2018 **LTC Harold D. Williams** *First African American Commander* *2nd Battalion, 153rd Infantry Regiment* *39th Infantry Brigade Combat Team*		
2019 **MSG Kira S. Sharkey** *First African American* *Female Personnel Services* *Noncommissioned Officer 39th* *Infantry Brigade Combat Team*		
	2020s	
2020 **COL Erica L. Johnson Ingram** *First African American Female* *Installation Commander*		**2020** **Lt. Col. Jacqueline Taylor** *First African American* *Female Commander*
2020 **LTC Sandra Y. Young** *First African American Female* *Commander 217th Brigade Support* *Battalion 142rd Field Artillery Brigade*		**2020** **Lt. Col. Jacqueline Taylor** *First African American Female to* *Command Arkansas Air National* *Guard Detachment National Guard* *Marksmanship Training Unit*
2021 **MSG Kira S. Sharkey** *First African American Female* *Awarded The 39th Infantry Brigade* *Combat Team Bowie Knife*		
2022 **LTC Noyal Brasfield** *First African American to Command* *The 777th Aviation Support Battalion* *77th Theater Aviation Brigade*		**2022** **CMSgt Regina L. Monk** *First African American Female* *Command Chief Master Sergeant* *189th Airlift Wing*
2022 **BG Leland Tony Shepherd** *First African American General* *Officer to Command the ARNG*		
2023 **CW5 Veronica Austin** *First African American Female* *Command Chief Warrant Officer*		
2023 **LTC Sharetta Glover** *First African American Female* *Commander 39th Brigade Support* *Battalion, 39th Infantry Brigade*		

BIOGRAPHIES OF ARKANSAS NATIONAL GUARD PIONEERS THEIR UNTOLD STORIES

Colonel James L. Abernathy

First African American Colonel
Arkansas Air National Guard

Colonel (Col.) James Abernathy was born in Van Buren, Arkansas, and graduated from Van Buren Senior High School in 1961. He was awarded a Bachelor of Science Degree in Elementary Education from Arkansas Polytechnic College in 1968. He received his Master's Degree in Elementary Education in 1973 from Northeastern State College/University.

In 1968, Col. Abernathy began his teaching career with the Fort Smith Public School System. For twenty-five years, he taught fifth and sixth graders at Howard Elementary School in a self-contained setting. During his teaching career, Col. Abernathy received numerous awards to include Teacher of the Month, Outstanding Teacher Award, Who's Who Among American Teachers and The Golden Apple Award, presented by the Fort Smith Classroom Teachers Association.

Col. Abernathy began his military career in the U.S. Army when he volunteered for the draft in 1961. He attended basic and advanced individual training at Fort Chaffee Military Reservation. After which, he served with the Army in Bamberg, Mannheim, and Berlin, Germany until he left active duty in 1963. After leaving active duty in 1963, he joined the 95th Training Division in Fort Smith, Arkansas where he remained until his discharge in 1968. His military education included Officer Education and Training Course, Air Command and Staff College, Reserve Forces Course, Public Affairs Officer Course, Air War College Course, National Security Course, and the Officer Personnel School.

Col. Abernathy's military service with the Arkansas Air National Guard began in 1974 in which he served as the Drug Abuse Education Non-Commissioned Officer as a traditional Guardsman at the 188th Fighter Group. After achieving the rank of Technical Sergeant, he was offered a commission. After receiving his commission, he served as the Base Education and Training Officer until 1990. In October 1990, he became the first African American and first Arkansas Air National Guard Commander of the newly formed National Guard Marksmanship Training Unit at Camp J.T. Robinson.

In 1993, Col. Abernathy also served as the Military Personnel Management Officer for Headquarters, Arkansas Air National Guard. In that position, he provided staff assistance, guidance, policy, and direction concerning Air National Guard personnel, administration, training, recruiting, retention, and budgetary matters to the executive support staff. He was also responsible for investigations and representing the department on congressional and other high-level inquiries.

In 1999, Col. Abernathy served as the Public Affairs Officer, Headquarters, Air National Guard, Little Rock Air Force Base. Col. Abernathy's outstanding professional skill, leadership and devotion to people resulted in major contributions to the effectiveness and success of men in the Arkansas Air National Guard's program. He led by example and paved the way for many recruiting opportunities among the youth of the state, and authored programs that greatly enhanced the civilian community's understanding of the National Guard's mission.

Col. Abernathy was promoted to the rank of Colonel on March 30, 2000, and became the first African American Colonel in the Arkansas Air National Guard. His maturity, leadership, loyalty, and dedication to duty were displayed at every level of assignment in the Enlisted Force and Officer Corps during his thirty-six-year military career. Col. Abernathy retired from the Arkansas Air National Guard on June 10, 2003.

Chief Warrant Officer Five Veronica Y. Alexander

First African American GS-11 Systems Analyst in the United States Property and Fiscal Office Supply & Services Division

First Female African American Property Book Officer for the National Guard Marksmanship Training Center Arkansas Army National Guard

Chief Warrant Officer Five (CW5) Veronica Y. Alexander was born on July 19, 1966, in Little Rock, Arkansas. She grew up in North Little Rock and graduated from Jacksonville High School in May 1984. She received her Bachelor of Arts Degree in Christian Studies from Grand Canyon University in May 2023.

In April 1984, CW5 Alexander enlisted in Company C, 38th Aviation Battalion, Arkansas Army National Guard. From June to October of 1984, CW5 Alexander completed her Basic Combat Training at Fort Dix, New Jersey and her Advance Individual Training at Fort Lee, Virginia, where she acquired military occupational skill 76C10, Equipment Repair Parts Specialist. On May 18, 2001, CW5 Alexander received her commission as Warrant Officer One, 920A, Property Accounting Technician.

At the beginning of her military career, CW5 Alexander worked on active-duty orders from 1984-1986 for the National Guard Bureau Professional Education Center, the Military Entrance Processing Station (MEPS) and the Facilities Management Office (FMO). In 1986, CW5 Alexander was hired in the Military Technician Program as a GS-4 Admin Clerk within the United States Property and Fiscal Office, where she worked twenty-three years in the Supply &

Services Division. On November 27, 2005, CW5 Alexander was promoted to the grade of GS-11 and assigned as the System Analyst in the Supply and Services Division. She was the first African American promoted as a GS-11, System Analyst in the USPFO Supply and Services Division.

During her career as a Warrant Officer, CW5 Alexander duties and assignments included Platoon Leader and Deputy Commander of Detachment 1, Company B, 935th Combat Support Battalion, Supply System Tech, 871st Troop Command, Property Accounting Tech in the 233rd Regional Training Institute, and Program Analyst, Surface Maintenance Office, Arkansas Army National Guard.

On June 16, 2009, CW5 Alexander transitioned from the Military Technician Program to Active Guard Reserve (AGR) status as the full-time Property Book Officer for the National Guard Marksmanship Training Center in the rank of CW3. She was the first Female African American Property Book Officer for the National Guard Marksmanship Training Center. CW5 Alexander remained in that assignment from 2009 to 2014. On May 7, 2014, CW5 Alexander was assigned to Joint Force Arkansas as the Property Accounting Officer and later assigned as the Property Accounting Technician in the G4 Plans and Policy Section. She was promoted to Chief Warrant Officer Five on November 8, 2021.

CW5 Alexander's military education includes the U.S. Army Basic Combat Training, Advanced Individual Training in MOS 76C, Primary Leadership Development Course, Arkansas Army National Guard Battle Skills Course, Basic Noncommissioned Officer Course, Advanced Noncommissioned Officer Course, Warrant Officer Candidate Course, Warrant Officer Basic Course, Warrant Officer Advance Course, Warrant Officer Staff Course, Warrant Officer Senior Service Education and the Master Resilience Trainer Course.

Because of her distinguished service, CW5 Alexander received awards and decorations that included the Meritorious Service Medal with two Oak Leaf Clusters, Army Commendation Medal with three Oak Leaf Clusters, Army Achievement Medal with three Oak Leaf Clusters, the Army Reserve Component Achievement Medal with one Silver Oak Leaf Cluster, one Bronze Oak Leaf Cluster, and numerous other Federal and State Service Ribbons.

In December 2022, CW5 Alexander retired from the Arkansas Army National Guard with over 38 years of military service. She is a volunteer teacher in the Kingdom Kids program at her local church and she enjoys exploring the beauty in nature's art by restoring old furniture pieces, traveling, and participating in activities with her four grandchildren.

Lieutenant Colonel Betty Anderson

First Female Commander to Deploy to Guantanamo Bay, Cuba in Support of the Global War on Terrorism with the 216th Military Police Guard Company Arkansas Army National Guard

Lieutenant Colonel (LTC) Betty Anderson was born in Hayti, Missouri. She graduated from South Pemiscot High School located in Steele, Missouri in 1986. In 1990, LTC Anderson received her Bachelor of Arts Degree in Political Science from Murray State University, Murray, Kentucky and in 1993, she received her Master's in Public Administration from Arkansas State University, Jonesboro.

Her military career started on December 31, 1985, when she enlisted in the United States Army Reserve. While attending college at Murray State University, she joined the Reserve Officer Training Corps Program and received her Commission as a Second Lieutenant in May 1990. After completing the ROTC Program, LTC Anderson was assigned to the United States Army Reserve's 207th Chemical Company in Blytheville, Arkansas.

LTC Anderson began her illustrious military career in the Arkansas Army National Guard on June 1, 1996, with her first assignment as the Rear Area Security Officer at the 25th Support Detachment (RTOC), North Little Rock. She served as Commander of the 216th Military Police Company, West Memphis from 2001-2004. As the Commander of the 216th Military Police Company, LTC Anderson deployed to Fort Leonard Wood, Missouri in support of "Operation Noble Eagle."

In 2003, the 216th Military Police Guard Company deployed to Guantanamo Bay, Cuba in support of the Global War on Terrorism. LTC Anderson was the first Female Commander to deploy the 216th Military Police Guard Company to Guantanamo Bay, Cuba in the history of the Arkansas Army National Guard.

After serving as Company Commander, LTC Anderson served in various other assignments in the Arkansas Army National Guard. In 2004, she was assigned as the Assistant Operations Officer for the 25th Support Center (RTOC) and she served as the Equal Opportunity Advisor for 87th Troop Command from 2006-2009. LTC Anderson served as Adjunct Faculty for (DEOMI) Defense Equal Management Institute from 2008-2011. In 2011, she deployed with the 77th Aviation Brigade as an Equal Opportunity Advisor/Deployable Sexual Assault Response Coordinator in support of Operation Iraqi Freedom Campaign. In 2012, LTC Anderson served as the Provost Marshal for the Institute Support Unit (ISU), Camp J.T. Robinson. She was assigned as a Selective Service Officer for Joint Force Headquarters Arkansas in 2014. In 2015, LTC Anderson was assigned as the Deputy Commander of the Marksmanship Training Unit Brigade Headquarters, Camp J.T. Robinson.

LTC Anderson's military education includes the Military Police Officer Basic Course, Military Police Officer Advance Course, Company/Battery Commanders Course, Corrections Internment and Resettlement Course, Equal Opportunity Reserve Component Course, Equal Opportunity Mediation Course, Combined Arms Exercise Training and the Command and General Staff Officer Course - Intermediate Level Education.

For her outstanding service, she has been awarded the following awards and recognition to include the Meritorious Service Medal, Army Commendation Medal, Army Reserve Achievement Medal, National Defense Service Medal, Armed Forces Service Medal,

Meritorious Unit Commendation, Army Service Ribbon, Parachute Badge, Armed Forces Reserve Medal with "M' Device, Global War on Terrorism Expeditionary Medal, Afghanistan Campaign Medal, Arkansas Service Ribbon, Arkansas Federal Service Ribbon and the Arkansas Emergency Service Ribbon.

LTC Anderson began her civilian career in 1993 as a Human Resources Generalist with the City of Jacksonville. To gain experience, she went on to work for several other Government Agencies. From 1995-1997 she worked as an Employment Services Coordinator for Pulaski County Government. In 1997-2001, she began her first Management position for Arkansas Rehabilitation Services as the Assistant Personnel Manager/Grievance Officer.

However, she found her perfect spot with the City of North Little Rock. In 2001, she was hired by former North Little Rock Mayor Patrick H. Hays, as the Equal Opportunity/Fair Housing Director and in 2008; she was promoted to Human Resources Director. LTC Anderson currently works for the City of North Little Rock under Mayor Terry C. Hartwick. She serves as the Human Resources Director, and she also manages the Equal Opportunity Division.

LTC Anderson retired from the military with over 27 years of distinguished service. She currently resides in Maumelle, Arkansas.

Chief Warrant Officer Five Veronica Austin

First African American Female Command Chief Warrant Officer Arkansas Army National Guard

Chief Warrant Officer Five (CW5) Veronica Austin was born in Little Rock, Arkansas. She attended Parkview High School and graduated in May 1985. She received her Bachelor of Business Administration in Computer Information Systems from the University of Little Rock at Little Rock in December 2003.

Her military career started in 1986 when she joined the 25th Rear Area Operations Center, Arkansas Army National Guard as a Private First Class (E3). She completed her Basic Combat Training at Fort Dix, New Jersey and her Advance Individual Training at Fort Benjamin Harrison, Indiana where she acquired the Military Occupational Skill 75B10, Personnel Administration Specialist. She was later promoted to Specialist (E4) in 1988. In 1991, CW5 Austin deployed with the 25th Rear Area Operations Center in support of Operations Desert Storm.

At the beginning of her military career, CW5 Austin worked on active-duty orders from 1988-1989 for the National Guard Bureau Professional Education Center, Camp J.T. Robinson, North Little Rock, Arkansas. In 1990, CW5 Austin was hired in the Federal Military Technician Program as a GS-5 Secretary at the Directorate of Logistics, Arkansas Army National Guard. She worked in the Directorate of Logistics for 9 years.

In 1998 CW5 Austin attended Warrant Officer Candidate School, at Fort Rucker, Alabama, where she was the honor graduate. On

September 26, 1999, CW5 Austin received her commission as Warrant Officer One (WO1), 420A, Military Personnel Technician and was promoted to the grade of GS-10. She was assigned as the Human Resources Specialist for the Institute Training Unit, Camp J.T. Robinson. CW5 Austin was later promoted to GS-11 and assigned to the 35th Aviation Brigade, Camp J.T. Robinson, where she served as the S1 Personnel Officer. Additionally, CW5 Austin was assigned to the Deputy Chief of Staff Personnel as the SIDPERS Chief. She served in the Federal Military Technician Program for 20 years.

In 2010, CW5 Austin was hired into the Title 10 Active Guard Reserve (AGR) Program at the Human Resources Training Center, National Guard Professional Education Center, where she served as the Senior Instructor. In 2013, CW5 Austin was hired into the Title 32 Active Guard Reserve (AGR) Program for Arkansas Army National Guard as the Administrative Officer for Joint Force Headquarters, Camp J.T. Robinson. While a member of the Title 32 AGR Program, she has served in a variety of positions to include Officer Personnel Manager at Deputy Chief of Staff Personnel and State Equal Employment Manager (SEEM), Human Resources Office. In May of 2023, CW5 Austin was promoted to Chief Warrant Officer Five (CW5) and was reassigned to the Deputy Chief of Staff Personnel as the Officer Personnel Manager. On August 22, 2023, CW5 Austin was selected as the 8th Command Chief Warrant Officer of Arkansas Army National Guard. She is the First Female in the history of the Arkansas National Guard that has been selected as the Command Chief Warrant Officer.

CW5 Austin's military education includes the Warrant Officer Candidate School, Warrant Officer Staff Course Phase II, Officer in Charge Course, Composite Risk Management Basic Course, Administrative Officer Workshop, Physical Security Inspectors Course, Homeland Security Liaison Officer Program, Warrant Officer Senior Service Education, and the United States Military

Entrance Processing Command (USMEPCOM) Antiterrorism Level 1 Course.

Her awards and decorations include the Meritorious Service Medal, Army Commendation Medal, Army Achievement Medal, Army Reserve Component Achievement Medal, National Defense Service Medal, Kuwait Liberation Medal, Kuwait Liberation Medal (Saudi Arabia), Noncommissioned Officer Professional Development Ribbon, Army Service Ribbon, Southwest Asia Service Medal, Army Reserve Overseas Training Ribbon, Armed Forces Reserve Medal with "M" device, Arkansas Emergency Service Medal, Arkansas Federal Service Ribbon, and the Arkansas Service Ribbon.

CW5 Austin currently resides in Sherwood, Arkansas. She has one son, Malique and a grandson Malique Jr.

Captain Oneida D. Battle

First Female Equal Employment Manager
Arkansas Army National Guard

Captain (CPT) Oneida D. Battle was born in Landstuhl, Germany. She graduated from Henry Foss Senior High School in 1977. CPT Battle graduated Summa Cum Laude from the Pacific Lutheran University obtaining her Bachelor of Arts in Political Science on May 23, 1982. She received a Master of Arts Degree from Pacific Lutheran University on August 23, 1991.

CPT Battle began her military career on February 13, 1981, when she enlisted in the Washington Army National Guard in Tacoma, Washington as a Still Photo Specialist (84B10) as part of the Split Option Training Program. During the same time period, she completed Basic Training and Advanced Individual Training and was awarded the Nuclear Biological and Chemical (NBC) Military Occupational Specialty (54E). In June 1983, CPT Battle attended Officer Candidate School (OCS) at the Washington Military Academy. On July 21, 1984, she completed the OCS Program and was commissioned as 2nd Lieutenant Transportation Officer Branch.

After receiving her commission, CPT Battle served as the Chemical, Biological and Radiological (CBR) Team Chief in the 116th Rear Area Operation Center (RAOC) at Camp Murray, Tacoma, Washington. During this assignment, she performed temporary duty in Brussels, Belgium. On May 12, 1987, CPT Battle was assigned as Platoon Leader, 1161st Transportation Company, Ephrata, Washington. That was a short-lived assignment and in July of the same year she was transferred to Headquarters and Headquarters Detachment (HHD), 248th Transportation Battalion in Montesano,

Washington. She served as Detachment Commander for nearly two years. In January 1989, she assumed the role of Executive Officer for the 541st Personnel Services Company at Camp Murray in Tacoma, Washington. On December 3, 1990, CPT Battle transferred from the Washington Army National Guard to the Arkansas Army National Guard and was hired as the first female Equal Employment Manager in the history of the Arkansas National Guard.

CPT Battle served with distinction in her role as State Equal Employment Manager. She was awarded a Memorandum of Appreciation from the Chief, Equal Opportunity Division, National Guard Bureau (NGB) for her participation in the second workshop of its kind focusing on equal opportunity challenges and opportunities in the National Guard. On August 31, 1994, CPT Battle transferred from the Arkansas Army National Guard to the Arkansas Air National Guard and was assigned to the 189th Mission Support Squadron, 189th Airlift Wing, Jacksonville, Arkansas.

CPT Battle's profession military education include the Transportation Officer Basic Course, Transportation Officer Advanced Course, the Department of Defense (DOD) Defense Equal Opportunity Management Institute, Patrick Air Force Base Phase 1-III course for Equal Opportunity Advisors and Equal Opportunity Representative Course.
CPT Battle's service was recognized for its excellence through the receipt of the following awards, decorations and honors to include the Army Commendation Medal, Army Achievement Medal, Army Reserve Components Achievement Medal, National Defense Medal, Army Service Ribbon, Army Reserve Component Training Ribbon and Arkansas Commendation Medal.

Master Sergeant Robert Bell

First African American to Enlist in the 188th Tactical Fighter Wing Arkansas Air National Guard

Master Sergeant (MSgt) Robert Bell was raised in Roland, Oklahoma. He served in three branches of the military. MSgt Bell served in the U.S. Navy Reserves from June 29, 1946, to April 29, 1948. He later served in the U.S. Army Reserves from June 14, 1955, to June 13, 1961. On March 5, 1965, MSgt Bell enlisted in the 188th Tactical Fighter Group, Arkansas Air National Guard, Fort Smith, Arkansas. He was the first African American to Enlist in the 188th Tactical Fighter Wing, Arkansas Air National Guard.

MSgt Bell's last duty position in the 188th Civil Engineer Flight was First Sergeant. He retired from the 188th Fighter Wing on July 18, 1977, with over 20 years of military service. MSgt Bell retired from the U.S. Postal Service and Stephens Production Company in Fort Smith, Arkansas. MSgt Robert Bell passed away on January 10, 2020.

Lieutenant Colonel Wayne E. Berger

First African American to Serve as Group Commander 189th Air Wing, Arkansas Air National Guard

Lieutenant Colonel (Lt. Col.) Wayne E. Berger was born in Fort Smith, Arkansas. He graduated from Lincoln High School, in Fort Smith in 1964, and from Wichita State University, Wichita, Kansas, with a Bachelor of Arts degree in journalism in 1974. His military service began in June 1965 in the United States Air Force, and his first assignment was Materiel Control Inventory Management Specialist at Vandenberg Air Force Base, California.

He had advanced to the rank of staff sergeant when he was honorably discharged from the USAF in August 1969. After a break in service, Lt. Col. Berger joined the 188th Tactical Fighter Group, Arkansas Air National Guard in Fort Smith, as a Staff Sergeant. He later received his commission as first lieutenant (USAF) upon graduation from the Academy of Military Science, McGhee-Tyson Air National Guard Base, Tennessee, in 1981. He was promoted to lieutenant colonel in October 1997.

Lt. Col. Berger has served in a variety of military assignments to include equal employment opportunity officer for the 188th Tactical Fighter Group, Arkansas Air National Guard, Fort Smith, State Military Equal Employment Opportunity Officer for the Arkansas Air National Guard, Little Rock Air Force Base, and Executive Officer for 189th Mission Support Squadron, 189th Support Group, and 189th Airlift Wing, all at Little Rock Air Force Base. In 1987, Lt. Col. Berger was assigned as the

Commander of the 189th Support Group, Little Rock Air Force Base. Lt. Col. Berger was the first African American to serve as Group Commander in the 189th Air Wing, Arkansas Air National Guard.

As 189th Support Group commander, Lt. Col. Berger was responsible for providing support through the 189th Mission Support Flight, 189th Communications Flight, 189th Services Flight, 189th Security Forces Squadron, and 189th Civil Engineer Squadron for the 189th Airlift Wing and other geographically separated units.

Lt. Col. Berger graduated from the Air Force Squadron Officer School in 1985, Air Command and Staff College (seminar) 1994, and Air War College (seminar) 1999. His military decorations include the Air Force Meritorious Service Medal, Air Force Commendation Medal, Air Force Good Conduct Medal, National Defense Service Medal w/1 device, Air Force Overseas Short Tour Ribbon, Air Force Longevity Service Award w/4 devices, Armed Forces Reserve Medal, and Air Force Training Ribbon w/1 device. Lt. Col. Berger retired from military service in 2003.

Lt. Col. Berger was active in many community affairs. He volunteered for Big Brothers and Big Sisters and was an alumnus of the Leadership Greater Little Rock, Little Rock Chamber of Commerce.

Lt. Col. Berger served as the fifty-first President of the National Guard Association of Arkansas 2001-2002.

Sergeant Major Robert Blue

First African American
Sergeant Major
Arkansas Army National Guard

Sergeant Major (SGM) Robert Blue was born in Mound Bayou, Mississippi and graduated from Mounds Bayou High School in May 1964. He earned a Bachelor of Arts Degree in Business Administration from Philander Smith College, Little Rock Arkansas, in May 1968.

SGM Blue began his military career when he enlisted into Headquarters and Headquarters Company, 39th Infantry Brigade (Separate), Arkansas Army National Guard on May 29, 1968. On June 23,1969, he completed Basic Training and Advanced Individual Training at Fort Jackson, South Carolina. His Military Occupation Specialties and assignments include 71H, Personnel Specialist, HHC, 39th Infantry Brigade (Sep), 94B, Food Service Sergeant, HHC, 39th Infantry Brigade (Sep), 11B, First Sergeant, HHC, 39th Infantry Brigade (Sep), 94B, Food Service Supervisor, State Area Command, Arkansas Army National Guard, 76Z, Audit Examiner, State Area Command, Arkansas Army National Guard and 75Z, Personnel Sergeant, 119th Personnel Service Company, Arkansas Army National Guard.

On March 1, 1993, SGM Blue was promoted to E9, Sergeant Major. He is the first African American promoted to Sergeant Major in the Arkansas Army National Guard. He was assigned as Sergeant Major for Headquarters and Headquarters Detachment, 125th Medical Battalion, North Little Rock. SGM Blue later served as Senior Supply Sergeant for 87th Troop Command, Camp J.T. Robinson, and

Operations Sergeant for 25th Support Detachment Rear Tactical Operations Center (RTOC), North Little Rock.

SGM Blue's military education includes the Noncommissioned Officer Academy, Food Service Management Course, Food Service Senior Technical Course, Senior Noncommissioned Office Course, and the Battle Staff Course. He is the recipient of several awards, medals and decorations ranging from the Meritorious Service Medal, Army Commendation Medal, Army Component Achievement Medal, Armed Forces Reserve Medal, National Defense Service Medal, Army Service Ribbon, Arkansas Commendation Medal, Arkansas Emergency Service Ribbon, and the Arkansas Service Ribbon.

After graduating from Philander Smith College, SGM Blue was employed by Worthen Bank and Trust Company in Little Rock and was subsequently employed by Humble Oil and Refinery Company in April 1970. His initial interview and selection for employment by Humble Oil and Refinery Company was the catalyst to what would become a successful career at Exxon Mobil where he worked for over 32 years in the areas of marketing, sales, and engineering. After his flourishing career with Exxon Mobil, SGM Blue retired from the company in October 2002. A short while after his retirement from Exxon Mobil, SGM Blue successfully owned and operated a small business in Mandeville, Louisiana from 2003 until he retired in October 2013.

SGM Blue attributes much of his success to the education, skills, and values he gained as a student at Philander Smith College. For that reason, he is committed to giving back to the institution that gave him so much. He thinks of it as "paying it forward." For more than two decades, he has been contributing financially to the College. Not only is he committed to the College financially, but he also gives generously of his time and talent. In 2015, SGM Blue was elected to the Philander Smith College Board of Trustees. As a Trustee Board Member, he served as Chairman of the Board of

Trustees' Development Committee and in 2019, SGM Blue served as Honorary Co-Chair for the Fourth Annual President's Scholarship Gala. He is an active member of the National Alumni Association and for his outstanding contributions to Philander Smith College, SGM Blue was featured as an *Outstanding Alumni* in the Fall 2018 Edition of *The Philanderian Magazine.* He is a lifetime member of Alpha Phi Alpha Fraternity, Incorporated and the Philander Smith College Alumni Association.

SGM Robert Blue retired from the Arkansas Army National Guard on January 1, 1999, with over 30 years of distinguished military service. He has been married to his wife Carolyn for 44 years.

Command Sergeant Major Ira Blueford, Jr.

First African American Command Sergeant Major 35th Aviation Brigade

First African American Command Sergeant Major 77th Aviation Brigade Arkansas Army National Guard

Command Sergeant Major (CSM) Blueford was born in Warren, Arkansas. He graduated from Warren High School in 1973. He received an Associate of Arts Degree from Arkansas State University at Beebe in 1979.

CSM Blueford enlisted into the United States Army as a 77W, Petroleum Specialist on July 13, 1973, and served in the 102nd Quartermaster Company, Fort. Campbell, Kentucky. After completing his enlistment in the Army, CSM Blueford joined HHC (-), 3rd Battalion, 153rd Infantry, 39th Infantry Brigade, Arkansas Army National Guard in August 1975.

On February 8, 1976, CSM Blueford started working full-time for the Arkansas Army National Guard at the Army Aviation Support Facility and transferred to 936th Aviation Company at Camp Robinson. He later attended the UH-1H Helicopter Repair School at Fort Rucker, Alabama. At the Aviation Support Facility, CSM Blueford served as an Airfield Service Supervisor and UH-1H Technical Inspector.

CSM Blueford served in various military assignments such as First Sergeant, Company B, 437th Attack Helicopter Battalion, First Sergeant, Co. B, 1-114th Aviation Battalion, and First Sergeant, HHC, 1-114th Aviation Battalion. In October 1996, First Sergeant

Blueford was promoted to Command Sergeant Major of HHD, 2-114th ATC. On November 1, 2002, CSM Blueford was assigned to the 35th Aviation Brigade, Arkansas Army National Guard as the Brigade's Command Sergeant Major. CSM Blueford was the first African American in the 35th Aviation Brigade assigned to that position.

His other assignments included Command Sergeant Major for the Institute Support Unit, Camp Robinson Maneuver Training Center, and the National Guard Marksmanship Training Center. On July 16, 2012, CSM Blueford was assigned to the 77th Aviation Brigade, Arkansas Army National Guard as the Brigade's Command Sergeant Major. He was the first African American in the 77th Aviation Brigade assigned to that position.

CSM Bluford's awards and decorations include the Legion of Merit, Meritorious Service Medal, Army Commendation Medal, Army Achievement Medal, Good Conduct Medal, Army Reserve Component Achievement Medal, Armed Forces Reserve Medal, Arkansas Distinguished Service Medal, Master Aircraft Crewman Badge, Army Lapel Button, Order of Saint Michael, and other Federal and State awards.

His military education includes the United States Army Sergeant Major Academy, First Sergeant Course, Senior NCO Course, Advanced NCO Course, Army National /guard Battle Skills Course, Instructor Training Course, Battle Staff Course, and the Alamo Safety Course.

CSM Blueford is a member of Mount Pleasant Baptist Church and has served as the Chairman of the Deacon's Ministry. CSM Blueford retired with on November 30, 2014, with over 41 years of military service.

Chief Master Sergeant Ronald O. Boston

First African American
Command Chief Master Sergeant
189th Airlift Wing
Arkansas Air National Guard

Command Chief Master Sergeant (CMSgt) Ronald Boston was born in Crossett, Arkansas. He attended Northeast Louisiana University in Monroe in 1982, and later received a Bachelor's Degree in Social and Criminal Justice in April 2014.

In 1988, he began his military career with the 189th Airlift Wing, Arkansas Air National Guard at Little Rock Air Force Base as a member of the Security Forces Squadron. He completed his Basic Training and Student Security Police Training at Lackland Air Force Base, Texas.

As a 189th Security Forces Leader, CCM Boston accepted a number of active-duty challenges to include numerous tours at Little Rock Air Force Base with the 314th and 19th Security Forces Squadron and abroad. In 1997, he served as a Security Force Member with the 39th SFS, Incirlik Air Force Base, Turkey. In 2003, he served as Team Leader, 732nd SFS, Baghdad International Airport, Iraq. In March 2005, he served as Flight Chief, 48th SFS, RAF Lakenheath, England. Also, CMSgt Boston served as Flight Chief of the 376th Expeditionary Security Forces Squadron while deployed to Manas Air Force Base, Kyrgyzstan in 2009.

In addition to his overseas deployments, CMSgt Boston deployed in support of Hurricane Katrina in New Orleans, Louisiana in 2005,

Operation Jump Start (Border Patrol) in Tucson, Arizona in 2006 and Operation Jump Start (Border Patrol) in Lordsburg, New Mexico in 2008. CMSgt Boston served as Operations Superintendent for the 189th SFS and Mission Support Group Superintendent for the 189th Mission Support Group, 189th Airlift Wing, Arkansas Air National Guard.

On February 1, 2014, CMSgt Boston was promoted to Chief Master Sergeant (E9) and assigned as Command Chief Master Sergeant for the 189th Airlift Wing, Arkansas Air National Guard. He is the first African American assigned as Command Chief Master Sergeant for the 189th Airlift Wing. As the Command Chief Master Sergeant, he works closely with the 189th Airlift Wing Commander, all commanders in the 189th Airlift Wing, as well as all Chief Master Sergeants to prepare the Enlisted force to best execute mission requirements. In 2019, CMSgt Boston was assigned as the Command Chief Master Sergeant for the Arkansas Air National Guard Headquarters, Camp J.T. Robinson.

CMSgt Boston has been awarded and decorated throughout his military career. He is the recipient of the Air Force Commendation Medal, the Air Force Achievement Medal, Air Force Outstanding Unit Award, the Humanitarian Service Medal, Air Reserve Forces Meritorious Service Medal, National Defense Service Medal, Armed Forces Expeditionary Medal, Global War on Terrorism Expeditionary Medal, Global War on Terrorism Service Medal, Air Force Overseas Ribbon-Short Tour, Air Force Expeditionary Service Ribbon, Air Force Longevity Service, Armed Forces Reserve Medal, and the Meritorious Service Medal. Additionally, CMSgt Boston is the recipient of the 2004, 189th Security Forces Squadron Colonel Jack H. Lykes Memorial Award and in 2010 he was the recipient of the 189th Security Forces Squadron Senior NCO of the Year.

In his civilian capacity, he served as Chief of the Information Protection Office, 19th Airlift Wing, Little Rock Air Force Base, where he was responsible for the development, maintenance, and currency of all security guidance and directives to meet current and long-range program goals and objectives. He also spent 11 years as a full-time member of the Pine Bluff Police Department. CMSgt Boston is currently self-employed and serves as the Chief Executive Officer for the Big Chief Transport Service.

CMSgt Boston retired from the Arkansas Air National Guard in January 2022, with over 33 years of outstanding military service.

Lieutenant Colonel Noyal Brasfield

First African American to Command the 777th Aviation Support Battalion 77th Theater Aviation Brigade Arkansas Army National Guard

Lieutenant Colonel (LTC) Noyal Brasfield was born in Dumas, Arkansas. He graduated from Dumas High School in 1994. He received a Bachelor of Science Degree in General Studies from the University of Arkansas at Pine Bluff in 2007.

As a product of a military family, LTC Brasfield began his military journey in the Arkansas Army National Guard in November 1993 as an 11B, Rifleman with Company C, 3rd Battalion, 153rd Infantry, 39th Infantry Brigade. LTC Brasfield attended Basic Training and Advanced Individual Training at Fort Benning, Georgia.

He obtained the grade of Specialist E4, before he entered the Arkansas Military Academy Officer Candidate School (Class 42). After receiving his commission, he was assigned as a Platoon Leader in Company D, 3rd Battalion, 153rd Infantry, 39th Infantry Brigade. Immediately upon completion of his Infantry Officer Basic Course, LTC Brasfield started deployment train-up for deployment to Bosnia.

During his 30-years career, he has served in various leadership positions including Anti-Armor Platoon Leader (Joint), D 3-153rd IN attached to 3rd Squadron, 7th U.S. Calvary, Bosnia; Platoon Leader, Detachment 1, Company B, 1st Battalion, 141st Infantry, Victoria,

Texas; Company Executive Officer, Company A, 2nd Battalion 142nd IN (Joint), Tallil, Iraq; Deputy Support Plans Operations/Transportation Officer, Headquarters and Headquarters Company (-), 2nd Battalion, 142nd Combat Sustainment and Support Battalion, Tallil, Iraq; Commander, Company B, 39th BSB and OWT Team Chief (Simultaneous Commands), S3 Battalion Operations Officer, HHC(-), 39th Support Battalion, Hazen, Arkansas; BDE Logistic Officer (S4) HHC, 77th Aviation Brigade (Joint) Kuwait.

LTC Brasfield entered the Arkansas National Guard Federal Technician program in 2019 as the Logistics Management Specialist (GS-11) for the National Guard Marksmanship Training Center. He has served as the Logistics Plans and Policy Officer (GS-11) for Deputy Chief of Staff Logistics. He currently serves as the Supervisory Logistics Management Specialist (GS-12) for the Deputy Chief of Staff Logistics. On August 3, 2022, LTC Brasfield assumed Command of the 777th Aviation Support Battalion, 77th Theater Aviation Brigade. He is the first African American to serve as the Commander of 777th Aviation Support Battalion.

LTC Brasfield's military education includes the Infantry Officers Basic Course, Infantry Officer Advanced Course, Ordinance Officer Branch Qualification Course, Composite Risk Management Basic Course, Intermediate Level Education Common Core Phase 1(Command and General Staff College), Intermediate Leaders Education Advanced Operations Course (CGSC), Support Operations Officer Course and Ground Safety Officer Course.

LTC Brasfield is the recipient of many awards, medals and decorations to include the Bronze Star Medal, Meritorious Service Medal, Army Commendation Medal, Army Achievement Medal, Army Reserve Component Achievement Medal, National Defense Service Medal, Armed Forces Expeditionary Medal, Armed Forces Reserve Medal, Meritorious Unit Medal, Army Service Ribbon, Overseas Service Ribbon, Armed Forces Reserve Medal with "M"

Device, Global War on Terrorism Expeditionary Medal, Global War on Terrorism Service Medal, and the Iraqi Campaign Medal.

Currently, LTC Brasfield is employed as a Full-Time Federal Technician for the Arkansas Army National Guard. He serves as the Supervisory Logistics Management Officer (SLMS) for the Deputy Chief of Staff, Logistics (DCSLOG).

LTC Brasfield is a member of the Alpha Phi Alpha Fraternity, Incorporated and he and his wife, Nickole and their two sons (Nubian and Nzion) and daughter (Nyla) live in Pine Bluff.

Major Eddie Brown

First African American to Complete Arkansas Military Department Officer Candidate School Arkansas Army National Guard

Major (MAJ) Eddie L. Brown was born in Gregory, Arkansas. He graduated from Carver High School in Augusta, Arkansas in 1968. In the fall of 1968, MAJ Brown enrolled in Arkansas State University, Beebe. On May 2, 1969, he enlisted into Company B, 2nd Battalion, 153rd Infantry, 39th Infantry Brigade, Arkansas Army National Guard. While in Company B, 2nd Battalion, 153rd Infantry, MAJ Brown served as a Light Weapons Infantryman.

MAJ Brown attended the Arkansas Military Academy Officer Candidate School in 1973 and he was commissioned as 2nd Lieutenant on June 29, 1974. MAJ Brown was the first African American to complete the Arkansas Military Academy Officer Candidate School in school's history.

After completing the Arkansas Military Academy, MAJ Brown was assigned to the 39th Infantry Brigade. As a member of the 39th Infantry Brigade, MAJ Brown dedicated over 24 years of military service. His many assignments included Liaison Officer, Rifle Platoon Leader, Mortar Platoon Leader, Tactical Intelligence Officer, Executive Officer, and Brigade Assistant S1. MAJ Brown also served as Company Commander of Headquarters and Headquarters Company, 39th Infantry Brigade from 1980-1984.

MAJ Brown served as the Computer Systems Programmer for the Directorate of Information Management and State Retention Officer for Recruiting and Retention Command. His military courses are the

Infantry Officer Basic Course, Infantry Officer Advanced Course, Military Personnel Officer Course, Advanced Computer's Course, Combined Arms Services and Staff School, Command and General Staff College, and the National Guard Professional Education Center Recruiting and Retention Managers Course.

MAJ Brown's awards consist of the Meritorious Service Medal, Army Commendation Medal, Army Achievement Medal, Army Reserve Component Medal, National Defense Service Medal Armed Forces Reserve Medal, and the Army Service Ribbon. MAJ Brown separated from the Arkansas Army National Guard on July 31, 1997, with over 29 years of military service.

Chief Warrant Officer Five Kenneth D. Brown

First African American State Command Chief Warrant Officer Arkansas Army National Guard

Chief Warrant Officer Five (CW5) Kenneth D. Brown began his military career on May 5, 1979, after graduating from East End Bigelow High School. He enlisted in the Arkansas Army National Guard split option program, and performed his basic training at Fort Jackson, South Carolina, and his Advanced Individual Training (AIT) at Fort Leonard Wood, Missouri the following years. His unit assignments were with the 439th Signal Company, Delta Company, 212th Signal Company, Bravo 39th Support Company, HHC 212th Signal Company, Golf Company 39th BSB, Alpha Battery 1/206th Field Artillery and Joint Force Headquarter.

His Warrant Officer Military positions and occupations held are, State Command Chief Warrant Officer (currently), Alpha Battery 1/206th Executive Officer, Battalion Maintenance Officer, Unit Maintenance Officer, Command Maintenance Evaluation Team (COMET) Chief and member, Battalion Special Staff Officer, Senior Maintenance Officer, Engineer Warrant Officer. Chief Brown's enlisted positions held are, Platoon Sergeant, Network Operator, Senior Generator Repair, and Heavy Equipment Repairer Supervisor. He holds five Military Occupation Specialty (MOS) 91B (63B), 52X, 31F, 915A, and 915E.

He was hired as a Military Technician in September 1984, and worked as a Mechanic, Automotive Mechanic Supervisor, Heavy Equipment Repairer Supervisor, Surface Maintenance Mechanic Supervisor, and Surface Maintenance Specialist Supervisor. On December 3, 2018, the Adjutant General of Arkansas selected CW5

Brown as the State Command Chief Warrant Officer for the Arkansas Army National Guard. CW5 Kenneth Brown is the first African American in the history of the Arkansas Army National Guard to hold that position.

His military schools are Primary Leadership Development School, Basic Non-Commission Officer School, Advance Non-Commission Officer School, Warrant Officer Candidate School, Warrant Officer Basic Course, Warrant Officer Advance Course, Warrant Officer Staff Course, Warrant Officer Senior Staff Course, Instructor Training Course, Master Fitness Course, and a Knowledge Management Course. He has numerous college hours toward a Homeland Security Bachelor's Degree, an Associate Degree in Applied Science from Vincennes University.

Chief Brown's awards received are Meritorious Service Medal, Army Commendation Medal, Army Achievement Medal, Army Reserve Component Achievement Medal, National Defense Service Medal, Iraq Campaign Medal, Global War on Terror Service Medal, Armed Force Reserve Medal, NCO Professional Development Ribbon, Army Service Ribbon, Army Reserve Component Overseas Ribbon, and numerous State Ribbon and Awards.

CW5 Brown retired from the Arkansas National Guard in 2023.

Chief Warrant Officer Three Ife Caldwell

First African American Female Pilot
Arkansas Army National Guard

Chief Warrant Officer Three (CW3) Ife Caldwell was born in Milwaukee, Wisconsin. She grew up in North Little Rock, Arkansas and graduated from North Little Rock High School West Campus in 1995. She received a Bachelor's Degree in Psychology from the University of Arkansas at Little Rock.

CW3 Caldwell joined the U.S. Army in 1995 after graduating high school, beginning her Army career as a Dental Hygienist (91EX2). In 2003, she got accepted into flight school through the Warrant Officer Candidate program. CW3 Caldwell began her aviation career as an OH-58D Scout Helicopter Pilot. She completed a combat tour in Iraq in 2005 with the 4th Squadron, 3rd Armored Calvary Regiment (4/3ACR) before moving to Fort Polk, Louisiana where she flew a different kind of mission that prepared her for the civilian occupation she holds today.

In 2010, CW3 Caldwell separated from active duty and moved from the Army National Guard to U.S. Army Reserves in support of her then spouse's continued Army career. Each move provided her an opportunity to fly a different airframe. She landed a place in the 5-159th General Support Aviation Battalion (GSAB) in Fort Eustis, Virginia., flying CH47 Chinooks before eventually returning to her hometown, North Little Rock.

On July 14, 2015, CW3 Caldwell joined Headquarters and Headquarters Company, 1/114th Aviation S & S Battalion, 77th

Aviation Brigade, Arkansas Army National Guard. CW3 Caldwell was first African American female UH60, Black Hawk Pilot in the Arkansas Army National Guard.

As a member of the 77th Aviation Brigade, CW3 Caldwell also completed assignments in B Company, $2\text{-}285^{th}$ Aviation Regiment, Co A (-), $2\text{-}149^{th}$ Aviation Regiment, HHC, 77th Aviation Brigade Headquarters, and Detachment 1, G Company, $1\text{-}168^{th}$ GSAB. On August 17, 2016, CW3 Caldwell deployed with the 77th Aviation Brigade to Kuwait.

CW3 Ife Caldwell retired from the Arkansas Army National Guard in 2018 after 23 years of military service but continues to serve her community as a helicopter EMS pilot for Air Evac Lifeteam in Greenville, Mississippi.

For her outstanding military service, CW3 Ife Caldwell earned numerous awards, accolades, and citations throughout her career to include the Meritorious Service Medal.

Staff Sergeant
Lillie Moore Carter

First African American Female
Full-Time Employee
Arkansas Army National Guard

Staff Sergeant (SSG) Lillie Moore Carter was born in England, Arkansas. She enlisted in the Arkansas Army National Guard in 1974, and was assigned to Company A, 39th Support Battalion, 39th Infantry Brigade. In December 1974, she was hired in a Full-Time Technician position with Co A, 39th Support Battalion, 39th Infantry Brigade. SSG Carter was the first African American Female hired full-time for the Arkansas Army National Guard. Later, she worked at the United States Property and Fiscal Office (USPFO) as an Accounting Technician. SSG Carter resigned from the Technician Program in 1980, but remained on drill status with the Arkansas Army National Guard until her discharge in 1982.

SSG Carter received a Bachelor of Arts in Elementary Education from Arkansas Baptist College in 1976. She later received her Master's Degree from Ouachita Baptist University and her Certification in Elementary Administration from the University of Central Arkansas. SSG Carter was hired as a teacher with the Pulaski Special School District, and she was later employed with the Little Rock School District. In the Little Rock School District, SSG Carter taught at Cloverdale Elementary School. She served as an Assistant Principal at Martin Luther King Kindergarten, Assistant Principal at Rockefeller Incentive School, and Assistant Principal at Pulaski Heights Elementary School. SSG Carter retired from the Little Rock School District in 2016.

Lieutenant Colonel Willie Chapple

First African American Officer to Serve as Aide-de-Camp for the Assistant Adjutant General-Army

First African American to Serve as Commander for the Sniper and Small Arms School National Guard Marksmanship Training Center Arkansas National Guard

Lieutenant Colonel (LTC) Willie Chapple was born in Cotton Plant, Arkansas. He graduated from Cotton Plant High School in 1989. LTC Chapple has several degrees including a Bachelor of Arts Degree in Agricultural Economics from the University of Arkansas at Pine Bluff. He has a Master of Arts Degree in Human Resources Development, and a Master of Arts Degree in Computer Resources and Information Management from Webster University.

His military career started by enlisting in the Arkansas Army National Guard in 1989. He served as an Indirect Fire Infantryman (11C) with the 2nd Battalion, 153rd Infantry in Brinkley, Arkansas. He served with the 3rd Battalion, 153rd Infantry as a 4.2 Mortar Chief Ballistic Operator and later as a Motor Transport Operator. LTC Chapple attended the Arkansas Military Academy Officer Candidate School and was commissioned as a Signal Corps Officer in 1997.

LTC Chapple served in various military command and leadership assignments throughout his career in the Arkansas Army National Guard, to include Deputy Chief of Staff Information Management Support Branch-Division Chief, Knowledge Manager - Information Management Support Branch, and Professor of Military Science,

Henderson State University. On July 7, 2012, LTC Chapple became the first African American to serve as the Commander for the Sniper and Small Arms School at the National Guard Marksmanship Training Center Commander in the history of the Arkansas Army National Guard.

LTC Chapple's other military assignments included Deputy Commander, 61st Civil Support Team (CST), Operations Officer 61st CST, Nuclear Biological and Chemical (NBC) Team Leader, 61st CST, Communications-Electronics Officer, 212th Signal Battalion and Commander, Headquarters & Headquarters Company, 212th Signal Battalion. On January 1, 2001, LTC Chapple was assigned as Aide-de-Camp for the Assistant Adjutant General – Army. He was the first African American to serve as the Aide-de-Camp to the Assistant Adjutant General-Army.

LTC Chapple served as a Platoon Leader at D Company, 212th Signal Battalion and Platoon Leader at C Company, 212th Signal Battalion. In 1992, he deployed to Honduras with the 39th Infantry Brigade and later deployed in support of Operations Enduring Freedom to Afghanistan from 2010-2011.

LTC Chapple's military education and certifications includes the Signal Officer Basic Course, Signal Officer Advanced Course, Combined Arms Services Staff School, the Command and General Staff College, Department of Defense Cyber Awareness Course, Level 1 Antiterrorism Awareness Training, Army National Guard Information Technology Project Management Course, Army National Guard System Center Configuration Managers Course, Knowledge Management Qualifications Course and the Network+ and Security+ Information Assurance Certifications Course.

For his outstanding and distinctive military service, LTC Chapple received awards and commendations to include the Meritorious Service Medal, Army Commendation Medal, Army Achievement Medal, Army Reserve Component Achievement Medal, National

Defense Service Medal, Afghanistan Campaign Medal, Global War on Terrorism Expeditionary Medal, Armed Forces Reserve Medal, Armed Forces Reserve Medal w/ M Device, Noncommissioned Officers Professional Development Ribbon, Army Service Ribbon, Overseas Service Medal, Army Reserve Components Overseas Training Ribbon, NATO Medal, Arkansas Federal Service Ribbon, Arkansas Service Ribbon, and the Meritorious Unit Commendation.

LTC Chapple retired on November 26, 2018, with over 29 years of distinctive military service. He and his family currently reside in Little Rock. He is a life member of the National Guard Association of Arkansas, National Guard Association of United States, Kappa Alpha Psi Fraternity, Incorporated and the Signal Corps Regimental Association. LTC Chapple is the owner of Will's Enterprise, LLC., where he specializes in Computer/Cell Phone repair, Bounce House Rentals, and Real Estate Investing. He is a Real Estate Agent, and he owns WE Care Contracting LLC where he builds and remodels houses.

Chief Warrant Officer Five Cornelius Charles

First African American S1/XO for the Recruit Sustainment Program

First African American to be the first Company Commander of B Company, Recruiting and Retention Battalion

First and First African American Warrant Officer to serve as Aide-de-Camp Arkansas Army National Guard

Chief Warrant Officer Five (CW5) Cornelius Charles was born on 16 July 1973. He graduated from McGehee High School in May 1991. In 2010, CW5 Charles graduated from South-Western College in Wichita, Kansas with a Bachelor of Science Degree in Criminal Justice and in 2014, he graduated from Webster University with a Master's Degree in Human Resources Management. CW5 Charles currently serves as the State Officer Personnel Manager (OPM) for the Deputy Chief of Staff/Personnel, Arkansas Army National Guard.

CW5Charles enlisted in the Arkansas Army National Guard on July 26, 1990, where he attended Basic Combat Training and Advanced Individual Training at Fort Benning, Georgia. He served as an infantry Fire Team Leader in Company C, 3rd Battalion, 153rd Infantry, 39th Infantry Brigade Combat Team (Cold Steel Charlie!).

In 1998, he entered the Active Guard/Reserve program at Detachment 1, Co A, 1st Battalion, 153rd Infantry, 39th IBCT. He was later promoted to Staff Sergeant in 3rd Battalion, 153rd Infantry, 39th IBCT in Fordyce, Arkansas. Later he was reassigned to HHC 3rd

Battalion, 153rd Infantry, 39th IBCT. After thirteen and half years in the 39th IBCT, he was promoted to Sergeant First Class in the 25th Rear Operations Center. He deployed with the unit to Iraq from 2005 – 2006. He served as the Operations NCO for five years until he was transferred to the 233rd Regional Training Institute Human Resources NCO position.

In April 2009, he attended Warrant Officer Candidate School and was appointed as a Warrant Officer one (WO1). His initial assignment started in the Installation Support Unit (ISU) as the Human Resource Technician. In 2009-2010, CW5 Charles was assigned to work as the S1 and Executive Officer for the Recruit Sustainment Program in the Recruiting and Retention Area Command. He was the first African American and Warrant Officer to serve in that position. In 2011, CW5 Charles served as the first Company Commander for B Company, Recruiting and Retention Battalion. He was the first African American to be assigned to that position. He commanded a full-time staff of over 36 Active Guard/Reserve soldiers with three Recruit Sustainment Sites that were responsible for over 350 new recruits.

In 2011, CW5 Charles was selected as the states' MacArthur Leadership Award Recipient Nominee. CW5 Charles served as an Officer Strength Manager that serviced the entire southern portion of the state from July 2011 to December 2011, and in December 2011, CW5 Charles was reassigned to the 233rd Regiment, Regional Training Institute to serve as the Human Resource Technician. Additionally, in 2011 CW5 Charles was not only selected as the states' first African American Warrant Officer Aide-de-Camp, but he was also the first Warrant Officer Aide-de-Camp in the Arkansas National Guard. He served as Aide-de-Camp to Brigadier General Patricia Anslow, the first female General Officer in the Arkansas National Guard.

In July 2014, CW5 Charles was assigned to the 39th IBCT Headquarters and served as the Brigade's Human Resources

Technician. CW5 Charles was deployed to Kosovo (KFOR23) in support of OPERATION JOINT GUARDIAN from July 2017 to March 2018. While deployed, he served as the Personnel Service Center OIC. Upon returning from deployment, in 2018, CW5 Charles was assigned to Joint Force Headquarters, Arkansas to serve as the State's Officer Personnel Manager. As the State Personnel Officer, he has responsibility for managing records for over 700 officers and warrant officers and he supervises the personnel security section which manages over 6000 security clearances.

His awards and decorations include the Bronze Star, Defense Meritorious Service Medal, Meritorious Service Medal with four Oak Leaf Clusters, Army Commendation Medal with six Oak Leaf Clusters, Army Achievement Medal with six Oak Leaf Clusters, The Army Good Conduct Medal, The Armed Forces Reserve Component Achievement Medal, The National Defense Service Medal with two bronze service stars, Armed Forces Expeditionary Medal, Armed Forces Reserve Medal with gold hour glass with M device and numeral 2, Army Reserve Component Overseas Training Ribbon, Army Service Ribbon, The Global War on Terrorism Service Medal, The Iraqi Campaign Medal, Military Outstanding Volunteer Service Medal, NATO medal, Noncommissioned Officer Professional Development Ribbon, Overseas Service Ribbon Joint Meritorious Unit Service Award, Meritorious Unit Commendation, Air Borne Badge, Air Assault Badge, and numerous other federal and state awards.

CW5 Charles' military education includes Warrant Officer Candidate Course, Warrant Officer Basic Course, Warrant Officer Advance Course, Warrant Officer Intermediate Level Education, Warrant Officer Senior Service College, ARNG G1 Staff, ARNG Senior Human Resource Noncommissioned Officer and Warrant Officer, Mission Command Digital Master Gunner, Sexual Harassment Assault and Response Program, Master Resiliency Trainer, Human Resources Plans and Operations Course, and Protocol Event and Management Course for the military.

In 2023, Charles was promoted to Chief Warrant Officer 5.

Sergeant Major Ester L. Crockett

First African American Female Sergeant Major

First African American Female Director of Logistic Sergeant Major Joint Forces Arkansas Army National Guard

Sergeant Major (SGM) Ester L. Crockett earned her Associate Degree in Applied Science in 2008 from Excelsior College with a major in Administration Management.

SGM Crockett began her military career in 1974, where she served on active duty with HHC, 15th S&T Battalion, 1st Cavalry Division in Fort Hood, Texas as a Clerk Typist. In February 1976, SGM Crockett joined the Arkansas Army National Guard and was assigned to the 1122nd Transportation Company in Monticello, Arkansas as a Repair Parts Specialist.

In April 1978, SGM Crockett transferred to HHD, 455th Transportation Battalion as a Personnel Admin Specialist and she held a variety of duty positions as she moved through the ranks with the 455th Transportation Battalion. Her last assignment in the 455th Transportation Battalion was Senior Personnel Sergeant. SGM Crockett was hired as a Full-Time Technician in 1985 and stayed with the Battalion until it was deactivated in 1996.

SGM Crockett transferred to HHD, 2-114th Aviation in September 1996 and served as the Senior Personnel Sergeant. In 2001, MSG Crockett was promoted to E8 (Master Sergeant) as the Personnel Service Sergeant with Detachment 1, 87th Troop Command. SGM Crockett was assigned to the Directorate of Logistics in 2006 as the

Traffic Management Specialist. SGM Crockett has worked in the Personnel and Transportation field for over 38 years. She was promoted to the rank of E9 (Sergeant Major) on September 8, 2012. SGM Crockett is the first African American Female Sergeant Major in the Arkansas Army National Guard. SGM Crockett retired on March 31, 2013.

Chief Master Sergeant Delphine D. Crumpton

First African American Female Chief Master Sergeant 189th Airlift Wing Arkansas Air National Guard

Chief Master Sergeant (CMSgt) Delphine D. Crumpton was born in Shreveport, Louisiana where she graduated from Fair Park High School in May 1985. She attended Central Baptist College in Conway, Arkansas and received a Bachelor Degree in Psychology in 2012 and a Bachelor Degree in Human Resource Management in 2014.

On June 16, 1986, CMSgt Crumpton enlisted in the United States Air Force as an administrative specialist. After she completed Basic Training and Technical School in September 1986, she was stationed at Barksdale Air Force Base, Louisiana. While at Barksdale, she was assigned to the 2nd Avionics Maintenance Squadron as an administrative specialist. She then moved to the 2nd Operational Maintenance Squadron where her Air Force Specialty Code (AFSC) was converted to personnel. In January 1990, she received orders to the 7th Mission Support Squadron, Dyess AFB, Texas where she held the positions of Orderly Room Manager, Assistant Noncommissioned Officer in Charge (NCOIC) Separations and Retirements, and Assistance NCOIC Customer Service. On June 30, 1995, she separated after serving 9 years and 15 days of active duty.

In July 1995, CMSgt Crumpton enlisted in the 189th Airlift Wing, Arkansas Air National Guard as a Personnel Specialist. In February 1996 she was selected for a full-time position in the Career Enhancement section. She served in numerous duty positions throughout her career including Personnel Relocations, Personnel Readiness, Assistant Base Education and Training Manager, Personnel Employment, and Personnel Systems Manager where she was promoted to the rank of Senior Master Sergeant. In February 2007, CMSgt Crumpton was selected as the Superintendent of Personnel for the 189th Mission Support Flight and promoted to the rank of Chief Master Sergeant. She was the First African American Female promoted to Chief Master Sergeant in the history of the 189th Airlift Wing, Arkansas Air National Guard.

Her military professional courses include the Air National Guard Chief Orientation Course, USAF Senior Noncommissioned Officer Academy, USAF Noncommissioned Officer Academy, Noncommissioned Officer Leadership School, Noncommissioned Officer Preparatory Course, Personnel Craftsman Course, Education and Training Apprentice Course, Personnel Systems Data Management Course, SORTS Data Handler Training Course, Train the Trainer Course, and the MANPER-B Systems Training Course.

During her exceptional military career, CMSgt Crumpton earned awards, medals, and decorations to include the Meritorious Service Medal with 1 device, Air Force Commendation Medal with 1 device, Air Force Achievement Medal with 3 devices, National Defense Service Medal with 1device, Global War on Terrorism Expeditionary Medal, Global War on Terrorism Medal, and Arkansas Distinguished Service Medal.

Other awards and recognitions earned by CMSgt Crumpton include the 189th Mission Support Flight Top Performer (1999), 189th Support Group Outstanding Non-commissioned Officer of the Year (1999), 189th Airlift Wing Non-commissioned Officer of the Year (1999), 189th Airlift Wing Outstanding Graduate of the Year (2000), 189th Airlift Wing Outstanding Service Award (2003) and Arkansas Air National Guard Enlisted Person of the Year (2004).

Her professional memberships and affiliations include the Enlisted Association of the National Guard of United States, Noncommissioned Officer Graduates Association, Residence Professional Military Education Coordinator (Secretary), President and Coordinator for the 1st Annual Senior Non-commissioned Officer Induction Ceremony, and she served as the 189th Airlift Wing Chief Council's Vice President and President.

CMSgt Crumpton currently works for the Little Rock School District as an Air Force Junior ROTC Aerospace Instructor at the Historic Little Rock Central High School. In July 2011, she retired from the Arkansas Air National Guard after serving 25 years and 15 days of outstanding military service. CMSgt Crumpton and her family resides in Redfield, Arkansas.

Sergeant First Class Stephanie Eddington

First African American Executive Assistant to the Adjutant General Arkansas National Guard

Sergeant First Class (SFC) Stephanie Eddington was born in Little Rock, Arkansas. She attended Parkview Arts and Magnet High School and graduated in June 1999. She attended Pulaski Technical College and received an Associate's Degree and is currently attending Liberty University to complete her Bachelor's Degree.

SFC Eddington's military career started on February 16, 1999, when she enlisted in Headquarters and Headquarters Company, 39th Infantry Brigade, Little Rock, Arkansas. In October 1999, she attended Basic Training at Fort Sill, Oklahoma. January 2000, she attended Advanced Individual Training at Fort Jackson, South Carolina where she was awarded the Military Occupation Specialty (MOS) 42A, Personnel Specialist. In 2002, SFC Eddington was reassigned to Detachment 4, Medical Detachment, State Area Command (STARC) as a Patient Administrative Specialist. On February 9, 2004, she was mobilized for 3 years in support of Operation Enduring Freedom with the Community Based Healthcare Organization (CBHCO) at Camp J.T. Robinson.

In 2007, SFC Eddington was hired into the Arkansas National Guard Federal Technician Program where she served in numerous positions to include Secretary (OA), Administrative Assistant to the State Command Sergeant Major, Sexual Assault Prevention and Response Victim Advocate Coordinator and Health Systems Specialist.

From 2010 to 2016, SFC Eddington served as the Executive Assistant to The Adjutant General of Arkansas. She was the first African American in the history of the Arkansas National Guard to serve in that position. She currently works as a Budget Analyst in the Title 5 Federal Employee Program. Militarily, she is assigned as the Senior Human Resource Noncommissioned Officer (NCO) at the Arkansas Medical Detachment and serves as the S1, Noncommissioned Officer in Charge (NCOIC) at Camp Robinson.

SFC Eddington's military training include the Primary Leadership Development Course, Advanced Common Core Course, Army National Guard Basic Human Resource and Administration Course, Sexual Harassment and Rape Prevention Certification Course, Army National Guard Unit Readiness NCO Course, Human Resources Specialist Advanced Leaders Course Phase I and Phase II, Human Resources Senior Leaders Course Phase I and II, Commander's Safety Course, Joint Medical Executive Skills Institute Personal and Professional Ethics Course and the Budget Analyst Course.

Her awards and decorations include the Meritorious Service Medal, Army Commendation Medal (3), Army Achievement Medal (4), Army Reserve Component Achievement Medal (8), Good Conduct Medal, National Defense Service Ribbon, Armed Forces Reserve Medal (2), Army Service Ribbon, Arkansas Emergency Service Medal, Arkansas Federal Service Ribbon, and the Arkansas Service Ribbon (4).

SFC Eddington is a member of the Enlisted Association of the Arkansas National Guard, and she has served as a volunteer with the Highway 365 Optimist Club. SFC Eddington has over 24 years of exceptional military service. She lives in Maumelle, Arkansas with her husband Kenneth and two daughters, Taylor and Logan.

Master Sergeant
Kenneth Renard Esaw

First African American Recruiter
Arkansas Air National Guard

Master Sergeant (MSgt) Kenneth Renard Esaw was born in Dumas, Arkansas. When he was five years of age, his family moved to Fort Smith, Arkansas. Later, his family moved to Albuquerque, New Mexico where in 1984 he graduated from Highland High School and began his military career by joining the New Mexico Army National Guard.

After two years in the New Mexico Army National Guard, he decided that he wanted to join the United States Air Force. His career in the Air Force started in food Services, however MSgt Esaw wanted more. As a result of his desire to expand and broaden his career goals, he later cross trained and entered the field of Accounting and Finance.

When his six years of active duty ended, he decided it was time to get closer to home and he moved to Fort Smith, and joined the 188th Fighter Group, Arkansas Air National Guard in 1992. MSgt Esaw obtained full-time employment with the 188th Fighter Group as a Military Pay Technician and when a Recruiter position became available, he applied and was accepted for the position in 1996, therefore, he became the first African American Recruiter in the Air National Guard.

MSgt Esaw was an active member in his community where he volunteered to work for the Mallalieu Community Center. He served as a volunteer instructor for the Rights to Passage Program that was designed to teach young African American males about their heritage, personal responsibility, self-respect and respect for the rights and property of others. MSgt Esaw's military career spanned over 29 years.

Colonel Alex Finger

First African American to Command 87th Troop Command

First African American to Command the 233rd Regiment, Regional Training Institute, Arkansas Army National Guard

Colonel (COL) Alex Finger was born October 28, 1958, in Palestine, Arkansas, and graduated from Palestine High School in 1976. He received an Associate Degree in Psychology from UALR in 1983, a Bachelor's Degree in Criminal Justice with minor in Sociology in 1984, and a Master's Degree in Public Administration and Human Resource Development in 1997 from Webster University.

COL Finger began his military career on active duty in 1976, when he enlisted with D Battery, 6-68th Field Artillery as a Crewman. He served in the 6-68th Field Artillery for three years as a 13B Section Chief. He later joined the Arkansas Army National Guard in October 1988, and enlisted in Company A, 39th Support Battalion, 39th Infantry Brigade. COL Finger entered the Arkansas Military Academy Officer Candidate School in 1988. He was commissioned as an Engineer Officer in 1989.

COL Finger served in various military assignments such as Unit Engineer Officer, Unit Physical Security Officer, Company Commander, Communication Electronic Operations Officer, Operations and Training Officer, Facility Maintenance Officer, Detailed Inspector General for the Arkansas National Guard, Commander, 2nd Battalion, 233rd Regiment, Regional Training Institute; Deputy Commander, 233rd Regiment, Regional Training Institute; Joint Force Headquarters Arkansas G4 and Deputy Chief of Staff, Engineers. Additionally, COL Finger served as Brigade Commander, 87th Troop Command from June 10, 2012, to July 31, 2014. He later served as Regiment Commander, 233rd Regiment, Regional Training Institute from March 1, 2016, to July 25, 2017. COL Finger was the first African American to serve as the Brigade Commander, 87th Troop Command and the Regiment Commander, 233rd Regiment, RTI.

COL Finger's awards include the Meritorious Service Medal, Army Commendation Medal, Army Good Conduct Medal, Army Reserve Components Medal, National Defense Service Medal, Army Service Ribbon, and the Arkansas Service Ribbon.

His military education includes the 21D, Combat Engineers Officer Basic Course, 95B, Military Police Advanced Course, Commander's Course, Military Criminal Investigation Course, Physical Security Officer Course, Unit Environmental Compliance Officer Course, Combined Arms and Services Staff College, and the Command and General Staff College.

COL Finger also retired from the Arkansas State Police with over 36 years of service. He worked in several divisions within the Arkansas State Police such as Highway Patrol Division, Criminal Investigation Division, Administrative Services Division, and he served as the Highway Patrol Commander for Troop A, which includes Pulaski, Faulkner, Saline, and Lonoke Counties.

COL Finger retired from the Arkansas National Guard with over 33 years of distinguished military service.

Sergeant Major Danny J. Fletcher

First African American
First Sergeant for the 106th Army Band
Arkansas Army National Guard

First Sergeant Major for the Army National Guard Bands of the United States

Sergeant Major (SGM) Danny J. Fletcher was born September 5, 1955, in Little Rock, Arkansas. He is a 1973 graduate of Little Rock Hall High School, received a Bachelor of Music Education Degree, a Master's Degree in Educational Leadership and a Doctoral Degree in Educational Leadership from the University of Arkansas at Little Rock. He currently resides in Little Rock, Arkansas.

SGM Fletcher began his military career when he enlisted as a private in the 106th Army Band, Arkansas Army National Guard on May 5, 1973. Throughout the years he served the 106th Army Band in a variety of leadership positions including Saxophone Section Leader, Woodwind Group Leader, Stage Band Leader, Jazz Combo Leader, Unit Retention NCO, Unit Recruiter, Unit Mobilization NCO, and Principal Drum Major.

On January 24, 2001, he was appointed First Sergeant and acting commander for the 106th Army Band. He served in this position until July 2006. On February 23, 2004, while serving as First Sergeant and acting commander for the 106th Army Band, he was appointed as Sergeant Major for 1st Army Bands West, Army National Guard, and he was the first Sergeant Major to hold that position. SGM Fletcher graduated from the United States Sergeants Major Academy, Class#1-06 in June 2006. In this capacity he served as a Senior Enlisted Leader on the Army Bands Strategic Council and served all Soldiers in the (51) Army National Guard Bands of the United States of America. SGM Fletcher retired in 2015 with over 42 years of service. He is currently the Arts Director for the Little Rock School District. The LRSD serves over 25,000 students.

Chief Warrant Officer Four Kenneth R. Franklin

First African American AH-1 Cobra Helicopter Pilot Arkansas Army National Guard

Chief Warrant Officer Four (CW4) Kenneth R. Franklin was born in Tunica, Mississippi. Six months after he was born, his parents moved to Chicago, Illinois. During his childhood, his family lived nearby Chicago's O'Hare's Airport. Hearing the frequent passing of the airplanes overhead, sparked his interest in aviation and motivating him to become a pilot.

Praying for the fulfillment of his dreams lasted throughout his school days, and upon graduation from high school, CW4 Franklin enrolled into Southern Illinois University at Carbondale, and received his Bachelor of Science Degree in Aerospace Systems at the School of Aviation.

Being more realistic of his dreams, CW4 Franklin decided he needed flying experience and that spawned the need for him to start his military career. In 1981, he joined the U.S. Air Force. After he reached his full potential in the Air Force, CW4 Franklin joined the U.S. Army in 1983. In 1984, he completed the OH-5A A/C Aero-Scout Pilot course and was assigned to Fort Polk, Louisiana. Upon completion of his active duty in 1988, CW4 Franklin joined Company A, 1/185th Aviation Battalion, Mississippi Army National Guard in Jackson, Mississippi. On March 26, 1992, CW4 Franklin joined the Arkansas Army National Guard and was assigned to Company A, 1/114th Aviation Battalion as an AH 1 Cobra Pilot. CW4 Franklin was the first African American AH-1 Cobra Attack Helicopter Pilot in the Arkansas Army National Guard.

In addition to serving as an AH 1 Cobra Pilot in Company A/1/114th Aviation Battalion, CW4 Franklin served as an Aeromedical Evacuation Pilot in the 172nd Medical Company (Air Ambulance) and an OH-58 Pilot for Company D, 2/135th Aviation Brigade, Arkansas Army National Guard. He was promoted to Chief Warrant Officer Four on May 2, 2001.

CW4 Franklin received numerous awards and medals to include the Army Commendation Medal, Army Reserve Component Achievement Medal, Army Achievement Medal, Armed Forces Reserve Medal, Air Force Good Conduct Medal, Army Service Ribbon, Air Force BCT Ribbon, Air Force Small Arms Ribbon and the Army Aviation Badge.

On April 14, 2003, CW4 Franklin retired from the Arkansas Army National Guard with over 20 years of military service.

Chief Master Sergeant Alwina "Collette" Freeman

First Female African American Chief Master Sergeant 188th Fighter Wing, Arkansas Air National Guard

Chief Master Sergeant (CMSgt) Alwina "Collette" Freeman was born in Fort Smith, Arkansas. She received a Bachelor's Degree in Education from Arkansas Tech University, Russellville; and later received Master Degrees in Human Resource Management and Special Education from Webster University.

Her military career started on March 7, 1983, when she enlisted into the 188th Fighter Wing, Arkansas Air National Guard, Fort Smith, Arkansas. She was assigned to the Public Affairs Office as an Administrative Clerk. She later entered the United States Air Force on August 27, 1984, and was assigned to the 27th Headquarters Squadron at Cannon Air Force Base, New Mexico. While assigned to the 27th Headquarters Squadron, CMSgt Freeman duties included Accounting and Finance Administrative Support Clerk, Aircraft Generation Squadron Orderly Room Personnel Clerk and Noncommissioned Officer-In Charge (NCOIC) Transportation Orderly Room.

CMSgt Freeman was reassigned to Lajes Field, Azores, Portugal in March 1990. While at Lajes Field, she served in several positions including INTRO Manager for the Air Force Base, NCOIC for the Security Police Orderly Room and NCOIC for Classification and Training. In January 1993, she returned to the United States and assigned to Frances E. Warren Air Force Base, Wyoming and was assigned as the NCOIC of the Operations Orderly Room. In October

1994, CMSgt Freeman completed her tour with the U.S. Air Force and returned to the 188th Fighter Wing, Arkansas Air National Guard in Fort Smith.

Her first assignment upon return to the 188th Fighter Wing was Accounting and Finance Clerk. Later she transferred to the Military Personnel Flight and served in the Customer Service Section. In August 1998, CMSgt Freeman was hired into the Active Guard/Reserve (AGR) Program as the Education and Training Manager for the 188th Mission Support Flight. She served in that capacity until March 1999, when she became Chief of Personnel Employments for the 188th Fighter Wing. On September 11, 2004, CMSgt Freeman was promoted to Chief Master Sergeant (CMSgt) and became the first African American Female in the history of the 188th Fighter Wing promoted to Chief Master Sergeant.

During her military career, CMSgt Freeman attended several military schools to including the U.S. Air Force Noncommissioned Officer Academy and the U.S. Air Force Senior Noncommissioned Officer Academy. In 1999, CMSgt Freeman was named the 188th Fighter Wing's Outstanding Active Guard/Reserve Employee of the Year and the Arkansas Air National Guard's Active Guard/Reserve Employee of the Year. CMSgt Freeman retired from the 188th Fighter Wing on March 31, 2012, with nearly 30 years of distinguished military service.

After retiring from the military, CMSgt Freeman taught in various schools in the Fort Smith community, however, she found her teaching home at Tilles Elementary School. CMSgt Freeman loved spending time with her family and teaching children. Sadly, she passed away in April 2023 surrounded by her family members.

First Sergeant Eugene Fultz

First African American First Sergeant
Company B, 212th Signal Battalion
Arkansas Army National Guard

First Sergeant (1SG) Eugene L. Fultz is the first African American First Sergeant of Company B, 212th Signal Battalion in Benton, Arkansas. He served in the U.S. Armed Forces for more than 22 years. At the age of 18, 1SG Fultz got married and joined the U.S. Navy, serving four years on active duty.

He joined the Arkansas Army National Guard as a Specialist in 1975 and was assigned to Headquarters and Headquarters Company, 212th Signal Battalion, North Little Rock. 1SG Fultz had no real military career goals set when he enlisted in the Army National Guard. After being a member of HHC 212th Signal Battalion for two years, he took advantage of the career opportunities within his military occupational specialty (MOS). 1SG Fultz soon progressed to the rank of Staff Sergeant.

In 1989, the 212th Signal Battalion was the first National Guard Signal Battalion, nationwide, to receive the Mobile Subscriber Equipment (MSE). This equipment was the Army's equivalent to what is commonly known today as the cellular telephone system. 1SG Fultz transferred to Company D, 212th Signal Battalion where he could excel in training himself, as well as others on this state-of-the-art communications equipment. He advanced to eventually become a team chief and continued to train his troops.

It was during this period of transition that he met 1SG Gregory Settles, who inspired him to set his goals higher and pursue them. During Operation Desert Storm, 1SG Settles become the first

African American Command Sergeant Major (CSM) of the 212th Signal Battalion and SSG Fultz was transferred to Company B, 212th Signal Battalion and promoted to Sergeant First Cass. In December 1992, SFC Fultz was promoted to First Sergeant of Company B, 212th Signal Battalion.

1SG Fultz's military education includes the Primary Development Course, the Basic NCO Course, and the Advanced NCO Course. He earned numerous awards throughout his military career such as the Army Achievement Medal, Vietnam Service Medal, Armed Forces Reserve Medal, NCO Professional Development Ribbon, Army Service Ribbon, Republic of Vietnam Campaign Medal, Navy Meritorious Unit Commendation, Army Reserve Component Achievement Medal, National Defense Service Medal, and Marksmanship Badge. 1SG Fultz has a Bachelor's Degree in Social Science with a minor in Psychology from Arkansas Baptist College.

In 1995, 1SG Fultz and his family moved to Orlando, Florida from Little Rock, and in 1996, he and his wife established Greater Grace Outreach Ministries of Orlando, a street ministry. They set up a corporation, and began feeding, clothing, and praying for people on the streets. In April 2001, they sold their dream home in Orlando, left their jobs, and moved to Lake Wales, Florida to start a cross cultural outreach ministry. He and his wife pastored for seven years in Lake Wales. As part of their ministry, they started an after-school program catering to at least 125 neighborhood children. They are currently the CEO & CFO of Greater Grace Outreach Ministries of Florida, Inc. (501c3 certified) currently serving an average of 450 hot meals per month to hungry people in Lake Wales, and Haines City. In addition to his ministry, 1SG Fultz served 4 terms as Mayor of the City of Lake Wales.

1SG Fultz retired from the Arkansas Army National Guard in 1995.

Command Chief Master Sergeant Normal Gilchrest

First African American Command Chief Master Sergeant

Frist African American Human Resource Advisor Arkansas Air National Guard

Command Chief Master Sergeant (CCM) Normal Gilchrest is a 1971 graduate of Brinkley High School. He attended the University of Central Arkansas and Philander Smith College.

CCM Gilchrest served the United States Air Force on Active Duty from 1972 to 1976. He was a member of the Arkansas Air National Guard from 1980 to 2009. CCM Gilchrist served his state and country in various positions.

His managerial skills, attention to detail, and his focus on diversity development led him to be selected as the first black human resource advisor at the state headquarters. He was among the original class of 37 HRAs in 1992, and he spent 8 years in this position.

In 2000, CCM Gilchrest was appointed as Command Chief Master Sergeant for the State of Arkansas, the highest enlisted position in the Arkansas Air National Guard. Not only was he the first African American Command Chief Master Sergeant in the Arkansas Air National Guard, but he is also the longest running Command Chief Master Sergeant in the history of the Arkansas Air National Guard; he held this position for 9 years. In this position he worked directly for the Adjutant General of Arkansas and the Commander of the Arkansas Air National Guard overseeing the activity of over 2,000 members of the Arkansas Air National Guard. During this time, as an influential leader, promoted the "Can do anything you set your mind to" atmosphere. He promoted and illuminated the Arkansas Air National Guard, which was not well known throughout the state. Chief Gilchrest also led a very successful civilian career path.

His favorite accomplishment from his military career was having established the annual Enlisted Symposium, which was a two-day joint conference of the top three senior enlisted ranks for both the Air and Army to discuss key issues affecting the enlisted force.

CCM Gilchrest began his postal career in January 1977, at the Arkansas Processing and Distribution Center in Little Rock. During his civilian career he held various positions, including Acting Manager of Post Office Relations, Diversity Development Coordinator, Supervisor of Customer Services, and acting Labor Relations Specialist. He also served in various OTC assignments in Sweet Home, Dewitt, and Magnolia, Arkansas. CCM Gilchrest served as Postmaster in the Arkansas cities of Devall's Bluff, England, Brinkley, and Forrest City. While representing the Postal Service for the United Way, he was selected Executive of the Year. In November 2004, he was selected as Customer Service Ambassador for the Southwest Area. As a Postal Ambassador, he represented the Postal Service in training films, publications, forums, and numerous activities promoting and fostering a positive image and effective avenues of communication for employees and customers of the USPS. CCM Gilchrest retired from his civilian career in April 2009, and later retired from his military career in October of the same year.

In addition, CCM Gilchrest is a business partner in the Branscomb, Johnson and Gilchrest Funeral Home located in Brinkley, Arkansas. In 2012, he was appointed to the Arkansas State Burial Board by then Governor Mike Beebe and in 2013-2014 served as the board president. He has been serving as a high school and college basketball official since 1985 and has officiated numerous state and regional tournaments. CCM Gilchrest has also formerly served as the Arkansas Director/Regional Developer with the Combined Federal Campaign of Greater Arkansas. Command Chief Master Sergeant Gilchrest retired from military service in October 2009.

Lieutenant Colonel Phylinthia Givens

First African American Female Lieutenant Colonel

First African American Female Inspector General of Dispute Resolutions, 189th Airlift Wing

First African American Female Inspector General Officer 188th Air Wing Arkansas Air National Guard

Lieutenant Colonel (Lt. Col.) Phylinthia Givens was born and raised in Little Rock, Arkansas. She graduated from Little Rock Central High School in 1984 and earned a Bachelor of Business Administration degree from the University of Arkansas at Little Rock in January 1992. Lieutenant Colonel Givens graduated in May 2018 from Webster University, George Herbert Walker School of Business & Technology with a Masters of Arts Degree in Management and Leadership.

On November 11, 1986, Lt. Col. Givens enlisted in the Arkansas Air National Guard as a traditional Guardsman. She completed Basic Military Training at Lackland Air Force Base, Texas and attended Technical Training School at Sheppard AFB, TX. She graduated in July 1987.

Her first assignment was as a Financial Specialist in the 189th Airlift Wing, Arkansas Air National Guard at Little Rock Air Force Base, Arkansas. In June 1997, Lt. Col. Givens graduated from the Academy of Military Science in Knoxville, Tennessee., where she was commissioned as a 2nd Lieutenant in the Arkansas Air National

Guard, at this time she transitioned from a Financial Specialist to the Budget Officer in the Finance office. In February 2005, Lt. Col. Givens was assigned as the Chief Military Equal Opportunity (MEO) Officer for the 189th Airlift Wing. To obtain the Air Force Specialty Code for MEO, she attended the Consolidated Base Personnel Officer School at Keesler AFB, Mississippi and the Defense Equal Opportunity Management Institute at Patrick AFB, Florida.

In June 2011, Lt. Col. Givens was assigned to the position of Inspector General of Dispute Resolutions for the 189th Airlift Wing, Arkansas Air National Guard. She was the first African American Female Officer in the 189th Airlift Wing assigned to this position. While assigned to that position, Lt. Col. Givens completed the Inspector General Course in Alexandria, Virginia. In August 2011, Lt. Col. Givens was promoted to Lieutenant Colonel. She became the first African American Female Officer in the Arkansas Air National Guard to obtain that rank.

In June 2017, Lt. Col. Givens was assigned as the Wing Inspector General at the 188th Air Wing, Arkansas Air National Guard in Fort Smith. She was the first African American Female Officer assigned to this position in the 188th Air Wing. In 2020, she was assigned to the Strategic Plans and Programming Office for Air Force at Joint Forces Arkansas Headquarters, Camp Joseph T. Robinson. In January 2022, Lt. Col. Givens was assigned as the Air Detachment Commander for the National Guard Marksmanship Unit at Camp Robinson.

Lt. Col. Givens' military education includes Squadron Officer School, Air Command and Staff College, and the U.S. Air Force Air War College.

Lieutenant Colonel Sharetta Glover

First African American Female Commander 39th Brigade Support Battalion, 39th Infantry Brigade

First African American Female Deputy Commander, 61st Civil Support Team Arkansas Army National Guard

Lieutenant Colonel (LTC) Sharetta Glover was born in Camden, Arkansas. She graduated from Camden Fairview High School in 2000. LTC Glover graduated with a Bachelor of Science Degree in Biology and a Minor concentration in Chemistry and Military Science from Henderson State University in 2004. She completed her Master's Degree in Public Health from the American Military University in 2017.

LTC Glover began her military career by enlisting in the Arkansas Army National Guard in July 2002, in Company A, 212th Signal Battalion, Arkansas Army National Guard. In August of 2002, she became a Reserve Officers' Training Corps (ROTC) Simultaneous Membership Program (SMP) Cadet at the Henderson State University and Ouachita Baptist University ROTC program. LTC Glover received her commission to Second Lieutenant as an Army Medical Department (AMEDD) Officer upon graduation.

LTC Glover completed the AMEDD Basic Officer Leadership Course in 2005, and the AMEDD Captain's Career Course in 2008. She attended the Human Resources Management Qualification Course in October 2015, and the Intermediate Level Education

Course in December 2015. She completed the Advanced Operations Course in September 2018, the Support Operations Course in November 2019, and the Medical Strategic Leader's Course in 2022.

LTC Glover has served in a variety of assignments throughout her career. She served as an Operations Officer at the Arkansas Army National Guard Medical Readiness Detachment and later became the unit commander for Arkansas Medical Readiness Detachment before joining the Active Guard/Reserve (AGR) program as the Medical Operations Officer for the 61st Civil Support Team (CST). In 2010, she became the Science Officer for the 61st CST and in 2014 she became the 87th Troop Command Brigade S1. In 2016, she was assigned as the commander of the 213th Medical Company (Area Support) while still filling the role as the Brigade S1 in a full-time capacity. In 2018, she returned to the 61st CST as the Deputy Commander. She was the first African American Female to serve as the Deputy Commander of the 61st Civil Support Team. LTC Glover served as the Personnel Services Branch Chief for the Deputy Chief of Staff- Personnel from June 2020 until June 2021. Her current full-time assignment is the Deputy State Surgeon at the Arkansas Medical Readiness Detachment. As the Deputy State Surgeon, she works with the State Surgeon to manage the medical readiness for all Soldiers in the Arkansas Army National Guard. On July 20, 2023, LTC Glover assumed Command of the 39th Brigade Support Battalion. She is the first African American Female to command a Battalion in the history of the 39th Infantry Brigade.

LTC Glover is a Past President and former legislative chair of the National Guard Association of Arkansas (NGAA). She is a lifetime member of the NGAA and National Guard Association of the United States. Additionally, LTC Glover is a lifetime auxiliary member of the Enlisted Association of Arkansas National Guard and a member of Association of United States Army. She currently serves as the Treasurer of the Arkansas National Guard Museum Foundation. She is also a member of the Governor's Challenge Team to prevent suicide among service members, veterans, and their families.

LTC Glover's awards and decorations include the Meritorious Service Medal (4th Award), Army Commendation Medal (2nd Award), Army Achievement Medal (5th Award), Army Reserve Component Achievement Medal, National Defense Service Medal, Global War on Terrorism Medal, Armed Forces Reserve Medal, Army Service Ribbon, Arkansas Service Ribbon (4th Award), Arkansas Emergency Service Ribbon, Tennessee National Guard Commendation Medal, and the Texas Adjutant General Individual Award.

Chief Warrant Officer Three Cassandra Green

First African American Female Warrant Officer 39th Infantry Brigade

First African American Female Warrant Officer Equal Opportunity Advisor Arkansas Army National Guard

Chief Warrant Officer Three (CW3) Cassandra Green was born in Altheimer, Arkansas. She graduated Salutatorian from Altheimer-Sherril High School in 1988. After high school, she attended the University of Central Arkansas in Conway, Arkansas where she graduated with a Bachelor of Science Degree in Psychology, and a minor concertation in Sociology in 1994.

CW3 Green began her military career in August 1995 by enlisting into the 39th Infantry Brigade, Arkansas Army National Guard as a Private First Class. In March 1996, she attended Basic Combat Training at Fort Leonard Wood, Missouri and continued Advanced Individual Training at Fort Jackson, South Carolina. CW3 Green decided to make a career in the Arkansas Army National Guard. In 1998, the Company Personnel Sergeant Active Guard Reserve (AGR) position was available; she applied for and was hired with the rank of Sergeant at Headquarters and Headquarters Company, 39th Infantry Brigade.

CW3 Green went on to serve in a variety of assignments during her enlisted career. She served as Personnel Admin Specialist, Training Noncommissioned Officer (NCO) and Senior Personnel Sergeant while assigned to the 39th Infantry Brigade. Later she transferred to

Joint Force Headquarters, Camp Robinson, North Little Rock, Arkansas as the Senior Personnel Sergeant.

CW3 Green was commissioned as Warrant Officer One (WO1) on September 18, 2009, and reassigned to the 39th Infantry Brigade as the Military Personnel Technician. CW3 Green was the First African American Female Warrant Officer in the history of the 39th Infantry Brigade. She served in that capacity from 2009 to 2014. In July 2014, she was reassigned to Joint Force Headquarters at Camp Robinson, North Little Rock as the State Equal Employment Manager. CW3 Green was the first African American Female Warrant Officer assigned as the State Equal Employment Manager for the Arkansas Army National Guard.

Her professional military training includes the Personnel Administrative Specialist Course, Basic Noncommissioned Officer Course Phase I and Phase II, Advanced Noncommissioned Officer Course Phase I and Phase II, Human Resource Warrant Officer Basic Course, and the Human Resource Warrant Officer Advance Course.

CW3 Green's awards and decorations include the Meritorious Service Medal (2nd Award), Army Commendation Medal, Army Good Conduct Medal (3rd Award), Army Reserve Component Achievement Medal, National Defense Service Medal W/ Bronze Service Star, Global War on Terrorism Medal, Armed Forces Service Medal, Non Commissioned Officer Professional Development Ribbon (3rd Award), Army Service Ribbon, Armed Forces Reserve Medal (2nd Award), Armed Forces Reserve Medal W/ M Device, Arkansas Service Ribbon (4th Award), Arkansas Emergency Service Ribbon (4th Award) and Arkansas Emergency Service Medal.

She retired on June 27, 2018, with over 22 years of distinguished military service. Currently, CW3 Green is employed as a Contractor for Joint Technology Solutions and serves as the Training Development and Support Technologist at the National Guard

Professional Education Center, Camp Robinson. CW3 Green is a member of Saint Mark Baptist Church in Little Rock. She is a Pulaski County Master Gardener, and she volunteers with community projects for the Ralph Bunche Neighborhood Association. She is also a member of Alpha Rho Omega Chapter, Alpha Kappa Alpha Sorority, Incorporated.

Technical Sergeant Julia Green

First African American Female to Enlist in the 189th Tactical Airlift Group Arkansas Air National Guard

Technical Sergeant (TSgt) Julia Green was the first African American Female to enlist in the Arkansas Air National Guard. She enlisted in the 189th Tactical Airlift Group on September 15, 1973. TSgt Green was also the first African American female hired as a full-time employee with the 189th Fighter Group as a supply technician.

Lieutenant Colonel Bridgette D. Griffin

First African American Female Bronze Star Recipient Arkansas Air National Guard

Lieutenant Colonel (Lt. Col.) Bridgette Delaine Scott Griffin graduated as Salutatorian from Blevins High School in May 1989. She received a Bachelor Degree of Business Administration Management from Henderson State University in 1996, Bachelor of Science in Nursing from Midwestern State University in 2008 and a Master Degree of Military Operational Art and Science from Air University in 2018. Since retirement Lt. Col. Griffin has earned her certification in Information Technology and is currently enrolled in the DeVry University Medical Billing and Coding program.

Her stellar military career started in December 1992, when she enlisted as an Airman First Class with the 188th Fighter Wing, Arkansas Air National Guard in Fort Smith, Arkansas. She attended basic training at Lackland Air Force Base, Texas and Technical School at Sheppard AFB, Wichita Falls, Texas where she excelled and achieved the red rope, the highest level a Tech School student leader can obtain. After training, Lt. Col. Griffin returned to the 188th Medical Group where she served as a Medical Service Specialist. In March 1998, Lt. Col. Griffin crossed trained and attended the training course for Clinical Laboratory Specialist at Sheppard AFB, Wichita Falls, Texas. In June 2005, Lt. Col. Griffin was pinned Second Lieutenant. She was enrolled in nursing school at Midwestern State University and working as the Assistant Manager of a Marriot Hotel chain. She was activated on orders during Hurricane Katrina and left her civilian life to become the Officer in Charge of Patient Administration during the evacuation of Hurricane Katrina victims to Fort Chaffee, Fort Smith, Arkansas.

In May 2006, Lt. Col. Griffin attended the Health Service Administration Course and was assigned as the 188th Medical Group, Medical Readiness Officer. In June 2010, she deployed to Bagram Airfield, Afghanistan where she was assigned to Task Force MED-East and 455th Expeditionary Medical Group, Craig Joint Theatre Hospital as the Air Force Commander and Army Staff Executive Officer and Public Affairs Representative. After four weeks, she was asked by the commander to stay in the position for one year versus the traditional six months for Air Force members. She was the point of contact for all government and foreign agencies congressional delegation, and distinguished visitors. In December 2010, she was hand selected by leadership to assist President Barack Obama present six Purple Heart Medals to Airmen and Soldiers. During this time, Lt. Col. Griffin was awarded the Bronze Star Medal becoming the first African American Female of the Arkansas Air National Guard to earn this medal.

In November 2013, she become the full-time 188th Medical Group Administrator where she had oversight of all members medical records as the Wing converted from a fighter unit to a remotely piloted aircraft unit. In June 2016, Lt. Col. Griffin accepted a position at the National Guard Bureau, Temple Army National Guard Readiness Center, Arlington, Virginia. She served as the Executive Officer to the Directorate of Domestic Operations. In June 2018, she returned to Arkansas and was assigned as the Deputy Director of Staff for two years at Camp Joseph T. Robinson, North Little Rock. In January 2020, she became the Executive Officer of the 189th Airlift Wing, Little Rock AFB, Jacksonville, Arkansas where she served during an unprecedented time of the nation amid a pandemic.

Lt. Col. Griffin's military education includes the Medical Service Specialist, Clinical Laboratory Specialist, Medical Laboratory Technician, Airman Leadership School, Reserve Commissioned Officer Training, Health Service Administration Course, Medical Readiness Officer Course, Squadron Officer School, and Air Command and Staff Course.

Her awards and decorations include the Bronze Star Medal, Defense Meritorious Service Medal, Meritorious Service Medal, Air Force Commendation Medal, Air Force Achievement Medal, National Defense Service Medal, Afghanistan Campaign Medal, Global War on Terrorism Expeditionary Medal, Global War on Terrorism Service Medal, Air Force Overseas Ribbon, Air Force Longevity Service and Armed Forces Reserve Medal. In 2014, Lt. Col. Griffin earned the NAACP Roy Wilkins Renowned Service Award.

Lt. Col. Griffin retired in January 2023, after 30 years of service. She enjoys spending time with her husband of three years Jonathan Griffin in their home in Missouri City, Texas. Lt. Col. Griffin travels back to Arkansas regularly to take care of her parents, Bennie and Sally Scott, ensuring their appointments are up to date and taken care of. She volunteers with Harris County Justice of the Peace Judge Wanda Adams Eviction Court as one of their resource advocates. She also finds time to substitute teach with Fort Bend Independent School District. She is a Lifetime Member of NGAA and Lifetime Associate of EANGUS. Lt. Col. Griffin is a member of New Faith Church in Houston, Texas.

Colonel Marcus R. Hatley

First African American
61st Civil Support Team
Commander

First African American
Counterdrug Coordinator
Arkansas Army National
Guard

Colonel (COL) Marcus R. Hatley was born in Prescott, Arkansas. He is a 1979 graduate of Gurdon High School. COL Hatley received Bachelor's Degrees from the University of Arkansas Dale Bumpers School of Agriculture and Excelsior College. He also received a Master's Degree in Strategic Studies from the U.S. Army War College.

COL Hatley received his commission as a Second Lieutenant, U.S. Army Chemical Corps in 1985 at the University of Arkansas in Fayetteville. He served continuously in various staff and command assignments culminating as the Arkansas National Guard Counterdrug Program Coordinator from June 2011 until May 2015. In 2011, COL Hatley became the First African American in the Arkansas National Guard to serve as the Counterdrug Program Coordinator. On June 5, 2000, COL Hatley was assigned as Deputy Commander of the 61st Civil Support Detachment, Arkansas National Guard. On May 1, 2005, COL Hatley was appointed as Commander of the 61st Civil Support Detachment, Arkansas National Guard. COL Hatley was the First African American in the Arkansas National Guard assigned to this position. On October 14, 2009, he served as Deputy J3, Arkansas National Guard.

COL Hatley's other assignments included but not limited to Cannon Crew Chief, Battalion CBRN NCO, Brigade Chemical Officer, 142nd Field Artillery Brigade during Operation Desert Storm Desert Shield; Service Battery Commander 2/142nd Field Artillery Battalion; Mobilization Officer, Arkansas Army National Guard; Executive Officer 87th Troop Command.

On November 15, 2015, COL Hatley reverted to an enlisted soldier to continue his military career as a Cannon Crew Chief, HHB 142nd FA BDE and later transferred to the 436th Chemical Company, Texas National Guard and deployed to the Horn of Africa with 1/141st Infantry Regiment, San Antonio Texas. COL Hatley retired November 19, 2019, after serving more than 34 years in the National Guard.

COL Hatley's certifications include but not limited to Criminal Analyst, HAZMAT Technician First Responder, OSHA Confined Space, OSHA Environmental Sampling, Installation Emergency Manager, FEMA Advanced Incident Command and General Staff, Joint Substance Abuse Prevention.

His military education includes the Army War College, Command and General Staff Course, Combined Arms Services Staff Course CAS3, Field Artillery Officer's Advanced Course, Chemical Officer's Basic Course, Defense Nuclear Weapons Course, Technical Escort Course, CBRN Joint Senior Leaders Course, CBRN Installation Emergency Management Course, CBRN Advanced Leaders Course.

COL Hatley received several medals and awards. Some of his decorations include Legion of Merit, Bronze Star Medal, Meritorious Service Medal, Army Commendation Medal, Army Achievement Medal, Armed Forces Reserve Ribbon, Armed Forces Service Medal, National Defense Medal, Army Reserve Components Achievement Medal, Overseas Service Ribbon, Saudi

Medal, Liberation of Kuwait Medal, and the Global War on Terrorism Medal.

COL Hatley worked as the Senior Representative for Military and Veteran Affairs Office of the Arkansas Attorney General from April 2015 to April 2016 and August 2019 to December 2022. While serving in this position, he coordinated with local, County, State, and Federal partners to advocate on behalf of Active Military, Guardsmen, Veterans, and their families.

He is a Master Mason, St. Johns Lodge 329, State of Arkansas, active member and Past Vice Polemarch Little Rock, Alumni, Kappa Alpha Psi; a member of American Legion Post 74 and a VFW Life member.

First Sergeant Jeff Hayes

First African American to Enlist Arkansas Army National Guard

First Sergeant (1SG) Jeff Hayes was born in Sterlington, Louisiana. He later relocated to Little Rock, Arkansas. He received a Bachelor of Arts Degree in English from Arkansas Baptist College in 1958.

He enlisted in the United States Army on April 27, 1951, and served until April 23, 1953. 1SG Hayes joined the United States Army Reserves on April 24, 1953, and remained until December 27, 1964. On December 28, 1964, 1SG Hayes enlisted in to the 148th Evacuation Hospital, Arkansas Army National Guard. He was the first African American to enlist in the Arkansas Army National Guard since reconstruction. His Military Occupation Specialties include 11B5M, Infantryman and 91B50, Medical Specialist. His duty assignments include Light Weapons Infantryman, Operating Room NCO, Chief Operating Room NCO, and First Sergeant, 148th Evacuation Hospital. In October 1986, Hayes was named the Deputy Commander and First Sergeant of the National Guard Battleskills Training Unit at Camp Robinson, North Little Rock.

1SG Hayes has received numerous awards, citations, and medals to include the Combat Infantry Badge, Vietnam Service Medal, Korean Service Medal, Armed Force Reserves Medal, Army Commendation Medal, Army Good Conduct Medal, National Defense Service Medal, NCO Professional Development Ribbon, Army Commendation Service Ribbon, Arkansas Commendation Medal, and the Arkansas Service Medal. In addition to his awards, citations, and medals, 1SG Hayes completed the AMEDD Medical Course, Arkansas National Guard Noncommissioned Officer Academy, and the U.S. Army Sergeant Major Academy's First Sergeant Course. First Sergeant Jeff Hayes retired on August 9, 1991, with over 40 years of military service.

Chief Warrant Officer Five Pamela Huff

First African American Female Chief Warrant Officer Five Arkansas Army National Guard

Chief Warrant Officer Five (CW5) Pamela Huff was born in Little Rock, and graduated from Hall High School in 1975, received a Bachelor's Degree in Organizational Management from John Brown University, and a Master of Arts degree in Human Resources Development.

She enlisted in the Arkansas Army National Guard (AR ARNG) in 1975 as a private (PV1). Throughout her career, she served in a variety of assignments. Her first duty assignment was with the 204th Dental Detachment, where she received the Humanitarian Service Medal for the Fort Chaffee Cuban Relocation Operation. She continued her assignments as a Personnel Clerk in the 39th Infantry Brigade, State Area Command (STARC) Arkansas Military Academy as an Admin Supply Clerk and Training Technician. She was the first African American female NCO Instructor at the Arkansas Military Academy. Her next assignment was with the 119th Personnel Service Company where she made a major decision to become a Warrant Officer. In 1990, she became a Warrant Officer and in 1991 was Mobilized with the 119th Personnel Service Company to replace Alpha Battery, Headquarters as the Personnel Records Chief and the OIC of the Mobilization Out-processing Center at Fort Sill, Oklahoma, mobilizing over 4,000 soldiers both active and reserve component. While there she received the Army Commendation Medal.

Chief Huff continued her military career and was promoted to Chief Warrant Officer Five in 2010, becoming the first African American

Female CW5 for the Arkansas Army National Guard. CW5 Huff's military awards include the MSM, ACM, AAM, ARCAM (11), NDSM (2), HSM, AFRM (4), AFRM with "M" Device, NCOPD (3), and the ASR. Chief Huff's State awards include the Arkansas Commendation Medal, Arkansas Federal Service Ribbon, and Arkansas Service Ribbon (7). Chief Huff retired from the Arkansas Army National Guard in 2017.

During Chief Huff's military career, she also became a full-time Federal Technician working for the AR ARNG in 1983. CW5 Huff moved up the ladder during her Federal Technician tenure from a GS-4 to a GS-13 where she retired in as the ARNG's Supervisor/Director over the Internal Review's Audit Division.

After retiring, Chief Huff returned in 2018 to work for the Arkansas Army National Guard as a Civilian Contractor as the Suicide Prevention Program Manager and Alcohol/Drug Coordinator.

Colonel Erica L. (Johnson) Ingram

First African American Female Battalion Commander

First African American Female Colonel

First African American Female Installation Commander Arkansas Army National Guard

Colonel (COL) Ingram was born in Wilmar, Arkansas, and is a 1990 graduate of Wilmar High School. She graduated from the University of Arkansas at Pine Bluff in May 1995, where she completed the four-year Army ROTC Scholarship program. She received her degree in Business Management with a minor in Administration. COL Ingram received her commission as a Second Lieutenant in the United States Army on August 15, 1995. While serving on Active Duty she was assigned as the Warrior Brigade Assistant Personnel Officer, 5th Personnel Services Battalion Operations/Training Officer and Headquarters Detachment Commander as well as Amarillo Military Entrance Processing Station (MEPS) Test Control Officer and Operations Officer. After serving four and a half years on active duty, she joined the Arkansas Army National Guard November 11, 1999.

COL Ingram served as Camp Joseph T. Robinson Maneuver Training Center (RMTC) Installation Commander until October 2021. Her previous positions within the Arkansas Army National Guard include serving as the 212th Signal Battalion Training Officer, Battalion Administrative Officer, Battalion Personnel Officer, Battalion Operations Officer, 87th Troop Command Brigade Personnel Officer, Recruiting and Retention Command Officer Strength Manager and Executive Officer, DCSPER Personnel Services Branch Chief, Deputy G-1, ARNG G-1, Deputy State

Surgeon - Administrative Officer, 87th Troop Command Brigade Administrative Officer, and 871st Troop Command Battalion Commander.

COL Ingram's awards and decorations include the Legion of Merit with one Oak Leaf Cluster, Meritorious Service Medal with eight Oak Leaf Clusters, Joint Service Commendation Medal, Army Commendation Medal with one Oak Leaf Cluster, Army Achievement Medal, Army Reserve Components Achievement Medal, National Defense Service Medal, Army Service Ribbon, Global War on Terrorism Service Medal, Arkansas Emergency Service Ribbon, and Arkansas Service Ribbon.

COL Ingram is a life member of the National Guard Association of Arkansas (NGAA) and the National Guard Association of the United States (NGAUS) and former NGAA President. In addition, she is a lifetime member of American Legion Post 74 and Military Officers Association of America (MOAA). She is also a Greater Leadership of Little Rock program alumnus.

COL Ingram has had the honor and privilege to serve as first African American female Arkansas Army National Guard Battalion Commander (2014), first African American female National Guard Association of Arkansas (NGAA) president (2014-2015), the first African American female colonel (2018) in the Arkansas National Guard's 215-year history and first female Camp Robinson Post Installation Commander (2020). She is also a 2022 Arkansas King Kennedy Lifetime Achievement Award recipient.

COL Ingram retired February 1, 2022. She previously served as the Chief of Staff- Assistant Director of the State of Arkansas Department of Veteran Affairs. Erica currently serves as the Integrated Primary Prevention Specialist for the Arkansas National Guard.

Chief Master Sergeant Sandra R. Jackson

First African American Female Cyber Operations Manager, 189th Airlift Wing Arkansas Air National Guard

Chief Master Sergeant (CMSgt) Sandra R. Jackson is a native of Pine Bluff, Arkansas where she graduated with honors from Dollarway High School in May 1984. She received an Associate Degree in Information Management from the Community College of the Air Force in July 1995. CMSgt Jackson received a Bachelor's Degree in Management from Park College. In October 2005, she received dual Master's Degrees in Computer Information and Resource Management and in Human Resource Development from Webster University. In February 2013, CMSgt Jackson received another Associate Degree in Applied Science from the Community College of the Air Force.

Her military career began when she enlisted in the United States Army Reserve in May 1983 and served until June 1990. The following month, she enlisted in the 189th Airlift Wing, Arkansas Air National Guard. While in the Arkansas Air National Guard, she was assigned to the 189th Medical Squadron, 123rd Reconnaissance Technical Squadron, 189th Mission Support Squadron, 189th Mission Support Flight and the 189th Communications Flight.

In October 2008, CMSgt Jackson assumed the role of Chief Cyber Operations Manager and became the First African American Female to achieve this position. She was responsible for directing the planning, development, management, and enforcement of the 189th

Airlift Wing's local information technology (IT) and communications architecture. Additionally, her passion for health and fitness led her to serve as Team Captain for the Arkansas Air National Guard Susan G. Komen Race for the Cure. She has deployed in support of Operations Southern Watch, Enduring Freedom, and Iraqi Freedom.

CMSgt Jackson has completed numerous military courses to include the Noncommissioned Officer Preparatory Course in 1993 and the Noncommissioned Officer Academy in 2003. She has received numerous Army Reserve and Air National Guard decorations, awards, citations, and accolades, to include the Meritorious Service Medal with two devices and the Military Outstanding Volunteer Service Medal.

CMSgt Jackson enjoys sharing her personal knowledge, skills, and experience to help improve the lives of others by volunteering her services across the full spectrum of life in her community. She is an active member of the Greater New Travelers Rest Missionary Baptist Church and an influential member of the Order of Eastern Stars - Lodge #145 in Pine Bluff. She is a member of Delta Sigma Theta Sorority Incorporated, Pine Bluff Alumnae Chapter (SP14). In addition, she presently serves as the Southeast Area Chair of Enlisted Support of Guard Reserve (ESGR) and regularly serves as a volunteer Assistant Director and Beginning Leader for Women Run Arkansas. Formerly, she also served as a volunteer Troop 1103 Unit Commander of Training for Boys Scout of America, Saracen District, Quapaw Area Council.

She retired on December 31, 2014, after thirty-three and a half years of outstanding military service. Chief Jackson and her husband, Isaiah, have four children and twelve adorable grandchildren, plus one added to the "Crue." She loves to spend quality time with her family, often traveling domestically and abroad to fulfill all her grandchildren's bucket lists.

Master Sergeant
Teresa James

First African American Female
189th Airlift Wing Base
Records Manager

189th Airlift Wing
Privacy Act Manager

189th Airlift Wing Freedom of
Information Act Manager
Arkansas Air National Guard

Master Sergeant (MSgt) Teresa James was born in Conway, Arkansas. She grew up in Damascus, Arkansas and graduated from Guy-Perkins High School in May 1983. In May 2001, she received a Bachelor of Science Degree in Management from Park University. Additionally, she received Associate Degrees in Allied Science and Information Resource Management in 1987 and 1999, respectively. From 1989 to 2003, by correspondence, she completed the Non-Commission Officer Preparatory Military Course, the Non-Commission Officer Academy, and the USAF Senior NCO Academy.

MSgt James enlisted in the Arkansas Air National Guard in May 1987 and was assigned to the 189th Military Personnel Flight at Little Rock AFB. After completing Basic Training at Lackland AFB in San Antonio, Texas, and Technical Training School at Keesler AFB in Gulfport, Mississippi, she served as a Reenlistment and Separations Personnel Specialist. She performed in this role for three years and then seized an opportunity to cross-train into an Information Management Specialist position with the 189th Maintenance Group until 1995.

In May 1995, MSgt James returned to the 189th Mission Support Group and assumed the role of the Base Records Manager for the 189th Airlift Wing where she became the first African American Female to hold this position. In addition, she served as the first African American Female Privacy Act Manager and Freedom of Information Act Manager. In May 2014, her position converted to a Knowledge Operation Management role.

MSgt James completed three tours overseas in support of several contingency operations. In July 2019-January 2020, while deployed to Kuwait in support of Operation Spartan Shield, she was coined by her squadron commander for her significant achievements and for her outstanding job performances.

Over the course of her military career, MSgt James volunteered as a mentor and counselor for the Annual Minuteman Youth Summer Camp held at Camp Joseph. T. Robinson, North Little Rock.

On October 3, 2021, MSgt James retired after faithfully serving 34 years of military service. She has received numerous Air National Guard and state awards, decorations, citations, and accolades, most notably, the Meritorious Service Medal with an Oak Leaf Cluster.

MSgt James is enjoying her retirement with her family. She is actively volunteering in her church and local community, and presently serving as a volunteer Outreach Director for the Arkansas Employer Support of the Guard and Reserve based at Camp J.T. Robinson.

Lieutenant Colonel Danny Johnson

First African American Helicopter Pilot

First African American Instructor Pilot Arkansas Army National Guard

Lieutenant Colonel (LTC) Danny Johnson was raised in Pine Bluff, Arkansas. He attended St. Peters Catholic School, Merrill Junior and Senior High School and Arkansas Mechanical and Normal (AM&N), currently University of Arkansas at Pine Bluff.

LTC Johnson entered the U.S. Army in January 1967 and attended the Officer Candidate Officer (OCS) School at Fort Benning, Georgia. He was commissioned a Second Lieutenant in the Infantry Branch on December 12, 1967. LTC Johnson was stationed at Fort Waters, Texas and Hunter Army Airfield in Savannah, Georgia. From May 1969 to May 1970, LTC Johnson served a tour in the Republic of Vietnam. He served as an Instructor Pilot at Fort Rucker, Alabama for three years prior to his attendance in the Infantry Officer Advanced Course and Airborne and Ranger School.

LTC Johnson served a tour of duty in the Republic of Korea as Commander of Company B, 38th Infantry Battalion. After leaving active duty, he joined the newly formed 936th Aviation Company, Arkansas Army National Guard in January 1976. LTC Johnson was the first African American helicopter pilot in the Arkansas National Guard.

In 1978, LTC Johnson transferred to the Washington, D.C. Army National Guard. In 1980, LTC Johnson became a Full-Time National Guard employee at the National Guard Bureau in Arlington, Virginia. He was assigned as the Directorate of Plans and Training as the Training Administrator, and he subsequently served as the Plans, Operations, and Military Support Officer. In 1982, LTC

Johnson returned to the Arkansas Army National Guard and served as a Helicopter Instructor Pilot at the Army Aviation Support Facility. LTC Johnson was the first African American to serve as an Instructor Pilot in the Arkansas Army National Guard.

In addition to his many other distinctions, LTC Johnson is a Master Aviator. He has qualifications as a Ranger and Military Parachutist. His military awards include the Bronze Star Medal with Oak Leaf Cluster, The Army Commendation Medal with "V" device (for valor) and Oak Leaf Cluster and 25 awards of the Air Medal.

Colonel Julius M. Johnson

Developed and Directed the First Tactical IT Academy Arkansas Army National Guard

First African American Commander of the Information Technology Training Center at the National Guard Professional Education Center

Colonel (COL) Julius M. Johnson was born in Chicago, Illinois. As a child, he grew up in Little Rock, Arkansas and attended the historic Little Rock Central High School and graduated in May 1983. After high school, COL Johnson attended the University of Central Arkansas in Conway and received a Bachelor's Degree in Business Administration and Computer Information Systems in 1990. He received a Master's Degree in Computer Information Systems from Webster University, St. Louis, Missouri in 1998. In 2002, COL Johnson received a Bachelor of Arts Degree in Biblical Theology from Arkansas Baptist College, Little Rock.

While attending college at UCA, COL Johnson enlisted in Headquarters and Headquarters Company, 39th Infantry Brigade (Separate), Arkansas Army National Guard in 1985. He attended Basic Training at Fort Leonard Wood, Missouri in May 1986, and Advanced Individual Training at Fort. Jackson, South Carolina in August 1986. While assigned in the 39th Infantry Brigade, COL Johnson served as a 71L Admin Specialist. He was later reassigned to the 119th Personnel Service Company, as a 74F Computer Programmer. In 1992, COL Johnson entered the Arkansas Military Academy Officer Candidate School at Camp Robinson. He was commissioned as a Second Lieutenant in the Signal Corps on June 20, 1994.

As a Commissioned Officer, COL Johnson was assigned to Company C, 212th Signal Battalion (MSE), Pine Bluff, Arkansas as a Nodal Platoon Leader. He was reassigned to Company A, 212th Signal Battalion as a Nodal Platoon Leader and later served as the Company Executive Officer. In May 1999, he was assigned to HHC, 39th Infantry Brigade as the Information Operations Planner. COL Johnson served as Company Commander, Headquarters and Headquarters Company, 1st Battalion, 153rd Infantry, 39th Infantry Brigade in August 2001. In January 2004, COL Johnson was assigned to HHC, 39th Infantry Brigade and deployed with the 39th Infantry Brigade in support of Operation Iraq Freedom for 18 months. During the deployment, he was assigned as the Deputy S6 with 3rd Brigade, 1st Calvary Division where he successfully managed Army tactical networks for over 900 users.

After the 39th Infantry Brigade's redeployment in January 2005, COL Johnson was assigned as the 39th Infantry Brigade's S6. While serving as the Brigade S6 in 2006, COL Johnson installed and fully connected the tactical networks of all five battalions and the Brigade HQs in a field environment as a complete Network Brigade for first time in history of the Brigade. Additionally, he was deployed as the Joint Task Force Communications Officer (J6) for Joint Task Force Razorback, Arkansas National Guard while supporting recovery and stability operations for Hurricane Katrina in Louisiana. He masterfully synchronized digital communications in his area of operations and worked with telecommunication companies at the federal, national, and commercial levels along with communications units from the Air Force, Army, Navy, and Coast Guard. Also in 2006, COL Johnson established and served as the director of the First Tactical IT Academy for the Arkansas Army National Guard. He was responsible for developing and providing Tactical IT training for the three Major Subordinate Commands (Infantry, Artillery and Aviation) of the Arkansas Army National Guard.

In 2007, the National Guard Bureau requested COL Johnson to leverage his leadership and training talents. He served as a Strategic Planner, writing the Strategic Plan for the Force Management Division of the National Guard Bureau. As a Force Manager, he successfully managed the structure of 94 ARNG Signal organizations with over 9,000 personnel spaces across 45 States and Territories, comprising 17% of the total Army Signal force structure. His efforts resulted in the reconsolidation of signal units that had been scattered with inadequate resourcing and training. By returning these units to the control of Signal commanders, enabled the States to effectively employ their capabilities in response to homeland security events and natural disasters. His vision and leadership created the first National Guard Signal Conference in 2008. This landmark event brought Signal units together from across the United States to organize, coordinate, and share ideas. This national conference continues today including both National Guard and Army Reserve Signal communities from across the country.

In 2012, he served as the first African American Commander of the Information Technology Training Center at the ARNG Professional Education Center (PEC). In this capacity, he was responsible for managing contracts of over $4.4M worth of building, IT, and sensitive equipment. He was responsible for the training and certification of IT, Cybersecurity, and Cyberspace operation professionals across the 54 states and territories of the National Guard. His dedication, drive, and training vision allowed his training center to become the first training center in the twelve-year history of PEC to achieve 100% TRADOC's first time full accreditation.

In 2013, COL Johnson created the first National Guard Cyber Exercise called "Cyber Shield" which continues today, hosting over 800 IT and cyber participants. He also developed a validation-training program to train and validate the first Army National Guard Cyber Protection Team. In 2014, COL Johnson served as the Operations Chief for the Capabilities, Development, Integration

Directorate at the United States Army Cyber Center of Excellence, Fort Gordon, Georgia. He was responsible for developing the concept and execution plan of the first CCoE Exercise called "Cyber Quest," an event that continues today as an exercise in cyberspace innovation that brings industry, education and military enterprise together providing expeditionary solutions to Army Signal and Cyber problems.

COL Johnson was promoted to the rank of Colonel in 2018 and was selected to serve as the Senior Advisor to the FORSCOM CIO/G6 General at Fort Bragg, North Carolina. There, he developed and led the Army Digital Integration proof of concept where he conducted four National Army Digital Integration Proof of Concept Exercises across the county which resulted in a reduction of time at the nine Mobilization Force Generation Installations improving mission command system readiness across the Army. COL Johnson served as the Army Cyber Command G3 Chief, Reserve Affairs Division from July 2020 to December 2022. His most recent noteworthy contributions are the writing of two key SOPs that provided techniques, processes, and tools to establish process improvement to deliver Reserve Component talent management to the command. He significantly improved unit relations between mobilized Reserve Component Cyber units and ARCYBER senior leadership enhancing the situational and operational awareness of Reserve Component civilian skills capabilities not achieved in the active component.

COL Johnson holds professional certifications in IT and Information Assurance; Lean Six Sigma Black Belt, Joint Cybersecurity Operations; Capability and Configuration Management; Strategic Leadership; and completed specialized certificate training in Project Management at Georgia Institute of Technology in Atlanta. Other military course completed includes Army Cyberspace Operation Planners Course, 1st IO Command School, Fort Belvoir, Virginia, Cyberspace 300 Course, Air Force Institute of Technology, Peterson

Air Force Base, Ohio, and the JPME II Joint Warfighting School, National Defense University, Norfolk, Virginia.

Among his many awards and decorations include the Arkansas Distinguished Service Medal and State Certificate of Appreciation awarded by the Governor of Arkansas; two Legion of Merit Service Medals, 4 Meritorious Service Medal (3OLC); 6 Army Commendation Medal (5OLC); 7 Army Achievement Medal, Army Reserve Component Achievement Medal (7OLC); National Defense Service Medal with Bronze Star; Global War on Terrorism Service and Expeditionary Medals; Humanitarian Service Medal; Armed Forces Reserve Medal with "M" Device and Silver Hour Glass; Combat Action Badge; and Army Staff Identification Badge. He is a member of the Signal Corps Regimental Association, the Armed Forces Communications and Electronic Association, Alpha Kappa Psi, National Professional Business Fraternity and Kappa Lambda Chi, Military Fraternity, Incorporated.

As a leader in the church community, COL Johnson has been a licensed and ordained minister for over 30 years and he currently serves as an Associate Minister at Beulah Grove Baptist Church in Atlanta, Georgia.

He is currently employed as a Joint Cyberspace Operations Planner II for the U.S. Cyber Command, Exigent Services LLC, Fort Meade, Maryland. COL Johnson retired from the Army on November 30, 2022, with over 37 years of distinguished military service to this great Nation.

Brigadier General William J. Johnson, Jr.

First African American General

First African American Deputy Adjutant General Arkansas Army National Guard

Brigadier General (BG) Johnson was born in Pulaski County, Arkansas. He graduated from Scipio A. Jones High School. He earned a Bachelor of Arts Degree in Organizational Management from Philander Smith College, and Master's in Strategic Studies from the United States Army War College in 2001.

BG Johnson enlisted into Headquarters, 212th Signal Battalion, Arkansas Army National Guard in 1976. He served in the Arkansas National Guard for more than 36 years in various leadership capacities. On January 1, 2008, BG Johnson was promoted to Brigadier General and assumed duties as Deputy Adjutant General, Arkansas National Guard. As the Deputy Adjutant General, he served as the full-time chief advisor and principal assistant to The Adjutant General and provided leadership to over 10,000 Army Soldiers and Airmen. Additionally, General Johnson served as one of the organization's strategic leaders who worked diligently to help guide the achievement of the Adjutant General's vision for the Arkansas National Guard. BG Johnson also oversaw the preparedness for domestic operations and homeland security.

BG Johnson is the first African American General in the history of the Arkansas National Guard and he was inducted into the Arkansas Black Hall of Fame in 2010 and the Arkansas National Guard OCS Hall of Fame in 2013.

General Johnson served as an enlisted Soldier in the Arkansas National Guard for five years prior to attending the Arkansas National Guard's Officer Candidate School at Camp Joseph T. Robinson, Arkansas, where he received his commission. General Johnson's military experience includes Platoon Leader, Company D, 212th Signal Battalion, TAC Officer, Arkansas Military Academy Officer Candidate School, Tactical Intel Officer, 1-153rd Infantry Battalion, 39th Infantry Brigade, Commander, Co B, 1-153rd Infantry Battalion, 39th Infantry Brigade, Aide-de-Camp to the Adjutant General, S1, 1-153rd Infantry Battalion, 39th Infantry Brigade, Battalion Executive Officer, 1st Battalion, 153rd Infantry, 39th Infantry Brigade; Personnel Officer, STARC(-), Chief Operations Officer, Marksmanship Training Unit, Deputy Military Personnel Director, STARC (-), Commander, 212th Signal Battalion and Chief of Staff, Arkansas Army National Guard. His most recent assignment was Director, Joint Staff, Arkansas Joint Force Headquarters.

BG Johnson is a member of the Michael Vann Johnson Post 74 American Legion, a member of the National Guard Association of Arkansas and he is past secretary for the 100 Black Men of Greater Little Rock Chapter, Inc. He is a Life Member of the U.S. War College Alumni Association and the Arkansas OCS Hall of Fame Association Executive Secretary. He is a member of Leadership Greater Little Rock Alumni. BG Johnson is also a member of Mu Beta Sigma Chapter, Phi Beta Sigma Fraternity, Incorporated and a member of The Worship Center in North Little Rock. Brigadier General Johnson retired from the military on December 31, 2012.

Colonel Walter L. Jones

First African American Commander
2nd Battalion, 233rd Regiment,
Regional Training Institute
Arkansas Army National Guard

Colonel (COL) Walter L. Jones was born on 8 July 1951, in Eudora, Arkansas. He graduated from G. C. Johns High School, Eudora in 1969. He received his Bachelor's Degree in construction engineering from the University of Arkansas at Little Rock. COL Jones has a Master of Art degree in Business from Webster University, and a Master's in Strategic Studies from the United States Army War College.

COL Jones entered military service in May 1971 as a draftee. After serving nineteen months (fourteen in Korea with 2nd Infantry Division), he received an honorable discharge in December 1972. COL Jones enlisted in to the 216th Medical Company, Arkansas Army National Guard in September 1977. Later, he entered the Arkansas Military Academy Officer Candidate School and received his commission as 2nd Lieutenant in March 1981.

As a member of the Arkansas Army National Guard, COL Jones served distinctively in various military assignments to include Platoon Leader, 216th Medical Company, Detachment Commander, Headquarters Detachment, 125th Medical Battalion, Commander, 216th Medical Company, S1, 125th Medical Battalion, S3, 125th Medical Battalion, Admin/Log Officer, 25th Rear Area Operations Center, Executive Officer, 125th Medical Battalion, Plans and Operations Officer, Marksmanship Training Unit, Safety Officer and S3/Executive Officer, Headquarters, 233rd Regiment Regional Training Institute.

COL Jones served as Commander, 2nd Battalion, 233rd Regional Training Institute from March 2002 to August 2004. He was the first African American to serve as Battalion Commander in the 233rd Regional Training Institute. He later served as Deputy Chief of Staff Logistics, Joint Forces Headquarters and culminated his career as Post Commander, Camp Robinson Maneuver Training Center.

COL Jones received the following awards and decorations: Legion of Merit, Meritorious Service Medal, with Oak Leaf Cluster, Army Commendation Medal, with Oak Leaf Clusters, Army Achievement Medal, Army Service Ribbon, National Defense Service Ribbon, Army Forces Expeditionary Medal (Korea), Korean Defense Service Medal, Army Reserve Component Achievement Medal, and the Army Physical Fitness Badge.

COL Jones' military education includes AMEDD Office Basic Course, AMEDD Officer Advance Course, Ordnance Officer Advance Course, Engineer Officer Advance Course, Combined Arms and Service Staff School, Command and General Staff Officer Course, National Defense Course, and the United States Army War College. COL Jones retired on March 31, 2011, with over 36 years of military service.

Master Sergeant
Margarett Amos (Linton)

First African American Female Assigned to the 172nd Maintenance Battalion

First African American Female Technician Hired Full-Time in the 142nd Field Artillery Brigade

First African American Female Hired in the Active Guard/Reserve Programs 142nd Field Artillery Brigade

First Female to Receive the Bronze Star Arkansas Army National Guard

Master Sergeant (MSG) Margarett "Margo" Linton was born in Simsboro, Louisiana. She attended Crawford High School and graduated from Arcadia High School, Arcadia, Louisiana. She received a Bachelor of Arts Degree in Business Management from Philander Smith College in 2002. MSG Linton is the only one of the 12 children in her family who received a college degree.

MSG Linton's remarkable military career started on September 12, 1973, when she joined the United States Marine Corps. She attended her Marine Corps Basic Training at Parris Island, South Carolina. After basic training, she was transferred to Camp Pendleton, California and worked in the Movement Corps Movement Coordination Center (MCMCC) as a Pay Transportation Clerk. MSG Linton was honorably discharged as a Sergeant (E5) from the U.S. Marine Corps on June 10, 1977. For her outstanding service in the Marine Corps, she received the Good Conduct Medal and a Letter of Appreciation.

Her career with the Arkansas Army National Guard began on September 12, 1978, when she enlisted into Detachment (Det) 1, 172nd Maintenance Company, Russellville. MSG Linton was the First African American Female assigned to Det 1, 172nd Maintenance Company. Her assignments included F-E System Repairman, Section Chief and Tank Turret Repairman. On March 1, 1983, she was reassigned to Headquarters and Headquarters Detachment, 217th Maintenance Battalion in Russellville as a Clerk Typist.

MSG Linton was hired as a Legal Clerk in the Arkansas Army National Guard Military Technician Program on March 1, 1983, and assigned to Headquarters and Headquarters Battery, 142nd Field Artillery Brigade, Fayetteville She was the first African American Female to work in a Full-Time status in the history of the 142nd Field Artillery Brigade. On January 1, 1984, MSG Linton was hired into the Active Guard/Reserve (AGR) Program. She was also the First African American Female hired in the AGR Program in the 142nd Field Artillery Brigade. While assigned to the 142nd Field Artillery Brigade, she worked as an Administrative, Supply and Training Specialist (AST), Legal Clerk and Senior Legal Noncommissioned Officer (NCO).

On September 20, 1990, MSG Linton deployed with the 142nd Field Artillery Brigade to Saudi Arabia in support of Operation Desert Shield/Operation Desert Storm. As a Sergeant First Class (SFC), she was the only female first-line leader during the deployment. MSG Linton has the honor of being the First Female in the Arkansas National Guard to receive the Bronze Star during Operation Desert Storm/Shield/Sabre.

On June 1, 1998, MSG Linton was transferred to the Arkansas Army National Guard Maneuver Training Center (ARARNG-MTC), Fort Chaffee, Arkansas. While assigned to ARARNG-MTC, she served as an Administration NCO and Range Scheduling NCO. On October 18, 1999, MSG Linton was assigned to Headquarters and Headquarter (-), 39th Infantry Brigade, Little Rock, and served as the Chief Legal NCO and Senior Administrative NCO for the 39th Infantry Brigade.

MSG Linton's professional military education includes 64C Vehicle Operator Course, Unit Administrators Course; Basic NCO Academy Course, Legal Specialist Course, Fort Benjamin Harrison, Indiana; Law for Legal Specialist Course, Judge Advocate General School, Charlottesville, Virginia; Primary Leadership Development Course, Camp Beauregard, Louisiana; Basic NCO Course, Fort Benjamin Harrison, Indiana; Automation Security Course, National Guard Professional Education Center, Camp Robinson, Arkansas; Field Artillery Combat Lifesaver Course, Fort Sill, Oklahoma; Advanced NCO Course, Fort Benjamin Harrison, Indiana; Personnel Services NCO Course, NGPEC and Equal Opportunity Advisor's Course, Camp Robinson; Equal Opportunity Advisor Reserve Component Course, Defense Equal Opportunity Management Institute, Patrick Air Force Base, Florida; and the Personnel Sergeant's Course, NGPEC, Camp Robinson.

Her awards, decorations and qualifications include the Bronze Star, Meritorious Service Medal (4th Award), Army Commendation Medal, Army Achievement Medal, Army Good Conduct Medal, Army Reserve Components Achievement Medal, Defense Service Medal, Kuwait Liberation Medal, Southwest Asia Service Medal, Armed Forces Reserve Medal, NCO Professional Development Ribbon, Army Service Ribbon, Sharpshooter Marksmanship Qualification Badge with Rifle Bar and the special skill identifier, "Q" for Equal Opportunity Advisor.

MSG Linton retired on September 30, 2002, with over 27 years of exceptional military service. She enjoys spending time with her husband, Harry Amos in their home in Kempner, Texas. She attends Christian House of Prayer Church (CHOP) where she serves as a member of the choir. She is a graduate of the church's Sonship School of the First Born and she volunteers her time by sewing robes for every new class and she sews robes for the 197 covenant churches that are located in Germany, Africa, and the United States. MSG Linton's hobbies are sewing and reading Christian fiction books.

Chief Warrant Four Barbara Lunon

First African American Female Personnel Branch Chief for the Deputy Chief of Staff-Personnel Arkansas Army National Guard

Chief Warrant Officer Four (CW4) Barbara Lunon was born in Little Rock, Arkansas. She is a 1975 graduate of Parkview High School in Little Rock, and in 1994, CW4 Lunon received her Bachelor of Arts Degree in Organization Management from Philander Smith College, which is now Philander Smith University, in Little Rock.

CW4 Lunon started her military journey on December 15, 1981, when she enlisted into the 204th Medical Detachment (Dental Service), Arkansas Army National Guard in North Little Rock. She completed Basic Combat Training and Advanced Individual Training at Fort Jackson, South Carolina in 1982. In 1987, she graduated from the Arkansas Military Academy Officer Candidate School (OCS) Class 30. Regulation prohibited her from accepting the officer commission because she was an enlisted technician which was not compatible. In 2002, CW4 Lunon entered the Warrant Officer Candidate Training Program at Fort Rucker, Alabama and on March 22, 2002, she was appointed as Warrant Officer One (WO1), 420A0 in the Adjutant General's Corps. CW4 Lunon at the age of 46 was the oldest candidate in her class, her perseverance and strong will gave her the strength to graduate. She helped pin the word and taught her class their "Hang That Hat" song, "We're Tracking."

While assigned to the 204th. Medical Detachment (Dental Service), CW4 Lunon served in a variety of positions such as Clerk Typist, Personnel Administrative Specialist and Chief Dental Facility Noncommissioned Officer. In 1997, she served as Senior Personnel Sergeant for Detachment 1, 87th Troop Command and later as Personnel Sergeant with Headquarters and Headquarters Service and Support Company, 1st Battalion, 114th Aviation Battalion in North Little Rock. As a Sergeant First Class (SFC), on December 4, 2000, CW4 Lunon was hired and assigned to Deputy Chief of Staff-Personnel (DCSPER) as a Military Personnel Technician. On March 27, 2002, CW4 Lunon was appointed and assigned to Joint Force Headquarters-Arkansas as a Human Resources Technician and Personnel Branch Chief, Joint Force Headquarters-Arkansas. She was the first African American Female assigned as the Personnel Branch Chief, in DCSPER. On October 4, 2009, CW4 Lunon was assigned to the State Education Office, and in 2013 assigned to the Arkansas Army National Guard Institute Support Unit as a Human Resources Technician. In 2015, she was assigned to the 77th Aviation Brigade as a Human Resources Technician.

She deployed in support of Operation Desert Storm and Operation Enduring Freedom/Spartan Shield. Her awards and decorations include the Legion of Merit, Meritorious Service Medal w/OLC, Army Commendation Medal with two Oak Leaf Cluster, Army Achievement Medal with one Oak Leaf Cluster, Army Reserve Component Achievement Medal with one Silver Oak Leaf Cluster and three Bronze Oak Leaf Clusters, National Defense Service Medal with a Bronze Star, Armed Forces Reserves Medal with gold hourglass and Mobilization Device, Noncommissioned Officers Professional Development Ribbon with Numeral 3, Army Service Ribbon, Overseas Service Ribbon, Arkansas Distinguished Service Medal, Arkansas Exceptional Service Medal, Arkansas Federal

Service Ribbon, Arkansas Emergency Service Ribbon, and Arkansas Recruiting Ribbon.

CW4 Lunon's military education includes the Human Resources Staff Course, Reserve Component General Officer Legal Orientation Course, Warrant Officer Staff Course Phase I, Warrant Officer Staff Officer Course Phase 2, Administrative Warrant Officer Advanced Course, U.S. Army Casualty Notification Training, Personnel Tech Warrant Officer Basic Course, Basic Noncommissioned Officer Course, Advance Noncommissioned Officer Course Phase 1 and 2, Unit Clerk Course, 75B Personnel Administrative Support Course, Primary Leadership Development Course, and the 71L Administrative Specialist Course.

CW4 Lunon volunteered numerous years with the Minuteman Youth Camp as a day counselor and night chaperone counselor. She also volunteered reading with the Arkansas READ Program at Amboy Elementary School, North Little Rock, and Baseline Academy, Little Rock. She was actively involved in the Camp Robinson Women's Group, the Camp Robinson "Voices of a Nation" Choir and the Black History Heritage Program. She also served as a member of the March Unit representing The National Guard of the United States in the Inauguration Parade of the 42nd President, William Jefferson "Bill" Clinton.

CW4 Lunon retired on September 30, 2017, with over 36 years of distinguished military service. After retirement CW4 Lunon continued to volunteer for the Arkansas Kids Read Literacy Program, On April 5, 2023, she received their Volunteer of the Year Award. She served as President of the Little Rock Alpha Gamma Chapter of Kappa Epsilon Psi Military Sorority, Incorporated for the last five years. Before the pandemic, the Alpha Gamma Chapter performed community service with Fishnet Ministry, preparing hot breakfast meals to serve homeless families in downtown Little Rock. The chapter also visits veterans' that reside at the Arkansas State Veterans Home in North Little Rock and volunteers at the

Arkansas Food Bank. She also volunteers with her Sorority with "My Vote is KEY," where she registers citizens to vote. She is an active member of the Little Rock Branch NAACP (6019-B). She has served as the Election Supervisor Chair, active At-Large Member on the Executive Board and is now currently serving as the first Vice President. She is a member of the Justice Now Coalition, Veterans of Foreign Wars Post 1316 (VFW), National Association for Black Veterans (NABVETS) Little Rock Chapter #0108, Ban the Box and Get out the Vote Campaign. As a member of the Women Veterans Freedom Sings USA-Trailblazer Songwriters Class, CW4 Lunon was able to tell her military story and a song was produced "Born to be A Soldier." Her vocalist is Ms. Hunter "Huntergril" Wolkonowski, who was one of the final two contestants on "American Idol." This was a great opportunity for women to come together via Zoom to write songs based on their military experiences.

She currently volunteers with her church in several ministries such as, Leading Ladies of Faith, Intercessory Prayer, Social Action Ministry (SAM) and the Youth Ministry at the 2nd Baptist Church, under the leadership of Senior Pastor, Dr., Maurice Watson, 1709 John Barrow, Little Rock. CW4 Lunon currently resides in Little Rock, with her husband, Darryl and they have three sons, 7 grandchildren, and 2 great grandchildren. Darry Lunon II, Charles Jones, and Roderick Lunon. Grandchildren, Raven Gregory-Haamid, (Son-in-Law Saudi Haamid), Veronica Johnson, Sana'a Lunon, Darryl Lunon III, Chardene' Jones, Lailiane Jones and Isaiah Jones. Great grandchildren; Camille Haamid and Tesla Howell.

Sergeant First Class Marilyn E. Matthews

First African American Unit Administrator 1122nd Transportation Company Arkansas Army National Guard

Sergeant First Class (SFC) Marilyn E. Matthews was born in Monticello, Arkansas. She attended Monticello High School and graduated from McKinley High School, St. Louis, Missouri in 1969. Upon graduating from High School, SFC Mattews studied at Fontbonne Women's College, St. Louis, State Community College, East St. Louis, Illinois and finally University of Arkansas at Monticello.

On June 8, 1982, SFC Matthews joined the 1122nd Transportation Company, Arkansas Army National Guard in Monticello. Her first assignment was Unit Clerk for the Company. In January 1983, she completed Basic Combat Training (BCT) at Fort Jackson, South Carolina, and Advanced Individual Training (AIT) in March 1983 at Fort Benjamin Harrison, Indiana.

On October 3, 1983, then, PFC Marilyn Matthews, was hired as the First African American Female to be employed as a Unit Administrator with the 1122nd Transportation Company, Arkansas Army National Guard. Shortly thereafter, the Unit Administrator's position titles were changed to Unit Clerks. She remained with the 1122nd Transportation Company until January 1988, and later transferred to the Department of Personnel Administration (DPA), STARC (-), Camp Robinson as a SIDPERS Data Analyst. Her military assignment was in Company A (Admin), 39th Infantry Brigade (Separate), Little Rock.

On September 12, 1989, SFC Matthews was transferred to the 119th Personnel Service Company, Camp Robinson and later mobilized with the 119th Personnel Service Company to Fort Sill, Oklahoma in support of Operation Desert Storm. In August 1993, she was reassigned to Deputy Chief of Staff, Personnel (DCSPER) as a SIDPERS Data Analyst, STARC (-). While assigned to STARC (-), SFC Matthews other duties included Personnel Records Specialist and Training Noncommissioned Officer (NCO). In 2000, SFC Matthews was transferred to the Arkansas National Guard Recruiting Command as an Administrative NCO.

SFC Matthew's professional military education includes Unit Administration Course, National Guard Professional Education Center (NGPEC), Camp Robinson, Primary Leadership Development Course (PLDC); Fort Sill, Oklahoma, 75F Personnel Information System Management Course, NGPEC, Camp Robinson, Basic Noncommissioned Officer Course, (BNCOC), Fort Jackson, South Carolina, and Advanced Noncommissioned Officer Course (ANCOC), Camp Ball, Louisiana.

Her awards and decorations include Meritorious Service Medal, National Defense Service Medal, Army Commendation Medal, Army Good Conduct Medal, Army Component Achievement Medal, Armed Forces Reserve Medal, Global War on Terrorism Medal, Army Service Ribbon, Army Reserve Component Overseas Training Ribbon, Noncommissioned Officer Professional Development Ribbon, Arkansas Service Ribbon, Arkansas Commendation Medal, Arkansas Emergency Service Ribbon, and the Recruiting Badge.

SFC Matthews retired on August 31, 2005, with over 23 years of distinguished military service. After retirement, SFC Matthews worked for the Arkansas Army National Guard Recruit Sustainment Program as a Civilian Contractor with SERCO Group. Currently, SFC Matthews serves as Chaplain of the Michael Van Johnson, Jr.

American Legion Post 74, North Little Rock. She is also a member of Calvary Baptist Church of McAlmont where she serves on the Mother's Ministry. Previously she has served as Sunday School Superintendent, Sunday School Secretary, Teacher, and former choir member for the Church. In the past, SFC Matthews volunteered with the Clinton Presidential Library. She enjoys reading and listening to music. SFC Mattews resides in Sherwood, Arkansas and she has a daughter and one grandchild.

Colonel Ronald W. McDaniel

First African American Colonel
189th Airlift Wing
Arkansas Air National Guard

Colonel (Col.) Ronald W. McDaniel was born and raised in Crossett, Arkansas and now resides in Jacksonville, Arkansas. He graduated from Crossett High School in 1970, and attended the University of Arkansas at Monticello, beginning in 1971, prior to entering the United States Air Force later in August 1972. Col. McDaniel has a Bachelor's Degree in Liberal Arts with Business Emphasis and a Master's Degree in Operations Management.

His first military assignment was with the 314th Medical Squadron at Little Rock Air Force Base as an enlisted member in 1972. His job title was Medical Administrative Technician apprentice, and he served until February 1979. Col. McDaniel separated from active duty and in 1979 he joined the 189th Medical Squadron, Arkansas Air National Guard at the rank of Staff Sergeant.

In 1984, Col. McDaniel received his commission as a Second Lieutenant and was assigned to the 189th Consolidated Aircraft Maintenance Squadron (CAM) in the Drill Status position of aircraft maintenance officer. In 1986, he was made executive officer for the squadron and served in this capacity until 1994. In this position he reached the rank of Captain.

In 1994, he was selected for a full-time position with the Arkansas Air National Guard as an aircraft maintenance officer and transferred from the Postal Service to the Air National Guard. At the same time, he was selected to be the Commander of the 189th Aircraft Generation Squadron. He was promoted to Major in 1995 and served as Commander of Aircraft Generation Squadron until assuming the dual position of Supply Management Officer and Chief of Supply in 1997.

In January 2003, he was selected for the position of Commander of the 189th Logistics Readiness Squadron. In April 2004, he assumed the position as Commander of the 189th Maintenance Squadron where he served until June of 2008, at which time he assumed the position as Commander of the 189th Maintenance Group. In May 2009, McDaniel made history in the wing by being the first African American Colonel in the 189th Airlift Wing. He retired in August 2012 at rank of Colonel after serving in the position of Commander, 189th Maintenance Group, Arkansas Air National Guard, Little Rock Air Force Base.

Col. McDaniel currently serves as member and former President and Vice-President, Jacksonville North Pulaski School Board (JNPSB). He is a former Community Advisory Board Member of the Pulaski County Special School District (PCSSD). Col. McDaniel is a member and current Secretary, Jacksonville Service to Mankind (SERTOMA) Club and served as past Chairman, Jacksonville, Civil Service Commission. He is the Board Secretary and volunteer, Jacksonville Senior Wellness and Activities Center (JSWAC) and Board Vice-President and volunteer, Jacksonville, Arkansas Military Museum of History (JMMH). Col. McDaniel is a Life Member, National Guard Association of the United States (NGAUS) and he is a Life member, National Guard Association of Arkansas (NGAA).

Colonel Nathaniel McGee

First African American Colonel

First African American to Command Camp Robinson Maneuver Training Area Arkansas Army National Guard

Colonel (COL) Nathaniel McGee is a native Arkansan. He is a graduate of William R. Golden High School in Turrell, Arkansas and received his Bachelor of Science Degree from Arkansas A. M. & N. College, Pine Bluff, (UAPB) with a Major in Chemistry and Biology and a Minor in Mathematics. His graduate degree was received at the Army War College in Carlisle, Pennsylvania in 1997.

He began his Military Service by enlisting in the Arkansas Army National Guard in July 1971, at Brinkley as an E-1 and upon completing Basic Training at Fort Jackson, South Carolina was promoted to Specialist Fourth Class (SPC-4). Shortly after returning from basic training, he enrolled in the Non-Commissioned Officer's Academy for Reserve Components at Fort Walters, Texas and in 1973, was promoted to Sergeant.

In May 1974, he was promoted to Staff Sergeant (E-6) and enrolled in the Arkansas Military Academy at Camp Joseph T. Robinson, North Little Rock, and after completing a 1- year Officer Candidate School was commissioned as a Second Lieutenant (2LT) in the Arkansas Army National Guard. COL McGee has completed such Military courses as the: Field Artillery Officers Basic Course, Communication Security School, Operations Training & Readiness Specialist Course, Special Staff Officers Refresher Courses, Towed Field Artillery Battalion Refresher Courses, Cannon Field Artillery Officer Refresher Course, FORSCOM/TRADOC BTMS Course,

Administrative Officer Course, Company Size Unit Commanders Course, Field Artillery Officer Advance Course, Organizational Maintenance Officer Course, Military Intelligence Officers Advanced Course, Battalion Training Management Courses, Command & General Staff College, Joint Fire Power Control Courses, Senior Officer Logistics Management Courses, and Ordnance Officer Advanced Courses. Since War College, Col McGee has graduated from the Senior Executive Development Course and the Garrison Commander Pre-Command course at Fort. Belvoir, Virginia.

Since receiving his commission, he has served in such positions as: Platoon Leader [both Field Artillery and Infantry], Forward Observer, Air Observer, Target Acquisition Platoon Leader, Air Defense Section Leader, Battery Commander, S-1, S-2, S-4, Motor Officer, Detachment Commander, Executive Officer, Maintenance Officer, Training Officer, Administrative Officer, Director of Maintenance, and Command Logistics Officer. While serving as the Director of Logistics for the State, LTC McGee completed a very successful 2-year tour as Battalion Commander, 5th Battalion, 1-206th Field Artillery Battalion. He served as Post/Garrison Commander, Robinson Maneuver Training Area, Camp Joseph T. Robinson, for 5-years [he held a total of four commands] and was last assigned as the Deputy Chief of Staff Logistics for the Arkansas Army National Guard.

COL McGee received his promotion to Colonel on November 2, 1995. As a result of his promotion, COL McGee became the first African American to be promoted to Colonel in the history of the Arkansas Army National Guard. In April 1997, he was assigned as the Commander of the Camp Robinson Maneuver Training Area. COL McGee was the first African American in the history of the Arkansas Army National Guard to Command at Brigade level.

COL McGee is the recipient of several awards, medals and decorations ranging from the Armed Forces Achievement Medal to the Army Commendation Medal with four Oak Leaf Clusters. His civilian education includes: graduate of OSHA Training and Certification - Fort Rucker, Alabama, Advance Executive Management Institute [Computer Literacy] - Dallas, Texas, Evaluation and Reporting Internal Controls - U.S. Department of Agriculture, Executive Management Institute for New Managers - Oak Ridge, Tennessee, Role of Supervisors and Management in EEO Training-Dallas, Applied Labor Management, Supervision and Group Performance, Executive Management Computer Literacy Course, Middle Management Institute, Staff Management Institute - Denver, Colorado., Senior Level Management Course, NGB-JA Fiscal Law Course - St Louis, Missouri, Senior Leader Equal Opportunity, Training (DEOMI), USDA's Graduate School, Building High Performing Teams, Advanced Management Seminar, APIC Course, Baldrige Self-Assessment and Continuous Improvement Workshops.

He is active in his community, serving on several Boards (Greater Little Rock UAPB/AM&N Alumni Chapter, Church, and Kappa Alpha Psi Fraternity) the Governor's Yellow Ribbon Task Force and currently enjoys retirement.

COL McGee retired on June 30, 2005, with over 34 years of military service.

Chief Master Sergeant
Regina L. Monk

First African American Female
Command Chief Master Sergeant 189th
Airlift Wing
Arkansas Air National Guard

Chief Master Sergeant (CMSgt) Regina L. Monk graduated from El Dorado High School in May 1982. She received an Associate Degree in Logistics Management from the Community College of the Air Force in 2011, and an Associate of Art Degree from Arkansas State University-Beebe in 2012. CMSgt Monk later received a Bachelor Degree in Professional Development-Criminal Studies from Arkansas Tech University, Russellville, in 2014.

Her dynamic military career started in September 1982, when she enlisted in the United States Air Force. She attended basic training at Lackland Air Force Base, Texas and Technical School at Sheppard AFB, Texas. In February 1983, CMSgt Monk was assigned as a Student Traffic Management Specialist at Sheppard AFB. She later served as a Passenger and Household Goods Specialist until August 1986 when she received a remote assignment to Comiso Air Station, Sicily. At Comiso Air Station, CMSgt Monk served as an Outbound Cargo Specialist. In October 1987, she received a follow-on assignment to Eaker AFB, Blytheville, Arkansas as the Noncommissioned Officer in Charge of Outbound Cargo. Chief Monk was later assigned to Taegu Air Base, South Korea in October 1989 as a Traffic Management Specialist. Her follow-on assignment in December 1990, was with the Royal Air Force Upper Heyford, United Kingdom.

In July 1992, CMSgt Monk separated from active duty at Charleston AFB, South Carolina and remained as an inactive reservist until

1994. In September 1998, she enlisted into the Air Force Reserve and was assigned to the 917th Logistics Readiness Squadron, Barksdale AFB, Louisiana. She remained with the Air Force Reserve unit until October 2000. In December 2000, CMSgt Monk enlisted into the Arkansas Air National Guard and was assigned to the 189th Logistic Readiness Squadron as a Cargo Movement Specialist. In March 2010, she became the Distribution Superintendent with the responsibility of overseeing cargo movement, passenger travel and ground operations. In October 2020, she was assigned as the Senior Enlisted Leader for the 189th Mission Support Group and in October 2022, CMSgt Monk was selected as Command Chief of the 189th Airlift Wing, Arkansas Air National Guard. With this assignment, she became the first African American Female assigned as the Command Chief Master Sergeant for the 189th Airlift Wing, Arkansas Air National Guard.

As the Command Chief for the 189th Airlift Wing, she advises commanders and staff on mission effectiveness, professional development, military readiness, training, utilization, health, morale,
and welfare of the wing's Enlisted Airmen and takes action to address shortfalls and challenges. She provides leadership to the enlisted force and is the functional manager for Group Superintendents and First Sergeants within the 189th Airlift Wing.

CMSgt Monk's military education includes the Traffic Management Apprentice Course, Noncommissioned Officer Leadership Course, Noncommissioned Officer Academy Course, Senior Noncommissioned Officer Academy, CMSgt Orientation Course and the CMSgt Command Chief Course.

Her awards and decorations include the Meritorious Service Medal, Air Force Commendation Medal, Air Force Achievement Medal, National Defense Service Medal, Global War on Terrorism Service Medal, and the Armed Forces Service Medal.

CMSgt Regina L. Monk currently works full-time for the 189th Airlift Wing, Arkansas Air National Guard. She is a member of the Top III which is an enlisted organization for E7-E9 members, and she serves as a member of the Little Rock Air Force Base Chief's Council. The Chief's Council is an organization in which its members are represented by every Air Force organization on LRAFB. CMSgt Monk is a member of EANGUS, and she served as a Volunteer Victim Advocate in 2019-2022. She also volunteers with the Special Olympics, Chief's Golf Tournament, the Arkansas Food Bank, the 5K Run for Fallen Soldiers and Senior Induction Ceremonies.

CMSgt Monk is a member of St. John Missionary Baptist Church where she serves as Chief Usher, and she serves as an Usher of the Union District of Arkansas.

Chief Warrant Officer Five Arthur Montgomery

First African American Warrant Officer Arkansas Army National Guard

Chief Warrant Officer Five (CW5) Arthur Montgomery was raised in Batesville, Arkansas. He attended public schools in Batesville and graduated from Ethel O. Miller High School on May 24, 1964. In September 1964, he entered Philander Smith College and graduated with a Bachelor of Arts Degree in Sociology on May 28, 1968.

On the same day of his graduation from college, CW5 Montgomery joined the Arkansas Army National Guard. He was assigned to Headquarters and Headquarters Company, 39th Infantry Brigade. He attended Basic Training and Advanced Individual Training at Fort Polk, Louisiana.

In 1980, CW5 Montgomery was the first African American to attend the Arkansas Army National Guard Officer Candidate School. Unfortunately, he was met with some adversity. After spending nine months at Camp Robinson, he was preparing to graduate from the academy. CW5 Montgomery said, "Saturday night, a fellow came to me and told me, 'When you leave here tomorrow, you won't be back,'" Montgomery said. "The commandant said he never graduated a [black man], and he wasn't going to start now."

Although CW5 Montgomery did not complete the course, on October 15, 1975, he was appointed to and commissioned as Warrant Officer by Brigadier Harold Gwatney, Commander of the 39th Infantry Brigade. CW5 Montgomery was the first African American Warrant Officer in the Arkansas Army National Guard.

CW5 Montgomery was assigned as the 39th Infantry Brigade's COMSEC Manager and served in that position until 1981. At that time, he was assigned to State Area Command (STARC) and served as the State COMSEC Officer/Inspector.

CW5 Montgomery worked for the Arkansas Unemployment Office in Batesville, and he retired as manager on December 31, 2006. While he was there, he served a five-county area: Independence, Sharp, Stone, Izard, and Fulton counties.

He has served as chairman of the Equalization Board, member of the Democratic Central Committee of Independence County and as a member of the Independence County Regional Museum Board. He also fulfilled his appointment by the governor to the state advisory board of the Department of Workforce Services and served on the board of trustees at Philander Smith College.

Sergeant Major
Lorine M. Mosley

First African American Active Guard/Reserve Sergeant Major

First African American G1 Sergeant Major Joint Force Headquarters Arkansas Army National Guard

Sergeant Major (SGM) Lorine M. Mosley was born in Dermott, Arkansas. She spent most of her youth in Detroit, Michigan. Later, returned to Dermott and graduated from Dermott High School in 1985. SGM Mosley received a Bachelor of Science Degree in Organizational Management in 2004 from Philander Smith College, Little Rock, Arkansas. She is a 2016 graduate of the United States Army Sergeants Major Academy, Fort Bliss, Texas.

SGM Mosley began her military career by enlisting in the Arkansas Army National Guard in March 1986 in Company C, 212th Signal Battalion where she served as a Network Combat Radio Operator. In October of 1989, she enlisted into the United States Army. Her initial duty station was at Fort Monmouth, New Jersey. She was assigned to the United States Military Academy Preparatory School Cadre as the Orderly Room Unit Clerk.

In 1994, SGM Mosley returned to the Arkansas Army National Guard and was assigned to the 87th Troop Command. While assigned to the 87th Troop Command, SGM Mosley served in various duty position assignments. In December 1999, SGM Mosley moved to Atlanta, Georgia and joined the U.S. Army Reserve in Decatur, Georgia. She was assigned to the 108th Instructional Training Command and received her certification as a Small Group

Instructor. She later transferred to the 4th RCS, Army Reserve Unit at Camp Pike, North Little Rock, Arkansas. During this assignment, she instructed Military Occupational Specialty (MOS) Training and Basic Noncommissioned Officer Training for Nuclear, Biological and Warfare Certifications.

In 2004, SGM Mosley returned to the Arkansas Army National Guard and was hired into the Active Guard/ Reserve (AGR) Program. She was assigned as a Recruiter in the Recruiting and Retention Command. During her tenure in the AGR Program, SGM Mosley served in various positions to include the Personnel Resources Noncommissioned Officer In Charge (NCOIC), 35th Aviation Brigade and the Plans Section, Deputy Chief of Staff Operations. In 2014, SGM Mosley was assigned to the 77th Aviation Brigade and mobilized with the Brigade to Kuwait.

Upon returning from deployment, SGM Mosley was assigned to the Deputy Chief of Staff, Personnel as the Enlisted Promotion Manager. In December 2017, SGM Mosely was promoted to Sergeant Major and assigned as the G1 Sergeant Major for the Deputy Chief of Staff, Personnel, Joint Force Headquarters, Arkansas. She was the first African American Female in the history of the Arkansas Army National Guard, in an AGR status, assigned to the G1 Sergeant Major position.

SGM Mosley's professional military education includes Basic Combat Training, Advanced Individual Training, Primary Leadership Development Course, Small Group Instructors Course, Basic Noncommissioned Officer Course, Advanced Noncommissioned Officer Course, First Sergeant Academy Course, Battle Staff Noncommissioned Officer Course, and the U.S. Army Sergeants Major Academy.

SGM Mosely retired from the Arkansas Army National Guard in August 2020 and currently resides in Austin, Arkansas.

Lieutenant Colonel Anderson Neal, Jr.

First African American Group Commander 188th Fighter Wing Arkansas Air National Guard

Lieutenant Colonel (Lt. Col.) Anderson Neal, Jr. served as State Diversity Officer for the Arkansas National Guard, Joint Force Headquarters, Camp J.T. Robinson, North Little Rock. He assumed this position in March 2015, with more than 29 years' service in the Arkansas Air National Guard.

Lt. Col. Neal was born in Fitzhugh, Arkansas on August 2, 1956, and graduated from Augusta High School in 1974. He received a Bachelor of Science Degree in Plant Science with emphasis on soils from Arkansas State University in Jonesboro, in 1978. Upon graduation he began a 37-year career with the United States Department of Agriculture (USDA). Neal has served in numerous positions and offices throughout the state of Arkansas from 1979 to 2009. He retired in 2015 as Deputy Director for the Office of Advocacy and Outreach, USDA, Washington, D.C.

Lt. Col. Neal enlisted in May 1985, with the 188th Fighter Wing, Fort Smith as Airman First Class. Neal completed Basic Military Training at Lackland Air Force Base, San Antonio, Texas and subsequently began technical training in aircraft maintenance as a crew chief at Sheppard AFB, Wichita Falls, Texas. He also served as senior student leader (Red Rope). He received his non-commissioned officer certification in April of 1988.

Lt. Col. Neal attended the Academy of Military Science, McGhee Tyson Air National Guard Base in Knoxville, Tennessee and was commissioned on April 4, 1989, as a Transportation Officer. He completed the Reserve Officer Transportation Training Course at Sheppard Air Force Base, Texas in 1990. Lt. Col. Neal completed Squadron Officer School by correspondence in 1994. In 1996, he was assigned Officer-in-Charge of the Management and Systems office in supply until January of 2001, when he was assigned as Chief of Supply until April 2001. Lt. Col. Neal assumed Command of the 188th Maintenance Squadron from April 2001 through 2005.

He was activated with the 188th for one year in support of Operation Noble Eagle following the September 11, 2001, attack on the World Trade Center in New York. Neal served as Inspector General for the 188th Fighter Wing from December 2005 until assigned as Aircraft Maintenance Squadron Commander, 189th Airlift Wing, Little Rock Air Force Base in Jacksonville, Arkansas in 2007. On May 14, 2011, he served as Director of Maintenance for the Joint Force Headquarters, Arkansas Air National Guard, located at Camp Robinson. Lt. Col. Anderson Neal Jr. assumed command of the 188th Maintenance Group at a ceremony at the 188th Fighter Wing December 2, 2012. Lt. Col. Neal was the first African American to serve as a Group Commander in the 188th Fighter Wing, Arkansas Air National Guard. He also served on the National Guard Association of Arkansas (NGAA) Board of Directors from 2005 to 2009 and presided as President from April 2008 to April 2009. Lt. Col. Anderson Neal retired from the Arkansas Air National Guard on July 1, 2016.

Staff Sergeant John Parker

First African American Hired at Combined Support Maintenance Shop Arkansas Army National Guard

Staff Sergeant (SSG) John Parker began his military career in November 1962. He was drafted into the military and spent two years on Active Duty. After being stationed in California for two years, SSG Parker returned home to fulfill a six-year obligation with the U.S. Army Reserves, but instead joined the Arkansas Army National Guard in 1964.

SSG Parker was the 3rd African American to join the Arkansas Army National Guard. During his enlistment, he became a member of the 148th Evacuation Hospital at Camp Robinson in North Little Rock. SSG Parker was assigned as a cook and four years later, he was promoted and became the dining facility Sergeant. He stayed in that capacity for 18 years.

SSG Parker was the first African American to be hired at the Combined Support Maintenance Shop (CSMS) in May 1972 as a Mechanic. He was the first African American to get promoted to the grade of WG-12 and the first to be hired in the Quality Assurance Section.

When asked what things he would change as a supervisor, SSG Parker responded by saying his objectives would be: helping people that he manages, providing better working conditions and better relationships between employees and management, and creating new ways to train his employees.

Chief Warrant Officer Four Marcellus Person

First African American Full-Time Military Technician Hired in a Supervisory Capacity Aviation Support Facility Arkansas Army National Guard

Chief Warrant Officer Four (CW4) Marcellus Person was born in Pulaski County, Arkansas. He graduated from Harris High School in 1967. He continued his education by attaining a Bachelor of Arts Degree from Arkansas Baptist College in 1979.

CW4 Person's life forever changed when he enlisted in the Army in 1967. He served two tours in the Vietnam War. In 1971, he enlisted into the Arkansas Army National Guard, and was the first African American full-time military technician hired in a supervisory capacity. He served as an aircraft systems foreman with the Arkansas Army National Guard Aviation Support Facility at Camp Robinson During the Staff Sergeant Corenna Taylor's discrimination lawsuit against Major General Jimmie "Red" Jones, CW4 Person served as an Advisor to plaintiff's counsel, throughout most of the second part of the trial. The *Taylor v. Jones* case was perhaps the most successful employment discrimination case in the state of Arkansas, and it prompted benefits to thousands of African American citizens throughout the state.

CW4 Person not only served as an Aircraft Mechanic and Equal Employment Manager, but in unofficial roles such as mentor, confidant, and friend. Throughout the course of his military career, CW4 Person, or "Mr. P," as his comrades called him, received many awards and decorations including the Legion of Merit, Bronze Star Service Medal, Meritorious Service Medal, Army Commendation

Medal, Good Conduct Medal, Army Reserve Components Achievement Medal, National Defense Service Medal, Armed Forces Expeditionary Medal, Vietnam service Medal, Commissioned Officer Professional Development Ribbon, Army Service Ribbon, Armed Forces Reserve Medal, Republic of Vietnam Campaign Medal, and the Armed Forces Reserve Medal.

CW4 Person retired with over 41 years of military service. He passed away on May 14, 2017.

Lieutenant Colonel William B. Phillips, II

First African American Public Affairs Officer Arkansas Army National Guard

Lieutenant Colonel (LTC) Phillips was born in Fairbanks, Alaska. He earned a Bachelor of Science Degree in Liberal Arts from Excelsior College and a Master's Degree in Strategic Leadership from the University of Charleston West Virginia in 2019. He enlisted in the United States Army in 1991 as a Physical Therapy Specialist in Atlanta, Georgia. He later joined the Georgia National Guard in 1999.

As a member of the Georgia National Guard, LTC Phillips held several enlisted military occupational specialties including intelligence analyst, medical records specialist, and combat medic before achieving the rank of Staff Sergeant. LTC Phillips was commissioned in 2003 through the Accelerated Officer Candidate Program at the Georgia Military Institute where he was selected as the Distinguished Honor Graduate. He attended his basic branch qualification at Fort Benning, Georgia where he graduated from Infantry Officer Basic Course on the commandant's list in 2004. LTC Phillips service in the Georgia National Guard includes a tour as a mechanized infantry company platoon leader, executive officer, and commander in Baghdad, Iraq.

In 2006, LTC Phillips joined the 39th Infantry Brigade Combat Team, Arkansas Army National Guard and served as rear detachment assistant brigade S3. Additionally, he commanded two troops in 1st Squadron, 151st Cavalry Regiment, held the Squadron-level staff positions of S3 and Executive Officer, and served as the first African American Operations Officer (S3) for the 39th Infantry

Brigade Combat Team. In 2017, LTC Phillips was assigned as the State Public Affairs Officer for the Arkansas Army National Guard. He was the first African American to serve in that capacity.

In 2019, LTC Phillips was assigned as the Legislative Liaison Officer for the Arkansas National Guard. LTC Phillips has been serving as Commander, 1st Battalion, 153rd Infantry Regiment, 39th Infantry Brigade Combat Team since September 2021, and as the State Public Affairs Officer.

LTC Phillips awards and badges include the Bronze Star, Meritorious Service Medal, Army Commendation Medal, Army Achievement Medal, Army Reserve Components Achievement Medal, National Defense Service Medal, Iraqi Campaign Medal, Global War on Terrorism Service Medal, Army Service Ribbon, Noncommissioned Officers Professional Development Ribbon, Combat Infantry Badge, Parachutist Badge, Laotian Combat and Special Skill Parachutist Badge, Order of Saint Maurice, Centurion and Order of Saint George, Bronze Award.

LTC Phillips is a lifetime member of the Infantry Officer's Association, the Military Officers Association of America, and the Enlisted Association of the Arkansas National Guard. He serves as a Friends of Reading board member for AR Kids Read, is a member of the 100 Black Men of Greater Little Rock, a graduate of Leadership of Greater Little Rock Class XXXV and Leadership Arkansas Class XVII and serves as a member of St. John's #329 Masonic Lodge.

Lieutenant Colonel
Lester Piggee

First African American Commander,
189th Security Police Squadron

First African American Officer to
Serve as Flight Commander
Arkansas Air National Guard

Lieutenant Colonel (Lt. Col.) Piggee joined the Arkansas Air National Guard's 189th Security Police Flight (SPF) in 1974 and continued his college career while serving in the Air National Guard. He was the first African American in this position. In 1976, he graduated from the University of Arkansas at Little Rock with a Bachelor's Degree in Business Administration and in 1978, he graduated from Webster University with a Master's Degree in Business Administration. He later qualified to attend the Academy of Military Science Program in Knoxville, Tennessee, where he received his commission as a First Lieutenant because of his prior military education and civilian education. Upon receiving his commission on December 18, 1980, he returned to the 189th Air Wing, Arkansas Air National Guard and assumed the position of Commander of the 189th Security Police Flight. Lt. Col. Piggee was the first African American Officer in the 189th Air Wing to command an organization.

Lt. Col. Piggee served as Commander of the flight for fourteen years. He was promoted to the rank of Lieutenant Colonel on October 15, 1997. He was instrumental in organizing the Minority Affairs Sub-Committee (MASC) within the 189th. Lt. Col. Piggee's Awards and Decorations include the Air Force Commendation Medal, Air Force Reserves Medal, Air Force Longevity Service

Award, National Defense Service Medal, Small Arms Expert Ribbon, and the Arkansas Service Ribbon.

Lt. Col. Piggee was an active participant in many community activities. He served as Superintendent of Sunday School at the Mt. Pisgah Baptist Church. He also served on the Jacksonville City Planning Commission. Lt. Col. Piggee was employed by the U.S. Treasury Department. He retired from the 189th Airlift Wing, Arkansas Air National Guard on December 13, 2000.

Chief Warrant Officer Four Timothy D. Pighee

First African American GS-12 Contract Specialist

First African American to receive Level III Certified Acquisition Professional Contracting Division United States Property and Fiscal Office for the Arkansas National Guard

Chief Warrant Officer Four (CW4) Timothy D. Pighee was born in Brinkley, Arkansas. He is a 1973 graduate of Brinkly High School. He received a Bachelor of Arts degree in Business Administration from the University of Arkansas at Pine Bluff in 1978.

CW4 Pighee's outstanding military career started in November 1980 when he enlisted in Company A (Admin), 39th Support Battalion, 39th Infantry Brigade (Separate). He completed Basic Training at Fort Jackson, South Carolina in April 1981, and the Advanced Individual Training at Fort Benjamin Harrison in June 1981. Upon completion of his AIT, he acquired the Military Occupational Skill (MOS) as a Finance Specialist (73C10). CW4 Pighee was hired in the Arkansas National Guard Military Technician Program as a GS-5 Military Pay Clerk for the United States Property and Fiscal Office (USPFO) for Arkansas in 1981. He worked in the Comptroller Division in USPFO for 3 years.

CW4 Pighee attended the Warrant Officer Candidate School and received his commission as Warrant Officer One, 920A, Property Accounting Technician in August 2001 at Fort Rucker, Alabama. As a Warrant Officer, he has been assigned as a Property Book

Officer for Headquarters and Headquarters Company, 2nd Battalion, 114th Aviation (ATS), 77th Theater Aviation Brigade, Property Book Officer, Headquarters Support Company, 777th Aviation Battalion, 77th Theater Brigade, Facility Supervisor, Property Accounting Tech and Contracting Officer for Joint Force Headquarters, Arkansas. CW4 Pighee deployed 12 months to Bilad, Iraq with the 2nd Battalion, 114th Aviation Battalion.

As a Federal Military Technician, CW4 Pighee was promoted to GS-12 Contracting Specialist in July 2005. In March 2006, he received the Level III Acquisition Certification. CW4 Pighee was the first African American Contracting Specialist and the first African American to receive the Level III Acquisition Certification in the Contracting Division, United States Property and Fiscal Office for Arkansas. As the Level III Acquisition Certified Contracting Specialist, he had sole authority to sign and award contracts not to exceed $10,000,000; sign and issue modifications not to exceed $10,000,000; issue notices of termination for the convenience of the Government; issue termination agreements not to exceed $10,000,000, and sign and issue delivery orders without monetary limitations against GSA schedule contracts.

CW4 Pighee's military and technician education include the Property Accounting Tech Basic Course, Property Accounting Tech Advanced Course, Warrant Officer Staff Course Phase I, Warrant Officer Staff Course Phase II, Organization Conflicts of Interest Course, Defense Small Purchase Advance Course, Principles of Contract Pricing Course, Government Contract Law Course, Intermediate Contracting Course, Intermediate Contract Pricing Course, Simplified Acquisition Procedures Course, Construction Contracting Course and Advanced Business Solution for Mission Support Course.

CW4 Pighee is the recipient of several medals, awards and decorations to include the Army Commendation Medal, Army Reserve Component Achievement Medal, National Defense Service

Medal, Armed Forces Reserve Medal, Meritorious Unit Commendation Medal, Army NCO Professional Development Ribbon, Army Service Ribbon, Armed Force Reserve Medal with "M" Device, Global War on Terrorism Expeditionary Medal, Global War on Terrorism Service Medal, Arkansas National Guard Service Ribbon and Arkansas National Guard Federal Service Ribbon.

CW4 Pighee was an active member of his community where he served as Deacon at Saint Mark Baptist Church, Little Rock, Scoutmaster of Boy Scout Troop 467, and Past President, Chief Executive Officer of the Board of Directors for the University of Arkansas at Pine Bluff/Arkansas Agricultural, Mechanical and Normal College (AM&N) National Alumni Association. He also served as President of the Arkansas National Guard Heritage Committee in 1994-1995. He retired from the military in 2015 with over 35 years of distinctive military service.

Chief Warrant Officer Four Celquetta D. Babb-Pride

First African American Female Property Book Officer

First African American Female Property Book Officer for the 39th Infantry Brigade Combat Team

First African American Property Book Officer for the 233rd Regiment Regional Training Institute Arkansas Army National Guard

Chief Warrant Officer Four (CW4) Celquetta Pride was born in Malvern, Arkansas. She graduated from Mountain Pine High School in 1979. CW4 Pride received an Associate Degree of Science from Vincennes University and a Bachelor of Science in Leadership and Ministry from Central Baptist College.

CW4 Pride military career started in the United States Army on July 2, 1979. She completed Basic Combat Training at Fort Dix, New Jersey. She received her Advanced Individual Training (AIT) at Fort. Lee, Virginia, where she acquired the Military Occupational Skill of 76C10, Equipment Records and Parts Specialist. Her first assignment was with the 227th Aviation Battalion at Fort Hood, Texas. She was honorably discharged from the U.S. Army in July 1982.

In September 1982, CW4 Pride enlisted into the Arkansas Army National Guard and was assigned to several units, the 212th Signal Battalion, Detachment 1, Company B, 935th Aviation Support Battalion, and Company C, 38th Aviation Battalion. Her duty assignments consisted of Equipment Records and Parts Specialist

(76C), Automated Logistical Specialist and Unit Supply Clerk (92Y30).

In April 1984, CW4 Pride was hired into the Full-Time Federal Technician Program at the Arkansas Army National Guard Combined Support Maintenance Shop (CSMS), Camp J.T. Robinson. During her tenure at CSMS, she worked in various positions such as a Surface Maintenance Dispatcher (GS-4), Supply Clerk (GS-6), Tools and Parts Attendant Supervisor (WG-4) and as a Senior Production Controller (GS-8). The highest position that CW4 Pride obtained in the Federal Technician Program was the GS-9, Equipment Specialist position in Deputy Chief of Staff, Logistic (DCSLOG), Camp J.T. Robinson, North Little Rock, Arkansas. CW4 Pride was the first female Supervisor assigned to the Arkansas Army National Guard Combined Support Maintenance Shop and the first female to serve as an Equipment Specialist for DCSLOG.

On August 28, 2002, CW4 Pride received her commission as a Warrant Officer and her duty assignment was with Headquarters and Headquarters Company, 233rd Regiment Regional Training Institute at Camp J.T. Robinson as the Property Book Officer. CW4 Pride was the first African American Female assigned to the Property Book Officer's position. Subsequent to the Property Book position, CW4 Pride retired from the Federal Technician Program with 20 years of Federal Service.

In May 2004, CW4 Pride was hired into the Active Guard Reserve (AGR) Program as a Property Book Officer (PBO) for HHC, 212th Signal Battalion, Arkansas Army National Guard. In 2006, she was assigned to the 39th Infantry Brigade Combat Team as the Brigade's Property Book Officer. CW4 Pride was the first African American Female to serve as the Property Book Officer for the 39th IBCT. The 39th IBCT is the largest Brigade in the Arkansas Army National Guard with approximately 4,000 soldiers assigned.

In 2009, CW4 Pride served as Property Book Officer for the 777th Aviation Support Battalion, Camp Robinson, Arkansas. In August 2013, she was assigned to Joint Force Headquarter-Arkansas, DSLOG, Camp Robinson, Arkansas. Upon Brigade's request, in August 2016, CW4 Pride was assigned to the 77th Aviation Brigade, Arkansas Army National Guard to serve as Property Book Officer. After completing her assignment with the 77th Aviation Brigade, CW4 Pride was reassigned to Joint Force Headquarter in 2019.

CW4 Pride's military education includes 76C, Equipment Records and Parts Specialist, AIT, National Guard Battle Skills Course, Basic Noncommissioned Officer Course, Warrant Officer Candidate Course, Warrant Officer Basic Course, Warrant Officer Advanced Course, Warrant Officer Staff Course, Property Accounting Technician Warrant Officer Advance Course, Material Control/Accounting Specialist Course, Standard Property Book System Course, Basic Property Accounting/PBUSE GGSS-Army Property Book Course, Supply Manager Course, Unit Supply Specialist Basic Technical Course, Unit Supply Enhancing Course, Surface Maintenance Management Support Course, SAMS-1 Course, OMS/UTES Supply Technician Course, Supervisory Personnel Management Office Course, Supervisor Personnel Management Office Supervisor Training Course, and the Food Operations Management Course.

CW4 Pride's military awards and citations include the Army Commendation Medal (2nd Award), Army Achievement Medal (2nd Award), Army Good Conduct Medal, Army Reserve Component Achievement Medal (8th Award), National Defense Service Medal w/ Bronze Service Star, Global War On Terrorism Service Medal, Noncommissioned Officer Professional Development Ribbon (2nd Award), Army Service Ribbon, Army Component Overseas Training Ribbon, Armed Forces Reserve Medal (3rd Award), Department of the Army Certificate Of Achievement, Certificate of Achievement, United States Army Quartermaster School Noncommissioned Officer Academy, 1st Cavalry Division

Certificate Of Achievement, Letter of Commendation's (3), and Letter of Appreciation (2).

CW4 Pride served as past board member for National Guard Association of Arkansas (NGAA), and she volunteers to read for Literacy Program at local schools. She enjoys traveling and spending time with her daughter and other family members. She is currently active in her church and serves as Treasurer for Grace National Apostolic Fellowship and Assembly of Churches.

CW4 Pride is very thankful to all the Pioneers that came before her and everyone that believed in her. She's most of all grateful to God. CW4 Celquetta Pride retired in August 2019 after over 40 years of distinguished military service.

Colonel Anthony Q. Sanders

First African American Legislative Liaison Arkansas Army National Guard

Colonel (COL) Anthony Sanders is a native of Carthage, Mississippi. He received his Bachelor of Science Degree from Mississippi State University in 1997. He holds two master's degrees: a Master of Arts Degree from Webster University in 2014 and a Master of Strategic Studies from The United States Army War College at Carlisle Barracks, Pennsylvania in 2020.

COL Sanders has served in a variety of positions with distinction to include two combat deployments in support of Operation IRAQI FREEDOM from 2004-2005 and 2008-2009. In 2012, he was assigned as the Assistant S3 for Headquarters, 39th Infantry Brigade Combat Team, Arkansas Army National Guard. In 2017, COL Sanders served as Battalion Commander, Headquarters and Headquarters Battery, 2nd Battalion, 142nd Field Artillery Brigade, Arkansas Army National Guard. He was assigned as the J3 Plans Officer, Joint Forces Arkansas in 2020.

COL Sanders is an Active/Guard Reserve Officer who currently serves as the Deputy G1 for the Arkansas Army National Guard and as the Brigade Commander for 87th Troop Command, Arkansas Army National Guard.

In 2015, COL Sanders was assigned as the Legislative Liaison Officer for the Arkansas National Guard. He was the first African American in the history of the Arkansas National Guard to be assigned to that position. In the Legislative Liaison Officer's position, COL Sanders developed, managed, and pursued The

Adjutant General's legislation action committee's actions and coordinated with the staff to educate, inform, and provide a timely response to congressional inquiries.

COL Sanders has received numerous awards and decorations including the Bronze Star Medal, Meritorious Service Medal, Army Commendation Medal, and the Combat Action Badge just to name a few.

Lieutenant Colonel David Savage, Sr.

First African American Battalion Commander
1st Battalion, 153rd Infantry
39th Infantry Brigade (Separate)
Arkansas Army National Guard

Lieutenant Colonel (LTC) David Savage Sr. was born in Little Rock, Arkansas. He graduated from Horace Mann High School in 1965. LTC Savage received his Bachelor's Degree from the University of Arkansas at Pine Bluff, Arkansas in 1986.

LTC Savage's military career started when he was drafted and served in the U.S. Army from April 19, 1968, to April 7, 1970. In May 1976, he enlisted into the Arkansas Army National Guard and entered the Arkansas Military Academy Officer Candidate School (OCS) Program. Upon completion of OCS, he was commissioned as a Second Lieutenant in the Army Medical Department (AMEDD) Branch. LTC Savage served in military assignments from Platoon to Brigade level in the 39th Infantry Brigade (Separate), Arkansas Army National Guard. From 1999-2001, LTC Savage served as the Commander, 1st Battalion, 153rd Infantry, 39th Infantry Brigade (Separate), Arkansas Army National Guard. He was the First African American to serve as the Battalion Commander in the history of the 1st Battalion, 153rd Infantry.

On June 1, 2004, LTC Savage separated from the Arkansas Army National Guard, however, on the same day, he was recalled to Active Duty by the Secretary of the Army in support of "Operation Noble Eagle" and assigned to the Pentagon Action Center's Crisis Action Team in Washington, D.C. for three years. LTC Savage retired on July 30, 2007, with over 34 years of distinguished military service to his state and nation.

His military education includes the Army Medical Branch Course, Infantry Officer Advance Course, Nuclear, Biological and Chemical (NBC) Officer/NCO Course, Communications Security (COMSEC) Custodian Course, Command and General Staff (CGSC) Course and the U.S. Army War College.

For his outstanding service, LTC Savage received several awards and medals to include the Legion of Merit, Meritorious Service Medal, Army Commendation Medal (2nd Award), Army Achievement Medal (2nd Award), Army Good Conduct Medal, Army Reserve Components Achievement Medal (7th Award), National Defense Service Medal with Bronze Star (2nd Award), Global War on Terrorism Service Medal, Army Service Ribbon, Armed Forces Reserve Medal (2nd Award), Overseas Service Ribbon, Armed Forces Reserve Medal with M-Device, Army Staff Identification Badge, Arkansas National Guard Service Ribbon, Arkansas National Guard Federal Service Ribbon and the Arkansas National Guard Service Ribbon.

LTC Savage also enjoyed a successful civilian career as a professional sales executive with companies such as IBM, Southwestern Bell, State Farm Insurance, and the Arkansas Democrat-Gazette Newspaper. His career achievements included Man of the Year, 100 Black Men of the Delta (1993) and Salesman of the Year, Southwestern Bell (1988). He was an ordained minister at the Rosedale Church of God in Christ in Little Rock, where he also served as a trustee and guitarist. Additionally, he served as the administrator for the Bishop J.O. Patterson Fine Arts Orchestra for the Churches of God in Christ and as a volunteer on the Greenville, Mississippi Arts Council.

LTC David Savage passed away on September 1, 2014, in Little Rock. He and his wife Jo Ann Fountain-Savage have four children and five grandchildren.

Chief Warrant Officer Four Gregory Settles

First African American First Sergeant, D Company, 212th Signal Battalion

First African American Command Sergeant Major, 212th Signal Battalion Arkansas Army National Guard

Chief Warrant Officer Four (CW4) Gregory Settles was born in Philadelphia, Pennsylvania. He graduated from South Philadelphia High School in June 1967. CW4 Settles attended UALR and the Arkansas College of Technology to study electronics and received an Associate Degree.

CW4 Settles military career started September 23, 1969, when he joined the United States Air Force. In the Air Force, he served as a Refrigeration and Air Conditioning Specialist where he received the Missile (ICBM) Master Technician Award.

In March 1978, CW4 Settles joined the Arkansas Army National Guard and was assigned to Training Site Unit, Camp J.T. Robinson, as a Utilities Repair Mechanic. He was later hired into the full-time workforce as an Electronic Mechanic for the 212th Signal Battalion at OMS-6. He later worked as a supervisor at CSMS Electronics Shop and as a database administrator at the United States Property and Fiscal Office (USPFO). CW4 Settles retired with 35 years of Federal Technician Service in 2004.

After retiring from the Federal Technician Program, he joined the Active Guard Reserve (AGR) Program in Aug 2004 as the Network Management Technician/COMSEC Custodian for HHC 212th

Signal Battalion. In June 2006, CW4 Settles was transferred to Company C, 39th BSTB, Pine Bluff, Arkansas as Unit Administrator. Once the 39th Infantry Brigade Headquarters discovered that they had a highly qualified COMSEC Warrant Officer working for the newly formed Signal Company, CW4 Settles was invited to be part of the 39th Infantry Brigade's Staff.

CW4 Settles served 8 years as the Tactical Network Technician and COMSEC Custodian for the 39th Infantry Brigade Combat Team, Arkansas Army National Guard. During his Deployment to Iraq in 2009, at Victory Base Camp, Iraq, he was instrumental in establishing the Brigade's COMSEC Account at the Base Defense Operation Center.

In March 1985, CW4 Settles was assigned as the first African American First Sergeant for D Company, 212th Signal Battalion, Arkansas Army National Guard. He was the first African American to be assigned as First Sergeant in the 212th Signal Battalion. In April 1988, CW4 Settles was selected as the Battalion Command Sergeant Major for 212th Signal Battalion, Arkansas Army National Guard. He was the first African American to serve as Command Sergeant Major in the 212th Signal Battalion.

CW4 Settles was appointed as a Warrant Officer on October 2, 1992, for Headquarters and Headquarters Company 212th Signal Battalion. CW4 Settles also served as the Electronic-Communication Inspector for the Command Evaluation Team, State Maintenance Office, and Joint Forces Headquarters.

CW4 Settles is past President and the first African American to serve as President of the Arkansas National Guard Noncommissioned Officer Association 1989-1990. He also served a member of the Moral, Welfare and Recreation Board (Canteen Board) and the Arkansas National Guard Museum. CW4 Settles served as President of the Arkansas National Guard Black Heritage Committee at Camp J.T. Robinson.

CW4 Settles military awards includes the Meritorious Service Medal (2), Operation Iraqi Freedom Medal, Global War on Terrorism Service Medal, Army Reserve Components Achievement Medal (7), Air Force Longevity Service Award, Air Force Overseas Ribbon, Arkansas Service Ribbon (5), Army Achievement Medal (4), National Defense Service Medal (2), NCO Professional Development Ribbon (4), Army Reserve Component Overseas Medal, Arkansas Emergency Service Ribbon, Air Force Good Conduct Medal (2), Armed Forces Reserve Medal (2), Army Service Ribbon (3), Arkansas Federal Service Ribbon, and Armed Forces Reserve Medal, Legion Of Merit. CW4 Settles retired on August 17, 2011, with 42 years of Military Service.

CW4 Settles has been serving the McAlmont Church of Christ since 1982 as Deacon, which he oversees Church Worship Services, Computer Networks, Digital Photography, Multimedia Consultant and Web-site Design. He also works with School of Religious Studies, Annual Capital Awards Program to recognizing Military Veterans for their Service to our Country. CW4 Settles was instrumental in establishing the Hero's Award to Honor all Branches of the Country's Military.

CW4 Settles' Values and Philosophy of Life is to Love God, Family, Country and to Do the Right Thing to and for all people.

Master Sergeant Kira S. Sharkey

First African American Female Personnel Services Noncommissioned Officer 39th Infantry Brigade Combat Team

First African American Female Awarded The 39th Infantry Brigade Combat Team Bowie Knife Arkansas Army National Guard

Master Sergeant (MSG) Kira S. Sharkey was born in Pine Bluff, Arkansas. She graduated from Little Rock Mills University Studies High School in 2000. She earned a Bachelor of General Studies degree from Columbia College in 2011.

MSG Sharkey joined the Arkansas National Guard on September 11, 2000. She attended Basic Combat Training (BCT) at Fort Jackson, South Carolina, and Advanced Individual Training (AIT) at Fort Huachuca, Arizona. MSG Sharkey started her military career as an Intelligence Analyst in Headquarters and Headquarters Company (HHC), 39th Infantry Brigade Combat Team (IBCT). She was deployed in support of Operation Iraqi Freedom II with HHC, 39th IBCT as an Intelligence Sergeant in 2004. In 2006, a year after returning to home station, she was hired in the Active Guard/Reserve (AGR) program as a Human Resources Sergeant in the 39th Infantry Brigade's S1 Section. In 2008, MSG Sharkey was deployed to Iraq for the second time as a Human Resources Staff Sergeant.

In March of 2017, MSG Sharkey was selected by the 39th IBCT Intelligence Officer (S2), Major Wesley Dumas, to serve a dual role as the First Sergeant for Company B, 39th Brigade Special Troops Battalion (MICO) and the Brigade Senior Intelligence

Noncommissioned (NCO) during their yearlong deployment to Kosovo; a Sergeants Major position that was performed by MSG Sharkey as a Sergeant First Class. After redeployment, she was reassigned to the 239th Brigade Engineer Battalion's S1 position. In September 2019, MSG Sharkey accepted the S1, NCOIC position in the 39th IBCT. She became the First African American Female assigned as the Personnel Services Noncommissioned Officer for the 39th Infantry Brigade Combat Team.

MSG Sharkey professional military training includes the Military Intelligence Analyst Course, TATS Primary Leadership Development Course, Human Resources Course; Information Assurance Security Officer Certification Course, Human Resources Basic NCO Course, Human Resources Specialist Senior Leader Course, DOD Sensitive Compartmented Information Security Official Course, Battle Staff NCO Course, Master Resilience Trainer Course, Senior Enlisted Joint Professional Military Education I and II, Unmanned Aircraft Systems Unit Commander and Staff Leader's Course, Mission Command Digital Master Gunner Course, Master Leader Course, and the Army Sexual Harassment Assault Response and Prevention Academy.

She has received numerous awards and decorations including the Meritorious Service Medal (2nd Award), Army Commendation Medal (3rd Award), Army Achievement Medal (2nd Award), Army Good Conduct Medal (6th Award), Army Reserve Component Achievement Medal (2nd Award), National Defense Service Medal (2nd Award), Armed Forces Expeditionary Medal, Armed Forced Reserve Medal, NATO Medal, Joint Meritorious Unit Award, Meritorious Unit Commendation, Noncommissioned Officers Professional Development Ribbon (4th Award), Army Service Ribbon, Overseas Service Ribbon (4th Award), Armed Forced Reserve Medal with M Device (3rd Award), Global War on Terrorism Expeditionary Medel, Global War on Terrorism Service Medal, Combat Action Badge, Iraq Campaign Medal with Campaign Star and the COL Robert L. Manning Achievement

Medal (AGCRA). In September 2021, she was the third in the state of Arkansas to receive the Military Intelligence "Thomas Knowlton Award" and first African American Female awarded the 39th Infantry Brigade Combat Team Bowie Knife.

MSG Sharkey's military memberships include Military Intelligence Corps Association, United Status Adjutant General's Corps, and the Enlisted Association of the National Guard (EANGUS). She is a member of Delta Sigma Theta Sorority, Incorporated and Kappa Epsilon Psi Military Sorority, Incorporated. Her hobbies are candle making, photography and reading urban fantasy novels.

Brigadier General Leland Tony Shepherd

First African American General Officer to Command the Arkansas Army National Guard

Brigadier General (BG) Leland Tony Shepherd is a graduate of Montgomery County Community College in Pennsylvania with an Associates in Electronic Engineering, a graduate of Philander Smith College, Little Rock, Arkansas with a Bachelor of Arts Degree in Organizational Management, he holds a Master of Arts in Information Technology (IT) Management from Webster University and a Master of Arts in Strategic Studies from the Army War College. BG Shepherd received his Doctoral degree in Executive Leadership from the University of Charleston. He is currently a Regional Vice President of Operations at PODS.

On June 12, 2022, BG Shepherd assumed overall command of the 6,500 members of the Arkansas Army National Guard. The Arkansas Army National Guard consists of four brigades: 39th Infantry Brigade Combat Team, 77th Theater Aviation Brigade, 87th Troop Command, and the 142nd Field Artillery Brigade. BG Shepherd is the first Black general officer to command the Arkansas Army National Guard and just the second Black general officer in the Arkansas Army National Guard.

BG Shepherd enlisted into the U.S. Army Reserves in Philadelphia, Pennsylvania, July 23, 1992. He attended Basic Combat Training at Fort Knox, Kentucky and Advanced Individual Training at Fort Sam Houston in San Antonio, Texas. He served two years as an X-Ray Technician at Blanchfield Hospital, Fort Campbell, Kentucky. BG Shepherd enlisted in the Arkansas Army National Guard in October 1995. In 1997, BG Shepherd enrolled into Officer Candidate School

Class 41 where he received his commission and was appointed as a Second Lieutenant in August 1998.

BG Shepherd's previous assignments include: Platoon Leader, Co B 212th Signal BN, Benton, Executive Officer, Co A 212th Signal BN, Hot Springs, S-6 Officer, 1-153rd INF BN, Malvern, Company Commander, HHC 1-153rd INF BN, Malvern, S-6 Officer, 39th IBCT; Executive Officer, 39th BSTB, Conway, Commander - 2nd Battalion, 233rd Regiment (RTI), Regimental Commander, 233rd (RTI) and currently serves as the Deputy Chief of Staff: G6.

BG Shepherd has served two combat tours in Iraq: with the 39th Infantry Brigade Combat Team. His first deployment was in 2004 where he served as the Signal Officer for the 1-153rd Infantry Battalion. His second deployment was in 2008 as the 39th IBCT Signal Officer. He has received the following awards and decorations: Bronze Star, Combat Action Badge, Meritorious Service Medal with 2 Oak Leaf Clusters, Army Commendation Medal, Army Achievement Medal, Overseas Service Ribbon, Operation Iraqi Freedom Service Medal, and numerous other Federal and State Service ribbons. BG Shepherd was awarded the prestigious Order of Mercury, Bronze; for the highest standards of integrity, moral character, professional competence, and selflessness, for those who have contributed significantly to the Army Signal Corps. BG Shepherd is also a recipient of the Army Legion of Merit award.

Colonel Sherman Tate

First African American Battalion Commander 39th Support Battalion, 39th Infantry Brigade Arkansas Army National Guard

Colonel (COL) Sherman Tate was born in Marvell, Arkansas. He graduated from Marvell High School in 1963. After graduating from High School, COL Tate enrolled into Philander Smith College in Little Rock, Arkansas. In 1970, he graduated from Philander Smith with a Bachelor of Arts Degree in Psychology.

COL Tate's stellar military career began in 1966-1968 when he was drafted into the United States Army. After completing Basic Training and Advanced Individual Training in 1967, he was ordered to Vietnam. While in Vietnam, he was later assigned near the Laotian border during the 1968 Tet Offensive. From September 6, 1968, to September 14, 1972, COL Tate served in the U.S. Army Reserve Control Group as a Sergeant E5. He later served in the U.S. Army Reserve as Sergeant First Class E7, Physical Security NCO.

On March 5, 1981, COL Tate started his outstanding military journey in the Arkansas Army National Guard. He received a Direct Appointment to the rank of Captain and commissioned in the Adjutant General Corps Branch. His first assignment was State Area Command (STARC), Arkansas Army National Guard, Camp J.T. Robinson. COL Tate was reassigned to Company A (Admin), 39th Support Battalion, 39th Infantry Brigade as the Company Executive Officer. In 1983, he was appointed as Company Commander, Co A (Admin), 39th Support Battalion. On February 5, 1988, COL Tate was appointed as the Battalion S1, Headquarters and Headquarters Company, 39th Support Battalion in Hazen, Arkansas.

COL Tate was reassigned to STARC (-), Arkansas Army National Guard from August 1, 1988, to July 29, 1990, and served in various duty positions such as Personnel Officer, Mobilization Plans Officer, and Chief Readiness/Force Integration Officer. On July 8, 1990, he was reassigned to HHC (-), 39th Infantry Brigade and served as the Recruiting and Retention/Equal Opportunity Officer. COL Tate was appointed as S1 for the 39th Infantry Brigade on July 1, 1991, and later selected as the Battalion Executive Officer for HHC (-), 39th Support Battalion. On September 1, 1994, COL Tate was assigned as Battalion Commander, HHC, 39th Support Battalion, 39th Infantry Brigade. COL Tate was the first African American assigned as Battalion Commander in the history of the 39th Support Battalion.

On August 3, 1996, COL Tate served as the Brigade Executive Officer for HHC, 39th Infantry Brigade, Little Rock. He later served as the Deputy Commander, Installation Support Unit, Camp Robinson, and Supply Management Officer, STARC (-), Arkansas Army National Guard.

COL Tate's military education includes the Officers Management Course, Fort Sam Houston, Texas, Adjutant General Officer Advanced Course, New Port News, Virginia and the Command and General Staff Course, Fort Leavenworth, Kansas.

His awards and decorations include the Bronze Star, Army Commendation Medal (2), Army Achievement Medal (6), Meritorious Service Medal (3), National Defense Service Medal (2), Good Conduct Medal, Armed Forces Reserve Medal (3), Vietnam Service Medal, Vietnam Campaign Medal, Arkansas Distinguished Service Medal, and the Arkansas Service Medal. Additionally, COL Tate participated in the Vietnam Tet Counteroffensive Operations phase I through phase V. COL Tate retired from the military with over 30 years of distinguished service.

He started his civilian career immediately after graduating from college. He was hired by the consulting firm, General Behavioral Systems. He then went to work for the Arkansas Office of Personnel Management in 1972 as a personnel analyst. He subsequently worked for the Arkansas Bureau of Legislative Research where he was the personnel director of the State Legislative Council, making him their first African American employee.

In 1974, COL Tate was hired by the University of Arkansas, Little Rock to develop and manage the office of non-academic personnel. At the request of Governor David Pryor, COL Tate returned to the Arkansas Office of Personnel Management and became the first African American to manage this department.

In 1980, he was named director of personnel for Arkla Gas Company's Arkansas Division, making him the first African American in a management position at the company. He was later promoted to Vice President of consumer and community relations, then Vice President of marketing; and two years later, he became Vice President of distribution and operations.

COL Tate joined Alltel Corporation in 1998 as Vice President and General Manager of operations, where he was responsible for human and fiscal resources for Alltel's telephone operations in Arkansas and Mississippi. He also served as President of the local telephone company and Vice President of external affairs for Alltel until the company was acquired by Verizon in 2009.

With Verizon, he served as Vice President from 2009 to 2011 and was responsible for legislative, regulatory, and public policy issues in Arkansas, Louisiana, Tennessee, Kentucky, and Ohio. In 2011, COL Tate left Verizon and established two management consulting firms, the Domino Effect and HT & Associates, now a part of the holding company Tate & Associates.

COL Tate was also the first African American to be elected chairman of the Little Rock Regional Chamber of Commerce in 1989 and has since served on numerous boards including for Philander Smith College, St. Vincent Health System, the United Negro College Fund, and the Pulaski County Facilities Board. Additionally, he served on the board of Arkansas Blue Cross and Blue Shield and Chairman of both, the Southern Bancorp Bank Governing Board, and the Urban League of the State of Arkansas. In 2017, COL Tate was nominated and selected to the Arkansas Business Hall of Fame. He is also a proud member of Alpha Phi Alpha Fraternity, Incorporated. COL Tate currently resides in Little Rock.

Lieutenant Colonel Alice Taylor

First African American Nurse
Arkansas Army National Guard

Lieutenant Colonel (LTC) Alice F. Taylor received her degree from the St. Vincent School of Nursing after majoring in pre-nursing at Philander Smith College in 1969. She worked at St. Vincent Infirmary until her transfer to the Veterans Administration Hospital in 1971. She was commissioned on September 17, 1971, as a Second Lieutenant in the Arkansas Army National Guard. In 1973, she completed the Army Medical Basic Officer Course at Fort Sam Houston, Texas. LTC Taylor was the first African American Nurse to join the Arkansas Army National Guard.

In 1974, LTC Taylor moved to Oklahoma City, transferring to the Veterans Administration Hospital. She worked in the emergency and outpatient department for six years. Although, she had a difficult time leaving her family unit, the Arkansas Army National Guard. LTC Taylor continued to be an active member of the Arkansas Army National Guard while performing extended duty in the 44th Army Reserve Unit in Oklahoma. After becoming more familiar and comfortable with the new changes and her new job, LTC Taylor separated from the Arkansas Army National Guard. She was assigned to the Headquarters and Headquarters Detachment, Oklahoma Army National Guard and attached to the 245th Medical Company in Midwest City. LTC Taylor became actively involved with the physical exams team and worked closely with the medics in the unit. She transferred from the 245th Medical Company in June 1982, and was assigned to Headquarters, State Area Command (STARC) and attached to the Oklahoma Military Academy. LTC Taylor's most challenging position in the Oklahoma Army National Guard was her assignment as the Medical Officer to support the

Non-Prior Service School. There she provided medical and emergency care to the Non-Prior Service recruits during their two-day weekend orientation program.

In 1988, LTC Taylor moved back to Arkansas where she worked in the emergency room at Baptist Memorial Hospital for 3 years. She transferred back to the Arkansas Army National Guard in 1988 and was assigned to STARC (-) and attached to 148th Evacuation Hospital Unit until 1990. In 1990-1992, she served in the position of Officer-in-Charge of the physical exam team at the Troop Medical Clinic at Camp Robinson. LTC Taylor completed the Command General Staff College Course in 1991. She served in the United States Nurse Corps for 28 years.

LTC Taylor, along with her husband, is the co-founder of the Zero to Ten Publishing Company where a number of pieces of their work have been published. She has also earned the title of Sales Director with Mary Kay Cosmetics, which illustrates her gift of connecting with people while inspiring them to accomplish their own dreams.

In her free time, LTC Taylor enjoys recreational activities such as cooking, fishing, reading, listening to music, and gardening. Also, at her church, Mosaic Central Church, she serves as a mentor to the youth.

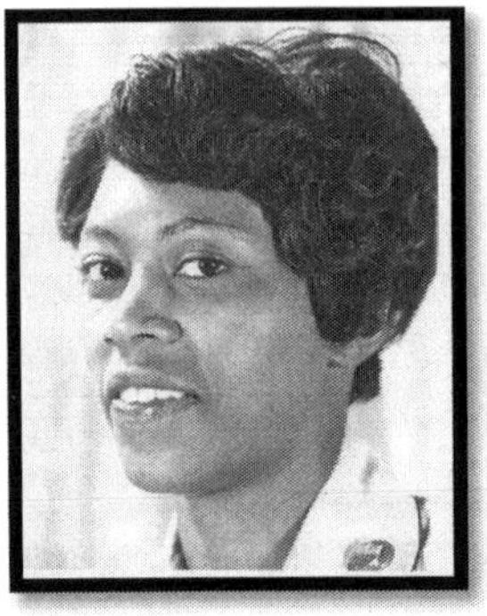

Staff Sergeant Correna Taylor

First African American Female Recruiter
Arkansas Army National Guard

Fought for Racial Justice in the Arkansas National Guard

Staff Sergeant (SSG) Correna Taylor was born in Searcy, Arkansas. She joined the Arkansas Army National Guard in 1973. SSG Taylor was hired by the Arkansas Army National Guard as a Recruiter March 1, 1974. She was the first African American female Recruiter in the Arkansas Army National Guard. SSG Taylor was also the third female to join the Arkansas Army National Guard. Her first unit of assignment was, Company B (Med) (-), 39th Support Battalion, 39th Infantry Brigade, in Lonoke.

She served in several 39th Support Battalion Detachments before transitioning to the 739th Ordnance Detachment in April of 1976. SSG Taylor held numerous military occupational specialties, General Clerk (71B), Post Clerk (71F), Card Punch Operator (74B) and Unit Clerk (75B) to name a few. She enlisted as Private (PV1/E1) and with excellent performance she was promoted to the rank of Staff Sergeant (SSG/E6) in a 12-year timeframe.

SSG Taylor was professional, competent, and consistently worked above her pay grade. She demonstrated high, ethical standards in the way she managed her career, and served as an example of the NCO creed. It was a teaching point for her NCOs to emulate. Her story is one of persistence, a continued fight for balance of race and gender inequalities.

In the *Taylor v. Jones* case, SSG Taylor maintained she was treated unfavorably because of her race. SSG Taylor had to work in uncomfortable and dangerous work environments before she filed her lawsuit. SSG Taylor served as a brave advocate in this case, not only for self-interest, but taking a stance to protect the rights of African Amcricans in the Arkansas National Guard against workplace discrimination. SSG Taylor fought for racial justice through various measures. The measures that brought significant change were, 1) escalating her complaint outside of the organization and, 2) endorsing legal representation for corrective action. She stood steadfast in her principles of fairness and lived by her favorite quote "It doesn't cost me anything to be kind."

On the 12th of March 1976, SSG Corenna Taylor filed a lawsuit against the Arkansas Army National Guard for alleged discrimination in two segments: first, on behalf of African American members as well as employees and, secondly, on behalf of the African Americans eligible for high-ranking positions. SSG Taylor was an employee with the Arkansas National Guard for less than one year, a period between the 1st of March 1974 and the 2nd of October 1974. From the first day of her employment, SSG Taylor served as a recruiter until June 30, 1974. She was demoted from her position as a recruiter to a clerk in the mailroom, a position from which she resigned following futile attempts at receiving a promotion or transfer to another Unit.

Throughout the period of her employment, SSG Taylor was a member of the National Guard and had been drilling one weekend per month to include a two-week training during summer. In the suit against her employer, SSG Taylor charged the Arkansas National Guard with two counts of discrimination, (1) under classification; and (2) being underpaid during her employment as a mailroom clerk.

She also alleged that the company had subjected her to racial epithets and that her employer had denied her both transfer and promotion opportunities despite her repeated requests. SSG Taylor also sought for relief at a wide range, with affirmative efforts by the Arkansas National Guard to offer employment opportunities to African American Guard members as well as civilian employees being an inclusion.

On February 20, 1980, the proceedings of SSG Taylor's trial were presented before the Honorable Judge Richard Arnold. Upon conclusion of the trial, it was found that the defendant, James Jones, the Arkansas Army National Guard Adjutant General, intentionally discriminated against the plaintiff based on her race, violating Title VII of the Civil Rights Act of 1964, as well as 42 United States Code of 1983. The court also found that the unauthorized transfer of SSG Taylor from her previous position as a recruiter to the mailroom clerk was racially motivated. Moreover, the court found that the resignation by SSG Taylor from her position as a clerk in the mailroom was the result of coercion and racially motivated prejudice.

Furthermore, MG Jones' lack of disciplinary actions toward any of SSG Taylor's supervisors and other perpetrators encouraged discriminatory behaviors throughout the organization. SSG Taylor's working environment had become extremely difficult for her to work free of worry. Fellow servicemembers and leadership subjected her to repeated and undue discriminatory gestures.

As a result, the court ordered MG Jones to reinstate SSG Taylor with retroactive pay. He was also ordered to place her in her previous recruiter position or a comparable position. The court made an injunction barring the defendant from recruiting any new employees for vacant positions, but later modified it to permit Arkansas National Guard to fill such positions if half of the newly recruited were African Americans.

Subsequently, the defendant, MG Jones, filed a motion calling for a new trial claiming that the recruiter position introduced into the case was an unfair surprise to him. The court granted the motion; however, the appeal addressed just two issues: whether the nonrenewal of SSG Taylor as a recruiter was within legal means and whether there was racial discrimination and the exact equitable relief that should be granted.

The new trial went before the United States Court of Appeals, Eighth Circuit. By August 8, 1980, the district court had not only entered its opinion but also the final judgment. There were no disturbances of the earlier findings by the court that the plaintiff had suffered constructive discharge from her position of recruiter to mailroom clerk due to her race, violating Title VII of the 1964 Civil Rights Act.

Moreover, the court reiterated the findings of deliberate discrimination by the defendant against the plaintiff based on the account of her race through failure to renew the appointment of SSG Taylor as a recruiter. In addition, the court found the basis of liability for the unlawful act was on 42 U.S.C. 1981. However, there was dissolution of the injunction during litigation, as the court directed the defendant to recruit at least one African American Soldier for every two white employees up to the point where the population of African American employees would be 16% of the total force.

In 1987, SSG Taylor received an honorable Discharge from the Arkansas Army National Guard. She also received a host of other awards, and decorations throughout her military career and from the community. SSG Taylor was an outstanding Black American and an exceptional Soldier. SSG Taylor passed in 1992.

Major Daryl A. Taylor

First African American Female
Assistant Staff Judge Advocate
189th Airlift Wing
Arkansas Air National Guard

Major (Maj.) Daryl A. Taylor was born in Northern Louisiana and graduated from Redwater High School in Redwater, Texas. She received her Bachelor of Science Degree in History, *Summa Cum Laude,* from Texas A&M University in 2004 and a Juris Doctor, from the University of Arkansas School of Law in 2007. In 2019, she received her Master of Laws in Cybersecurity and Data Privacy, *Summa Cum Laude,* from Albany Law School. In 2021, she received a Technical Master of Business Administration and a Master of Science, both in Cybersecurity, from Capital Technology University in Laurel, Maryland.

Major Taylor secured a direct commission as a First Lieutenant into the Arkansas Air National Guard on December 14, 2012. She was assigned as an Assistant Staff Judge Advocate for the 189th Airlift Wing, Little Rock Air Force Base, and became the first African Female to serve in this role. The following year, in 2013, she completed the Commissioned Officer Training School and the Judge Advocate Staff Officer Course at Maxwell Air Force Base, Alabama. By correspondence, she completed the Squadron Officer School from Maxwell AFB in 2016.

As the first African American Female Assistant Staff Judge Advocate at the 189th Airlift Wing, she assists in providing legal advice to the wing commander, subordinate commanders, and legal services to over 800 wing members.

In her civilian capacity, Major Taylor serves as the Attorney Advisor for the 189th Airlift Wing. Prior to serving as Attorney Advisor, she was the Managing Attorney with the Professional Licensure Standards Board (PLSB) for the Arkansas Department of Education, and the Assistant City Attorney for Pine Bluff.

Major Taylor said she was motivated to join the military while working as a law clerk for Judge Berlin C. Jones, a retired Jefferson County Circuit Judge in Arkansas. She said, "Judge Jones was an Air Force veteran who served in the Vietnam War. He operated a veteran focused 'Drug Court' that served as a drug intervention program within the criminal justice system. I developed wonderful relationships with the Veteran Affairs representatives in support of the Veteran's Drug Court. These relationships, along with the encouragement of Judge Jones, inspired me to join the military."

In reflecting back on her humble beginnings, Major Taylor said she calls herself a "mill brat." She laughingly explained and said, "I call myself a 'mill brat' because my father has worked for paper mills my entire life, and with my father's job, we moved several times within the Tri-state areas of Arkansas, Louisiana, and Texas, so I simply call myself a 'mill brat' instead of a military brat."

Her awards and decorations include the Air Force Commendation Medal, Air Force Outstanding Unit Award, Air Reserve Forces Meritorious Service Medal, National Defense Service Medal, Global War on Terrorism Service Medal, Air Force Longevity Service, and Air Force Training Ribbon.

Major Taylor is a member of the Arkansas Bar and admitted to practice law before the United States Air Force Court of Criminal Appeals, United States Court of Appeals for the Armed Forces and the U.S. District Court for the Eastern and Western Districts of Arkansas. She is also a member of the Alpha Kappa Alpha (AKA) Sorority, Incorporated.

She enjoys traveling, entertaining and cooking, particularly when it involves smoking meats on her Big Green Egg (BGE) grill. She typically spends her weekends in her backyard around her fire pit.

Lieutenant Colonel Jacqueline K. Taylor

First African American Female Commander In The Arkansas Air National Guard

First African American Female to Command Arkansas Air National Guard Detachment National Guard Marksmanship Training Unit Camp J.T. Robinson

Lieutenant Colonel (Lt. Col.) Jacqueline Taylor was born in Gary, Indiana. Her family moved to Blytheville, Arkansas when she was about 5 years old. Lt. Col. Taylor graduated from Blytheville High School with honors in 1988. She received an Associate of Applied Degree in Physical Therapist Assisting in 1990 from the University of Central Arkansas, Conway. She later received a Bachelor of Science Degree in Health Education and Community Health Promotion in 2001 from the University of Arkansas at Little Rock. In 2004, Lt. Col. Taylor received a Master of Arts Degree in Health Services Management from Webster University, St. Louis, Missouri. In 2007, she received a Master of Business Administration from Webster University, St. Louis. Lt. Col. Taylor obtained a Doctor of Physical Therapy Degree in 2014 from the University of Findlay, Findlay, Ohio.

Her distinctive military journey began in 1989 when she enlisted in the United States Air Force. She was assigned to the 189th Airlift Wing, Arkansas Air National Guard located at the Little Rock Air Force Base. Lt. Col. Taylor attended Basic Military Training at Lackland Air Force Base, Texas and Technical Training at Lowry Air Force Base, Colorado. Lt. Col. Taylor worked as a traditional Guardsman in the 189th Services Squadron and later with the 189th

Logistics Support Flight (part of the 189th Maintenance Group) until she received her officer commission from the Academy of Military Science in 2003 at McGhee-Tyson Air Force Base, Tennessee. Lt. Col. Taylor was assigned as an Equal Opportunity Officer and later became the Director of Equal Opportunity for the 189th Airlift Wing. In this role, she was responsible for analyzing data, demographics, and trends for the wing regarding issues that could affect the human relations climate. Lt. Col. Taylor was also instrumental in advising and recommending recruitment efforts with an emphasis on targeting underrepresented demographic groups. For her efforts as Director of Equal Opportunity for the 189th Airlift Wing, Lt. Col. Taylor was lauded as a Top Performer by the Headquarters, Air and Education Training Command during its 2012 and 2014 base inspections.

Later, Lt. Col. Taylor was assigned as the Planning and Programming Officer for Headquarters, Arkansas Air National Guard located at Camp Robinson, Arkansas. She was part of a team that coordinated and monitored peacetime and wartime planning during execution of programs for the Commander of the Arkansas Air National Guard. Lt. Col. Taylor's responsibilities included coordinating the strategic and long-term planning processes for the Arkansas Air National Guard to meet federal and state missions. She served as a liaison to all Arkansas Air National Guard units with the Director of Military Support and Arkansas Department of Emergency Management in the establishment, operations and training for state emergencies and advising Joint Force Headquarters Staff on Air and Army National Guard initiatives. During this assignment, Lt. Col. Taylor also analyzed emergency programs that supported the state of Arkansas and provided corrective actions to Joint Force Headquarters Staff.

On August 2, 2020, Lt. Col. Taylor made groundbreaking history as the first African American Female to become a commander in the Arkansas Air National Guard. Lt. Col. Taylor assumed Command of the Arkansas Air National Guard Detachment for the

National Guard Marksmanship Training Unit (NGMTU), Camp Robinson. As Commander, Lt. Col. Taylor's focus was to lead as the Air Component's representative for the joint mission of the Marksmanship Training Center. She was responsible for coordinating NGMTU functions and matters with other units, military services, and civilian agencies. Lt. Col. Taylor also aimed at ensuring competitors received the best training and skills development beyond basic proficiency to enhance combat survivability and capability.

Lt. Col. Taylor's military professional education includes the Academy of Military Science, McGhee-Tyson Air Force Base, Tennessee; Personnel Officer Course, Keesler Air Force Base, Mississippi; Squadron Officer School and the Air Command and Staff College Course, both located at Maxwell Air Force Base, Alabama.

Her major military awards and decorations include the Meritorious Service Medal, Air Force Commendation Medal, Air Force Outstanding Unit Award with three oak leaf clusters, Air Force Organization Excellence Award, Air Reserve Forces Meritorious Service Medal with one silver and three bronze oak leaf clusters, National Defense Service Medal with bronze star, Global War on Terrorism Service Medal, Air Force Longevity Service Award with three oak leaf clusters and the Armed Forces Reserve Medal with silver hourglass.

Lt. Col. Taylor retired from the Arkansas Air National Guard in 2022 after serving 32 years and 8 months of distinguished military service. Since retiring from the Arkansas Air National Guard, she currently holds the distinction of being the first African American Female to command the Air Force Junior Reserve Officer Training Corps (AFJROTC) at the Historic Little Rock Central High School. As the Senior Aerospace Science Instructor for this program, Lt. Col. Taylor has the responsibility of managing the AFJROTC unit in accordance with military regulations and the

Little Rock School District's policies and procedures. She has a personal commitment to instill in the cadets the values of community, personal responsibility, sense of accomplishment, all while stressing the importance of true self-esteem, teamwork, and self-discipline. Lt. Col. Taylor sets the standards by encouraging her cadets to commit to the core values of the United States Air Force… integrity first, service before self and excellence in all we do.

Lt. Col. Taylor is a life member of the National Guard Association of America, a proud member of Alpha Kappa Alpha Sorority, Incorporated; licensed as a Doctor of Physical Therapy, and a certified Air Force JROTC instructor. Additionally, she serves as a board member of Advocates Needed Today, Inc., a non-profit organization whose mission is to provide emotional support and information to those with developmental disabilities and behavioral health concerns. This organization is especially dear to Lt. Col. Taylor's heart since her son has diagnoses that include autism spectrum disorder. In her spare time, she enjoys running, volunteering with her sorority, and enjoying time doing activities such as road trips and attending sporting events with her family. Lt. Col. Taylor and her family live in Sherwood, Arkansas.

Senior Master Sergeant Harold Terry

Advisor, Minority Affairs Sub-Committee 189th Air Wing, Arkansas Air National Guard

Senior Master Sergeant (SMSgt) Harold Terry was born in Pine Bluff, Arkansas and graduated from Pine Bluff High School in 1978. He later attended the University of Arkansas at Pine Bluff in 1978-79.

SMSgt Terry enlisted into the United States Air Force in November 1979. He attended Basic Training at Lackland Air Force Base, Texas. In February 1980, he attended Technical School at Keesler Air Force Base, Mississippi. SMSgt Terry's first duty station was Tinker Air Force Base, Oklahoma. He served as an Administrative Specialist. In 1982, SMSgt Terry entered the Palace Chase Program where he was given the opportunity to voluntarily transfer from Active-Duty Air Force in to the 189th Air Wing, Arkansas Air National Guard.

In February 1983, SMSgt Terry was selected for the Active Guard/Reserves (AGR) Program for the 189th Air Wing. During his tenure with the 189th, he served as an Administrative Specialist, an Airfield Management Specialist, and an Air Operations Superintendent. SMSgt Terry retired from the 189th Air Wing, Arkansas Air National Guard in March 2000.

As a member of the 189th Air Wing, SMSgt Terry volunteered for many activities such as the United Way, The Water Shed, 189th Air Wing Open House Committee, 189th Air Wing Informal Commander's Call Committee, and the 189th Air Wing Christmas

Party Committee. SMSgt Terry also led the 189th Air Wing Men's Softball Team to two Base Championships.

SMSgt Terry's most significant accomplishment was his participation on the 189th Air Wing's Minority Affairs Sub-Committee. In 1991, he served as Vice President of the committee and served as an advisor to the Wing Commander on diversity matters. The Minority Affairs Sub-Committee advised minority Airmen and Officers on available promotion opportunities, provided guidance to ensure all were in compliance with Career Development Courses, Technical Schools, and Physical Fitness Requirement.

Colonel Burthel Thomas

First African American Battalion Commander
39th Infantry Brigade (Sep)
Arkansas Army National Guard

Colonel (COL) Burthel Thomas was born in Dumas, Arkansas and attended the University of Arkansas at Pine Bluff where he received his Bachelor of Science Degree in Agriculture in 1971. He received his Master of Science Degree in Agriculture from Arkansas State University in 1974.

After receiving his degree in 1974, COL Thomas served four years on active duty in the Army at Fort Benning, Georgia. He served as a Company Executive Officer and taught tactical communications at the United States Army Infantry Center. In 1978, COL Thomas' active duty ended, and he entered the Arkansas Army National Guard.

As a member of the Arkansas Army National Guard, he was assigned various duties within Company A, 39th Infantry Brigade Support Battalion and Headquarters and Headquarters Company, 3rd Battalion, 153rd Infantry, 39th Infantry Brigade. COL Thomas was later transferred to the State Area Readiness Command (STARC), as the State Marksmanship Coordinator where he was promoted to Lieutenant Colonel. In 1992, COL Thomas was selected to command the 3rd Battalion, 153rd Infantry, 39th Infantry Brigade in Warren, Arkansas. COL Thomas was the first African American to serve as Battalion Commander in the 39th Infantry Brigade.

COL Thomas' military assignments in the Arkansas Army National Guard also consisted of the Installation Support Unit, Director of Plans and Training, Director of Housing and Engineering, Deputy

Commander Installation Support Unit, and he served as the State Inspector General. He received his promotion to Colonel in 2004.

COL Thomas has received numerous distinguished awards and medals, which includes the Army Commendation Medal, three Army Achievement Medals, Army Reserves Components Achievement Medal, two National Defense Service Medals, and an Army Service Ribbon.

COL Thomas worked at the USDA as the Assistant State Conservationist for Field Operations, and he retired from this position in 2014.

Master Sergeant Willie Tyiska

First African American to Enlist
First African American Hired into the National Guard Technician Program
Arkansas Air National Guard

Master Sergeant (MSgt) Willie Tyiska was born in Jefferson, Texas, and later moved to North Little Rock, Arkansas. As part of "Greatest Generation," MSgt Tyiska served in the U.S. Army from October 26, 1942, to December 15, 1945, as a Radio Operator and Telephone Lineman. In addition to serving during World War II, he served in Korea and Vietnam. MSgt Tyiska enlisted into the 189th Combat Support Squadron, 189th Tactical Airlift Group on July 13, 1964, as an Airman 1st Class. He was assigned as a General-Purpose Vehicle Repairman. He was the first African American to enlist in the Arkansas Air National Guard.

In 1976, MSgt Tyiska was also the first African American hired into the National Guard Technician Program as a vehicle mechanic for the 223rd Combat Communications Squadron in Hot Springs. His Awards and Decorations include the Air Force Commendation Medal, Air Force Achievement Medal, Air Force Outstanding Unit Award, Air Force Longevity Award, and the Small Arms Expert Marksmanship Ribbon. MSgt Tyiska retired on July 29, 1985, with over 24 years of service. MSgt Willie Tyiska passed away on July 20, 2004.

Chief Warrant Officer Three Courtney E. Wallace

**First African American
Surface Maintenance Supervisor
Army National Guard Consolidated
Maintenance Facility
Arkansas Army National Guard**

Chief Warrant Officer Three (CW3) Courtney Wallace was born in Conway, Arkansas. He graduated from North Little Rock Oak Grove High School in 1981, and he received an Associate Degree in Science degree in 2004 from Vincennes University.

CW3 Wallace's illustrious military career began on July 29, 1981, when he enlisted in the Army under the delayed entry program. He completed Basic Combat Training at Fort Jackson, South Carolina. He received his Advanced Individual Training (AIT) at Fort Jackson, South Carolina, where he acquired the Military Occupational Skill (MOS) of 63B10, Wheeled Vehicle and Power Generator Mechanic. His first duty assignment was with Service Battery, 1/17th Field Artillery Battalion, Fort Sill, Oklahoma. While on active duty, CW3 Wallace had follow on assignments with the 26th Service and Supply Company (Germany), C Battery, 2/2 Field Artillery Battalion, Fort Sill, Headquarters and Headquarters Battery, 2/43rd Air Defense Artillery (Germany), and Company B, 4th Engineer Battalion, Fort Carson, Colorado.

On October 8, 1992, CW3 Wallace enlisted into the Arkansas Army National Guard and was assigned to several units to include the 148th Evacuation Hospital, North Little Rock, 936th Air Traffic Control Platoon, Camp J.T. Robinson, Company D, 114th Aviation Battalion and Det 1, Company B, 935th Combat Support Battalion. His duty assignments consisted of Wheeled Vehicle Mechanic, Motor

Sergeant, and Shop Foreman. CW3 Wallace deployed in support of Operation Enduring Freedom and Operation Iraqi Freedom.

On August 4, 1996, CW3 Wallace was hired into the Full-Time Federal Technician Program at Field Maintenance Shop (FMS) 7, as a Heavy Mobile Equipment Repairer. In June 1998, he was assigned to the Arkansas Army National Guard Combined Support Maintenance Shop (CSMS) as a Heavy Mobile Equipment Mechanic. While working at CSMS, CW3 Wallace entered the Warrant Officer Candidate School (WOCS) Program. He completed Warrant Officer Candidate School on March 22, 2002, and was Commissioned as Warrant Officer One, 915A, in the Ordnance Branch. He was later assigned to the Arkansas Army National Guard Surface Maintenance Office on July 23, 2004, as an Equipment Specialist (GEN). On July 6, 2009, CW3 Wallace was selected as the Surface Maintenance Mechanic Supervisor for the Consolidated Maintenance Facility at Fort Chaffee, Arkansas. He was the first African American to serves as the Surface Maintenance Mechanic Supervisor for the Consolidate Maintenance Facility at Fort Chaffee.

The Consolidated Maintenance Facility is the second largest maintenance facility in the Arkansas Army National Guard. It is a state-of-the-art facility that has over 150,000 S.F., and its employees maintain and service vehicles and other equipment that is assigned to the Arkansas Army National Guard units in the western part of the state.

CW3 Wallace additional military assignments include Unit Maintenance Officer, Company B, 935th CS Battalion (Forward), Support Staff Maintenance Tech, Joint Force Headquarters-Arkansas, Support Auto Maintenance Officer, Company F, 39th Brigade Support Battalion, 39th Infantry Brigade Combat Team, Support Auto Maintenance Officer, Headquarters and Headquarters Company, 2nd Battalion, 153rd Infantry, 39th Inf. BCT, and Support Auto Maintenance Officer, Company B, 217th Brigade Support Battalion, 142nd Field Artillery Fires Brigade.

His military education includes 63B, Wheeled Vehicle and Power Generator Mechanic (AIT), Military Vehicle Troubleshooting Course, Drivers Training and Vehicle Maintenance Course, Primary Leadership Development Course, Basic Noncommissioned Officer Course Phases I and II, Advanced Noncommissioned Officer Course Phases I and II, Total Army Instructor Training, Warrant Officer Candidate Course, Warrant Officer Basic Course, Warrant Officer Advanced Course, Battalion Motor Officer Course, Maintenance Leader Course, Commanders Safety Course, Action Officer Development Course, FMTV Training Course, Material Readiness Course, and the Support Maintenance Shop Supply Course.

CW3 Wallace has obtained civilian certificates and licenses in the following: ACE certification in Engine Repair, Suspension and Steering; Brakes and Engine Performance, Certified Chevrolet Technician, NRI Achievement Award, Master Course in Automotive Servicing and Servicing Motor Vehicle Air Conditioning.

During his military service, he has received awards and decorations to include the Meritorious Service Medal, Army Commendation Medal (5th Award), Army Achievement Medal (7th Award), Army Good Conduct Medal (4th Award), National Defense Service Medal, Overseas Ribbon (2), Army Service Ribbon, Southwest Asia Medal, Global War on Terrorism Medal, Liberation of Kuwait Medal, Iraqi Campaign Medal, Army Overseas Training Ribbon, Army Reserve Component Achievement Medal (4th Award), Arkansas Federal Service Ribbon, Arkansas Service Ribbon, Arkansas Emergency Service Ribbon, Army Meritorious Unit Commendation Medal and the Mechanic Badge with Component Bar.

CW3 Wallace retired from the Arkansas Army National Guard on November 26, 2010, with over 29 years of distinguished military service. He currently lives in North Little Rock. CW3 Wallace served as President of the Usher Board for 6 years at Trinity Grove Missionary Baptist Church in North Little Rock.

Sergeant First Class Tasheenia L. Wallace

First African American Female and First Female in the Arkansas Army National Guard to Graduate From the 11B Infantry Transition Course

Sergeant First Class (SFC) Tasheenia Wallace was born in Denver, Colorado. She grew up in Morrilton, Arkansas and graduated from Wonderview High School in 2004. She received a Bachelor's Degree in Business Administration in 2015 from Philander Smith College in Little Rock, Arkansas and she is currently working on her Master's Degree in Human Resources and Leadership, and she is scheduled to graduate in May of 2024.

SFC Wallace joined the Arkansas Army National Guard in 2004 after graduating high school, but had a break in service until 2006, where she then attended Basic Training and Advanced Individual Training at Fort Leonard Wood, Missouri. She started her Army career as a Chemical Specialist (74D) at Headquarters and Headquarters Company, 39th Brigade Special Troops Battalion. In 2007, she started her premobilization for the 2008-2009 Iraqi Freedom Deployment with the 2nd Battalion 153rd Infantry, 39th Infantry Brigade.

In 2010, SFC Wallace was hired to work full-time in the Active/Guard and Reserve (AGR) Program as an NBC Team Member for the 61st Civil Support Team (WMD) at Camp J.T. Robinson, North Little Rock. She was later promoted CBRN NCO and Team Chief on the Survey Team. In 2015, SFC Wallace transferred to the 1-151 Calvary Squadron as the Human Resources Sergeant. As the results of 1-151 Calvary Squadron deactivation, she was transferred to 1st Battalion 153rd Infantry and served as the Human Resources Sergeant.

In 2017, SFC Wallace made history for the Arkansas National Guard when she became the first female as well as the first African American Female to graduate from the 11B, Infantry Transition Course (ITC), at the Robinson Maneuver Training Center. In 2018 SFC Wallace was promoted to Sergeant First Class and then assigned to Company B, 1-153rd Infantry Battalion, Texarkana, Arkansas as a Platoon Sergeant during the JRTC training at Fort Polk, Louisiana. In 2021, she was reassigned to HHC (Det 1), 1st Battalion, 153rd Infantry as an Assistant Operations NCO. Later in 2021, SFC Wallace was assigned to the 61st Civil Support Team (WMD) as an Operations NCO. In 2022, she was assigned to 2nd Battalion, 233rd RTI as a Senior Instructor Writer where she is currently serving.

SFC Wallace's military courses includes the Advanced Leader Common Core Course, ARNG Basic Human Resources and Admin Course, Human Resources Senior Leaders Course Phase I, Human Resources Senior Leaders Course Phase II, Master Leader's Course, 11B Infantry Transition Course and Retirement Services Training.

For her outstanding service, SFC Wallace has received the following medals and awards: Meritorious Service Medal, Army Commendation Medal, Army Achievement Medal, National Defense Service Medal, Non-Commissioned Officer Professional Development Ribbon, Army Service Ribbon, Overseas Service Ribbon, Driver Mechanic Badge/Driver Wheeled Vehicle Badge, Armed Forces Reserve Medal, Global War on Terrorism Medal, Afghanistan Campaign Medal, Arkansas National Guard Service Ribbon, Arkansas National Guard Federal Service Ribbon, Arkansas National Guard Service Ribbon, and the COL Robert L. Manning Achievement Medal.

Staff Sergeant John C. Watson

First African American Male
Hired as a Full-Time Employee
Arkansas Army National Guard

Staff Sergeant (SSG) John Watson was born in Batesville, Mississippi. He attended Horace Mann High School in Little Rock, Arkansas and graduated in 1967. He began his military career with the 189th Consolidated Aircraft Maintenance Squadron, Tactical Reconnaissance Group, Arkansas Air National Guard. While a member of the Arkansas Air National Guard, SSG served as a Pneumatic Repairman. On October 6, 1971, SSG Watson enlisted into the 148th Evacuation Hospital (-), Arkansas Army National Guard.

On January 8, 1972, SSG Watson was reassigned to Headquarters and Headquarters Detachment, 125th Medical Battalion in North Little Rock. During his assignment with the 125th Medical Battalion, SSG Watson performed various military duties. He was reassigned to the 936th Aviation Company on November 23, 1975, where he was hired in the Arkansas Army National Guard Technician Program as an Aircraft Hydraulics Repairman and later as an UH-1 Helicopter Repairman/Crew Chief. SSG Watson was the first African American Male to work Full-Time for the Arkansas Army National Guard Technician Program.

SSG Watson had a desire to advance and progress within the Arkansas Army National Guard system. He applied for numerous full-time positions within the Full-Time Technician Program but found that it was not an easy task for a Black man to move in an all-white male domain. SSG Watson began to seek his rights under Title VII of the 1964 Civil Rights Act and the local union contract.

In 1975, he filed a discrimination complaint with the Arkansas National Guard and the Union, Local 1671. SSG Watson prevailed as the Court found in June 1984 that the Arkansas National Guard had discriminated against him in not promoting him while promoting less qualified white employees. SSG Watson's efforts greatly enhanced the ability of African Americans to have opportunities for advancement in the Arkansas National Guard.

SSG Watson was Honorably Discharged from the Arkansas Army National Guard on October 5, 1983, with over 14 years of military service. His awards and badges consist of the Army Reserve Achievement Medal and the Aircraft Crew Member Badge.

Chief Warrant Officer Four Heath A. Welch

First African American Property Book Officer Headquarters and Headquarters Company 39th Infantry Brigade

First African American Property Book Officer 77th Combat Aviation Brigade Arkansas Army National Guard

Chief Warrant Officer Four (CW4) Heath Welch was raised in Beebe, Arkansas and graduated from Beebe High School in 1985. He received his Bachelor of Science Degree in Health Education from the University of Central Arkansas and a Master of Arts Degree in Human Resources Development from Webster University.

CW4 Welch's outstanding military career began in May 1984 when he enlisted under the delayed entry program in the 820th Signal Company, U.S. Army Reserves, Camp Pike, North Little Rock, Arkansas. He completed Basic Training in August 1984, and later transferred to Headquarters and Headquarters Company, 2nd Battalion, 153rd Infantry, 39th Infantry Brigade, Arkansas Army National Guard. After completing high school, he completed his Advanced Individual Training where he acquired the Military Occupational Skill (MOS) 76C10, Equipment Parts Specialist.
From 1985 to 1992, CW4 Welch served as a Prescribed Load List (PLL) Clerk. His duties consisted of maintaining records of services performed, ordering, and managing repair parts, dispatching parts, and equipment. In 1987, he transferred to the 936th Air Traffic

Control (ATC) unit as a (76V), Material Storage and Handling Specialist.

In August 1993, CW4 Welch was hired into the Active Guard/Reserve (AGR) Program as a (68W) Medical Logistic Specialist and assigned to the 204th Dental Detachment, Arkansas Army National Guard. He was later reassigned to Detachment 4, STARC (-), Camp Robinson, Arkansas as the (68J) Medical Logistic Specialist. In 1997, he was assigned to STARC (-), Camp Robinson, Arkansas, where he served as the (92A), Unit Supply Specialist. While assigned to STARC (-), CW4 Welch entered the Warrant Officer Candidate School Program. Upon completion of the Warrant Officer Candidate School Program on November 2000, CW4 Welch accepted his commission as a Warrant Officer One and was assigned to Headquarters and Headquarters Company, 39th Support Battalion in Hazen, Arkansas as the Property Accounting Technician (920A). While deployed with the 39th Infantry Brigade Combat Team in support of Operation Iraqi Freedom II (2004-2005), CW4 Welch served as the 39th Infantry Brigade's Property Book Officer. He was the first African American to serve as the Property Book Officer in the history of the 39th Infantry Brigade.

In 2009, CW4 Welch was reassigned to Headquarters and Headquarters Company, 77th Combat Aviation Brigade, Camp Robinson, Arkansas. He was assigned as the Property Accounting Technician (920A) and served as the Property Book Officer. CW4 Welch was the first African American to serve as Property Book Officer in the history of the 77th Combat Aviation Brigade, Arkansas Army National Guard. He deployed with the 77th Combat Aviation Brigade in support of Operation New Dawn in 2011.

CW4 Welch's military education consist of U.S. Army Basic Training, Fort Dix, New Jersey, Advanced Individual Training, Fort Lee, Virginia, Primary Leadership Development Course, Camp Ball, Louisiana, Basic Noncommissioned Officer Course, Fort Lee, Virginia, Warrant Officer Candidate School, Fort Rucker, Alabama,

Warrant Officer Basic Course, Fort Lee, Virginia, Warrant Officer Advanced Course, Fort Lee, Virginia and the Warrant Officer Staff Course, Fort Rucker, Alabama.

For his distinguished military service, CW4 Welch has received the following awards and commendations to include the Iraq Campaign Medal w/2 Campaign Stars, Bronz Star Medal, Meritorious Service Medal, 2nd Award, Army Commendation Medal, Army Achievement Medal, Joint Meritorious Unit Award, Meritorious Unit Commendation, Army Good Conduct Medal 2nd Award, Army Reserve Component Achievement Medal 4th Award, National Defense Service Medal w/Bronze Service Star, Global War on Terrorism Expeditionary Medal, Global War on Terrorsm Service Medal, Noncommissioned Officer Professional Development Ribbon 2nd Award, Army Service Ribbon, Overseas Service Ribbon, Armed Forces Reserve Medal w/M-Device, Armed Forces Medal 2nd Award, Army National Guard Recruiter Badge, Combat Action Badge, Physical Fitness Excellence Badge, Arkansas Federal Service Ribbon, Arkansas Service Ribbon and the Arkansas Emergency Service Ribbon.

CW4 Welch retired from the Arkansas Army National Guard in May 2014, with over 30 years of dedicated service to this great Country and the State of Arkansas. He currently serves as a mentor with the Little Rock Public School District Volunteers in Public Schools (VIPS) Program. Additionally, he is a member of the Arkansas Officials Association of which he serves as a basketball official. He is a Life Member of Alpha Phi Alpha Fraternity, Incorporated, Life Member of the National Guard Association of the United States (NGAUS), Life Member of the National Guard Association of Arkansas, (NGAA), Life Member Porsche Club of America and a member of Prince Hall Mason of Arkansas. He also enjoys traveling and spending time with his grandchildren. CW4 Welch currently resides in Little Rock, Arkansas.

Lieutenant Colonel (CH) J. Dawson Williams

First African American Chaplain in the 212th Signal Battalion

First African American Full-Time Chaplain in the National Guard U.S.

First African American Chaplain Arkansas National Guard

Lieutenant Colonel (LTC) J. Dawson Williams was born in Sparkman, Arkansas, and graduated from Sparkman High School in 1975. He earned a Bachelor of Science in Secondary Education from Ouachita Baptist University in 1984 and a Master of Divinity from the School of Theology, Virginia Union University in 1987. LTC Williams earned a Doctor of Ministry from Midwestern Baptist Theological Seminary in 1996. In 1998, LTC Williams was recognized as Williams Baptist College's Outstanding Alumni, and he earned a Master of Clinical Counseling from Henderson State University in 2014.

LTC Williams served in the Arkansas Army National Guard and the U.S. Navy for more than 23 years in various capacities. In June 1996, he was hired into the Active Guard/Reserves (AGR) Program as The Adjutant General's Staff Chaplain for the Arkansas Army National Guard. This assignment was a first-of-its-kind military assignment, in which LTC Williams was asked to assist in establishing the first-ever full-time support Army National Guard Chaplain program in any state, district, or territory under the National Guard Bureau. Each year, long-range strategies were established to ensure those goals and objectives were met by clients. In those duties, he developed Government and Civilian community partners, provided specialized training, and advised commanders at all levels regarding personal and organizational development, supervised Military and Civilian employees as well as volunteer staff at the installation chapel level, and managed chapel funds in accordance with the appropriate regulations. He also delivered spiritual fitness activities with specialized training on topics such as stress and anger management, marriage enrichment, conflict resolution, and diversity appreciation, and he provided critical incident stress management and debriefing in numerous settings.

LTC Williams served in the U.S. Navy for five years as a Petty Officer Second Class. In 1990, he received his commission as an Officer in the 56A Branch, Army Chaplain with the Arkansas Army National Guard. His first assignment was in the 212th Signal Battalion where he served as the Battalion Chaplain. LTC Williams was the first African American Chaplain in the 212th Signal Battalion. His other military experience includes Battalion Staff Chaplain, 455th Transportation Battalion, Battalion Staff Chaplain, 39th Support Battalion, 39th Infantry Brigade, Joint Forces Headquarters Deputy Staff Chaplain, Arkansas Army National Guard, 1/206th Field Artillery Battalion Staff Chaplain, 39th Infantry Brigade (Operation Iraqi Freedom), 39th Infantry Brigade Staff Chaplain. LTC Williams retired in 2007.

LTC Williams's awards and badges include the Legion of Merit, Global War on Terrorism, the Combat Action Badge, and the Arkansas Distinguished Service Medal.

In December 2016, LTC Williams was hired by the Arkansas Army National Guard as a Department of the Army Civilian, GS-11, as the Arkansas Army National Guard's Resiliency, Risk Reduction, and Suicide Prevention Program Manager. In this position, he served as a Major Command Community Health Promotion Council Coordinator with oversight of Civilian Contractors and Military personnel who worked as program specialists in each of the three cited specialty areas. He provided vision based on Headquarters guidance, Project Management and Supervision.

Dora J. Williams

First African American Female Civilian Supervisor 189th Security Forces Squadron 189th Airlift Wing Arkansas Air National Guard

Miss Dora Williams graduated from Bald Knob High School in Bald Knob, Arkansas in 1978. She earned a Bachelor of Science degree in Journalism and Public Relations in 1985 from Arkansas State University at Jonesboro.

Miss Williams entered the 189th Airlift Wing, Air National Guard in September of 1987. She served 14 years in the enlisted ranks. In January 1989 she became a full-time State employee at the 189th Security Forces Squadron where she served in various positions. She was the first African American female to serve as a full-time Civilian Supervisor in the 189th Security Squadron. Additionally, she served as a member of the Commander Support Staff and the Administrative Assistant at 189th Security Forces Squadron. Other assignments included the 189th Airlift Wing Information Security Program Manager, Personnel Security Manager, Unit Deployment Manager, Unit Career Advisor, Personnel Craftsman and as an Administrative Specialist.

In 2009, she was chosen as the Outstanding Air Reserve Component Security Forces Civilian Employee for both the Air National Guand and the United States Air Force.

Lieutenant Colonel Harold D. Williams

First African American Commander
2nd Battalion, 153rd Infantry Regiment
39th Infantry Brigade Combat Team
Arkansas Army National Guard

Lieutenant Colonel (LTC) Harold D. Williams was born in Little Rock, Arkansas. He attended Sylvan Hills High School in Sherwood, Arkansas and graduated in 1991. LTC Williams has a Bachelor of Science Degree from Excelsior College and a Master's Degree in Management and Leadership from Webster University.

LTC Williams enlisted in the Arkansas Army National Guard on February 24, 1992, into 2nd Battalion, 114th Aviation in North Little Rock, Arkansas. He attended Officer Candidate School (OCS) at the Arkansas Military Academy and received his commission as a Second Lieutenant on July 8, 1997, as an Infantry Platoon Leader with B Company, 2nd Battalion, 153rd Infantry Regiment, 39th Infantry Brigade Combat Team.

LTC Williams' previous assignments include Rifle Platoon Leader, B Company, 2nd Battalion, 153rd Infantry Regiment (Batesville), Signal Platoon Leader, B Company, 212th Signal Battalion (Benton), Executive Officer, B Company, 212th Signal Battalion (Benton), Battalion S6, 3rd Battalion, 153rd Infantry Regiment (Iraq), Commander, D Company, 2nd Battalion, 153rd Infantry Regiment (Newport), S3 Air, 2nd Battalion, 153rd Infantry Regiment (Searcy), Battalion S3, 39th Brigade Special Troops Battalion (Conway), Battalion Executive Officer, 39th Brigade Special Troops Battalion (Conway), Battalion Executive Officer, 1st Battalion, 153rd Infantry Regiment (Malvern), Brigade S1, 39th Infantry Brigade Combat

Team (Little Rock), Commander, Joint Forces Headquarter Detachment (Ricks Armory - Little Rock), Deputy Chief of Staff Operations – Force Integration Readiness Officer, Joint Forces Headquarters Detachment (Camp Robinson), Legislative Liaison and Joint Forces Headquarters Detachment (Camp Robinson).

On July 1, 2018, LTC Williams assumed the duties as Commander, 2nd Battalion, 153rd Infantry Regiment (Searcy). He was the first African American to serve as the Commander of this Battalion. His culminating assignment was Antiterrorism Force Protection Officer, Joint Forces Headquarters Detachment (Camp Robinson).

His operational deployments include Operation Southern Watch, Kuwait (1999), Operation Noble Eagle, Little Rock Air Force Base, Jacksonville, Arkansas (2003), Operation Iraqi Freedom II, Baghdad Iraq (2004-2005), Humanitarian Relief Efforts in Support of Hurricane Katrina, New Orleans (2005), Operation Iraqi Freedom (2008), Camp Korean Village and Al Asad Air Base, Iraq.

LTC Williams' military education include the Infantry Officer Basic Course, Infantry Captains Career Course, Signal Officer Advance Course, Human Resources Management Course, Intermediate Level Education (ILE) Advanced Operations Course, and the Army National Guard Strategic Planning and Management Course.

LTC Williams received the following awards and decoration to include the Bronze Star Medal, the Meritorious Service Medal, the Army Commendation Medal, the Army Achievement Medal, the Army Reserve Component Achievement Medal, the National Defense Service Medal, the Armed forces Expeditionary Medal, the Armed Forces Service Medal, Military Outstanding Volunteer Service Medal, the Armed Forces Reserve Medal, the Joint Meritorious Unit Award, Meritorious Unit Commendation, the Army Service Ribbon, the Overseas Service Ribbon, the Global War on Terrorism Expeditionary and Service Medals, the Iraqi Campaign Medal, the Combat Infantryman Badge, National

Infantry Association Order of Saint Maurice – Centurion, the Signal Corps Order of Mercury, and the Adjutant General's Corps Colonel Robert L. Manning Achievement Medal.

He is a lifetime member of Kappa Alpha Psi, Fraternity, Incorporated and a lifetime member of the National Infantry Association. LTC Williams is a member of the Masonic Lodge Saint John 329 and a graduate the Leadership of Greater Little Rock Class of XXXIII and was selected the program's first Student-Graduate Keynote Speaker.

LTC Williams retired on August 31, 2022, with over 29 years of distinguished military service. He and his family currently reside in New Market, Alabama.

Chief Warrant Officer Four Paul Williams

First African American Unit Administrator

First African American First Sergeant 39th Infantry Brigade Arkansas Army National Guard

Chief Warrant Officer Four (CW4) Paul Williams was born in North Little Rock, Arkansas, and graduated from Scipio A. Jones High School in 1969. He enlisted in the United States Army in 1969 at the age of 17. He attended basic training and his job specialty training at Fort Polk, Louisiana, his MOS was in supply and logistics.

His first overseas assignment was Southeast Asia in Thailand, and he also served a tour in Germany. In December 1972, he enlisted in the Arkansas National Guard as a Specialist 4. He started working with the National Guard in 1977, and in 1978 he became the first black unit administrator for the 39th Infantry Brigade, Arkansas Army National Guard. In 1980, he was appointed to the rank of Warrant Officer 1.

Additionally, in 1980, he decided to return to active-duty status and in that same year, he was promoted to the rank of First Sergeant and was recognized as the first African American First Sergeant in the 39th Infantry Brigade.

In 1980, when the Arkansas Active Guard Reserve program was started, he was instrumental in getting black soldiers into the Active Guard/Reserve (AGR) program. He provided help with the application process and was present on job panels to assist with other required paperwork.

In 1986, CW4 Williams was transferred to Camp Robinson as the Accounting Supervisor. Of the 54 entities on Camp Robinson, he was one of four blacks in a leadership role. After a few years, he was promoted to Budget Officer and became Staff Accountant for the Arkansas National Guard until his retirement in 2002.

For his outstanding service, CW4 Williams was awarded the Legion of Merit, the Meritorious Service Medal, the Army Achievement Medal, the Army Accommodation, the Good Conduct Medal, the Vietnam Service Medal, the Vietnam Campaign Medal, and numerous other awards and decorations.

CW4 Williams believes that one of his greatest accomplishments was after being promoted to accounting supervisor, he was told that the department he had acquired was one of the worst in the nation. Within two years CW4 Williams, along with his staff, became one of the top five departments in the National Guard.

Major Magnolia Winkler

First African American Female Officer
Arkansas Air National Guard

Major (Maj.) Magnolia Winkler was born in Little Rock, Arkansas and raised in Wrightsville, a small rural town south of Little Rock.

She graduated from Wilbur D. Mills High School in 1977 with honors and earned a Bachelor of Business Administration in Management degree from the University of Arkansas at Little Rock in May 1994. She became the first African American officer in the Arkansas Air National Guard and the 189th Airlift Group. She is also a proud lifetime member of the UALR Alumni Association.

After high school, Maj. Winkler attended Philander Smith College as a part-time student while working at Blue Cross Blue Shield Insurance Company and at Southwestern Bell. On August 12, 1978, Magnolia enlisted in the Air National Guard as a traditional Guardsman for military tuition assistance. She completed Basic Military Training and attended Technical Training School, graduating from Keesler Air Force Base, Mississippi in January 1979.

Her first assignment as an Administrative Specialist was in the 189th Air Refueling Group at Little Rock Air Force Base. In November 1981, she transferred to the 189th Security Flight to perform similar duties until assuming an Active-Duty Guard Reserves (AGR) role as an Air Operations Resource Management Specialist in Current Operations, Scheduling and Plans section in the 189th Operations Group in October 1986. While faithfully serving in this position, she balanced her other roles as mother, wife, and student. In February

1992, she resigned her full-time position in the Air Command and Control section to finally pursue her goal of becoming an Air National Guard officer.

Maj. Winkler faced several unexpected challenges along the way, from impending age restrictions to AFOQT score modifications, and even the possibility of not being placed for an officer job assignment (an important prerequisite for enrolling in an officer training school). Despite these hurdles, she and her military colleagues and superiors remained persistent when others might have given up. Their dedication paid off on September 30,1993, when Maj. Winkler graduated from the Academy of Military Science in Knoxville, Tennessee becoming the first African American female officer in the Arkansas Air National Guard and the 189th Airlift Group. She was commissioned a second lieutenant. A personal letter she received from former governor of Arkansas, Jim Guy Tucker, recognized this memorable occasion.

Maj. Winkler's groundbreaking efforts to become an officer began in 1987 when she learned there were no Black female officers in the Arkansas Air National Guard. In 1988, after attending a Total Quality Management (TQM) training course, she spearheaded and organized an informal group of Black co-workers to create unity among each other and their families. Two years later, the Minority Affairs Subcommittee (MASC) evolved as an official organization operating under the Social Actions section in the 189th Airlift Group until 1994. MASC's two-fold agenda served to promote minority recruitment by emphasizing the need for minority male and female officers and to create awareness of career opportunities in the Arkansas Air National Guard in the local minority communities. As a result of these efforts, minorities rose through the ranks as officer and enlisted in the Air National Guard.

In March 1995, Maj. Winkler completed the Joint Public Affairs Officer Course at the Defense Information School, Fort George G. Meade, Maryland, allowing her to serve as Chief of Public Affairs in duty assignment for the 189th Airlift Group, October 1993-June 1995, the National Guard Marksmanship Training Unit, July 1995 - January 2006, and the 189th Airlift Wing, February 2006-August 2008.

During this same period, Maj. Winkler began a career as an insurance claims representative with State Farm Insurance Company, working there until 2000. In May 2000-April 2002, she worked ADSW at Camp Robinson with the National Guard Marksmanship Training Unit where she aggressively led both Air and Army NG PA activities for media coverage and provided back up support for other positions.

In 2000, she conducted an internal audit of the NGMTC's Weapons Security Requirement Home Storage Program and created new standards in accordance with Gen. Schultz's guidelines. Her analysis report received an "outstanding" rating from the MTC commander and the PEC commandant.

In MTU Public Affairs, specifically, she left an indelible footprint. She replaced 10–15-year-old antiquated media equipment with new digital equipment to allow MTU photojournalist access to high-quality images more quickly and more cost effectively than ever. In addition, she received her Level II Network Security Certification and planned, supervised, and implemented the "first-ever" Armed Forces Skill-at-Arms Meeting and Winston P. Wilson Online Registration, making it possible for over 800 competitors to register online from either a personal computer or a military component system prior to the October 2001 marksmanship events.

Shortly thereafter, Winkler assumed the role of MTC's Website Manager and assisted in establishing guidelines and procedures for submitting and posting match programs, match results and press releases to the marksmanship website in a timely manner, thus increasing overall readership by 40%.

In October 2001, she planned and coordinated both civilian and military media visits to MTC during the ANG Counter-Sniper Course. This coverage resulted in worldwide media exposure for the MTC Sniper course.

In December 2001, she personally contributed to the success of LTG Davis's Year of Diversity *Together We Can* CD-ROM project with the National Guard Bureau. The CD was used at the ANG Senior Leadership Conference in Washington, D.C. to highlight LTG Davis's declaration of the year 2002 as the National Guard's Year of Diversity, and 6000 copies were produced for distribution to every Air National Guard and Army National Guard installation.

By 2002, Maj. Winkler felt a nudge to return to the insurance profession, assuming a role as Master Claims Specialists for Nationwide Insurance in Houston, Texas. She quickly progressed to the state claims trainer position for the Texas Operation in Dallas in 2003 where she eagerly trained new hires and created a "first-ever" claims recorded interview guide for all loss types for companywide distribution. Her appointment as Nationwide's United Way Chair also led to a significant increase in charitable donations for the Texas operation.

In 2005, she assumed a role as claims manager in Houston for four years and successfully managed claims personnel in the fourth largest city in the nation. In 2009-2016, she transferred to the Elite Catastrophe Team for national deployments as a Catastrophe Field Specialist and often travelled to disaster-riddled areas to resolve catastrophe claims. While handling claims in the Catastrophe unit, she was tapped as a spokesperson by Nationwide's media personnel and assisted in making tornado and hurricane safety videos co-produced by The Weather Channel. These videos were featured in companywide publications as well as on other media platforms. She has received numerous insurance claims and volunteer awards during her tenure in the insurance industry, including the Mayor's

Hurricane Ike Cleanup Volunteer Award and Nationwide's Texas Diversity and Inclusion Award in Houston.

Over the course of her military and civilian careers, Maj. Winkler devoted her time to a variety of charitable organizations to help those in need.

When the COVID-19 pandemic plagued the world in March 2020, she became restless when she heard cries for help from family members and friends in several small rural communities where she grew up. Many people living in rural areas south of Little Rock were suffering from a lack of food and COVID-19 immunizations. With God's leading and her strong desire to help, she discussed the matter with her children and through much prayer, and God's divine intervention, the Magnolia Tree of Hope (MTOH), Inc. was born in Texas.

In May 2020, with the help of the Arkansas Food Bank, MTOH formed a partnership with We Care of Pulaski County. Working together, these two non-profit organizations purchased bulk food items from the food bank, and from local grocers, to distribute to needy families and churches along the highway 365 S corridor in Southeast Pulaski County. To date, WCOPC, MTOH, and several board members and volunteers have successfully distributed over 283,931 pounds of food to needy families living in underserved rural communities.

Winkler loves to quote Dr. Maya Angelou's "**When you learn, teach; when you get, give,**" since it so closely aligns to 17 passages in the Bible, most notably, Acts:20:35, "In everything I did, I showed you that by this kind of hard work we must help the weak, remembering the words the Lord Jesus himself said, "**It is more blessed to give than to receive**."

Maj. Winkler has two children, Dawn Renee and Raymond, Jr., and four grandsons, Noah, Raymond III, Yoel, and Ezra. As a Texas resident, she regularly visits Little Rock to spend time with family and to attend Saint Mark Baptist Church where she is a member. She credits her success to God's Grace, her father, and all her family members who, individually and collectively, have been her support and inspiration, encouraging her to "Just Do It."

Maj. Winkler retired from the Arkansas Air National Guard in August 2008, with over 30 years of military service.

Lieutenant Colonel Claudell Woods

First African American Judge Advocate General Arkansas Army National Guard

Lieutenant Colonel (LTC) Claudell Woods is a native of McNeil, Arkansas. In 1979, he received a Bachelor of Science Degree in Mathematics and Political Science from Southern Arkansas University at Magnolia. He later attended the University of Arkansas at Fayetteville where he received a Juris Doctorate Degree in 1982.

LTC Woods practiced as staff attorney with East Arkansas Legal Services in West Memphis, Arkansas from 1982 to 1984. He began his military career in February 1975, as a member of Combat Support Company, 3rd Battalion, 153rd Infantry, 39th Infantry Brigade. LTC Woods later attended the Arkansas Military Department Officer Candidate School Class #20. Upon completion, he was assigned to the 3rd Battalion, 153rd Infantry as a Rifle Platoon Leader, Redeye Section Leader, Chemical Officer/Assistant S3 and S1.

In 1984, LTC Woods was the first African American Full-Time Judge Advocate General (JAG) Officer for the Arkansas National Guard. His primary duty was to advise the Adjutant General on all legal matters. Additionally, he aided the National Guard Bureau with litigation pertaining to Arkansas. He reviewed contracts and rendered legal opinions on other military matters.

In 1990, LTC Woods left the Judge Advocate General position to reenter private practice. He also served as chairman of the Department of History, Political Science and Geography at Southern Arkansas University.

LTC Woods retired from the Arkansas Army National Guard in 1990 with over 25 years of military service.

Lieutenant Colonel Sandra Y. Young

First African American Female Commander 217th Brigade Support Battalion 142nd Field Artillery Brigade Arkansas Army National Guard

First U.S. Army African American Soldier to complete the International Staff Course under the Canada National Defense Training Center

Lieutenant Colonel (LTC) Sandra Y. Young is a native of Dermott, Arkansas. She graduated from Dermott High School in 1993. Upon graduation, LTC Young attended the University of Arkansas at Little Rock. In 2004, she completed her Bachelor of Science in Organizational Management from Nyack College, New York, and her Master of Science in Emergency Disaster Management from Trident University.

LTC Young began her outstanding military career in the Arkansas National Guard on July 15, 1992. She attended basic training in Fort Jackson, South Carolina, and Advanced Individual Training in Fort Gordon, Georgia, where she graduated from the Signal Corps as a Signal Support System Specialist (31U). LTC Young's enlisted career started in the 1122nd Transportation Company, Monticello, Arkansas, 205th Medical Support Company, Lake Village, and Company C, 212th Signal Battalion, Pine Bluff.

LTC Young received her officer commission from the Arkansas National Guard, 233rd Regional Training Institute's Officer Candidate School on August 19, 2000. Upon commissioning, she was assigned to the 1123rd Transportation Company in Marked Tree. LTC Young attended her Officer Basic Course in Fort Eustis, Virginia, where she graduated from the Transportation Corps on March 2, 2001. She was assigned to the Washington, D.C. National Guard as a Transportation Officer Platoon Leader with the 140th Transportation Company on May 8, 2021. Her additional assignments included: Executive Officer, 140th Transportation Company; Company Commander, 140th Transportation Company; Company Commander, 547th Transportation; International Affairs Officer, J5/J7; S1, 74th Troop Command; Secretary, General Staff, Headquarters-District of Columbia; G4 Plans and Policy Officer, Headquarters-District of Columbia Army National Guard; G4, Operations Officers, U.S. Army Central Command; Deputy G4, Headquarters-District of Columbia National Guard; G4 Senior Logistics Staff Officer, National Guard Bureau and Deputy G4, Joint Force Headquarters-Arkansas, Camp J.T. Robinson, Arkansas.

On August 20, 2020, LTC Young was selected as the Battalion Commander, 217th Brigade Support Battalion, 142nd Field Artillery Brigade, Arkansas Army National Guard. She was the first African American Female assigned as a Battalion Commander in the history of the 142nd Field Artillery Brigade. LTC Young has deployed to Jamaica to support U.S. Southern Command and Kuwait/Jordan in support of U.S. Army Central Command.

LTC Young's professional military education includes the Transportation Officer Advance Course (2003), Combined Armed Exercise Course (2007), IMCOM-Lean Six Sigma Green Belt (2007), Human Resource Management Qualification Course (2009), Intermediate Level Education (2014), Advanced Operation Course (2017), and How the Army Run Course (2018).

LTC Young's military awards include the Army Superior Unit Award (2nd Award), Meritorious Service Medal (4th Award), Army Commendation Award (4th Award), United States Air Force Commendation (2nd Award), Army Achievement Medal (2nd

Award), Air Force Achievement Medal (2nd Award), Army Reserve Component Achievement (4th Award), National Defense Service Medal, Global War on Terrorism Expeditionary Medal, Global War on Terrorism Service Medal, Army Service Ribbon (2nd Award), Armed Forces Reserve Medal (2nd Award/with M Device), U.S. ARCENT Combat Badge, and Army Staff Identification Badge. LTC Young received the Arkansas Officer Candidate School (Class 43) Graduate Leadership Award and the 87th Troop Command Academic and Leadership Award. She was awarded the District of Columbia National Guard Major General Charles Southward Leadership Award.

One of LTC Young's highest achievements was when she was selected to be the first United States Army Soldier to attend the Caribbean Junior Staff and Command Course, where she successfully graduated on December 9, 2004, in New Castle, Jamaica. LTC Young has been recognized as the only United States Army African American Soldier to complete the international staff course under the Canada National Defense Training Center.

LTC Young is a member of the National Guard Association of the United States. Currently, she supports the Urban League for the State of Arkansas as she assists with providing resources for economic and social development. Her new journey as the President and Chief Executive Officer of RCY Professional and Management Training, Incorporated, allows her to share her military leadership experience with others.

LTC Sandra Young retired on April 30, 2023, after completing over 30 years in the Army National Guard and 22 years of Active Federal Service. LTC Young and her family now reside in Benton, Arkansas.

Interviews from *Taylor vs. Jones* Conducted by MAJ Browning

Appendix I

Date: March 17, 2018
Name: COL(R) Nathaniel McGee
Joined: 1971
Status: Federal Technician, Active Guard Reserve (AGR)
Service Time: Technician (35 years); AGR (4 years)
Key Positions Held:
Highest Command Position: RMTC Brigade Commander (06)
Highest Directorate Position: Deputy Chief of Staff Logistics (G4) (GS-14)
Retirement Date: June 2005
Interviewer: CPT Krystle F. Browning
Interviewee: COL(R) Nathaniel McGee

Sir, you joined the Army in 1971, two years before SSG Corenna Taylor enlisted in the Arkansas Army National Guard. I've researched her story, tell me your story!

Q1. What were some of the challenges that you encountered being a member of the Arkansas Army National Guard? What was it like to be a minority male in the Arkansas Army National Guard?

Joining the military was a challenge for me, back in the 70s you couldn't stop by a recruiter's station to express interest, someone had to vouch for you to enter. I was fortunate to have a prominent male from Crittenden County vouch for me and was able to get me a scheduled appointment with a unit in Brinkley, Arkansas. Back then, the units were picked for you. I was currently living in West Memphis, and I was sent to a unit in Brinkley, Arkansas to take the

ASVAB test. I had to travel from West Memphis to Brinkley to the unit a half dozen times before the Unit Administrator would see me, I would arrive to a locked building with a note on the door stating someone would return in 30 minutes. I would sit outside in the parking lot for at least two hours for no one to show up. After several attempts, a Caucasian Colonel drove down to Brinkley while the staff was there and called for me to come interview and take the ASVAB. After I took the ASVAB, the Unit Administrator stated I only qualified for two jobs, cook or truck driver and they didn't have any trucks for me to drive. Nonetheless, I enlisted! The swearing in of my enlistment consisted of myself, the Unit Administrator, and the Detachment Commander. The Detachment Commander swore me in between two doors because he didn't want to see no Negros joining his detachment! Yep!

Now, after a very interesting enlistment, I'm serving as an enlisted Soldier! About three years later, around 1974 I enrolled in the Arkansas Military Academy (AMA). I attempted to join in 1973, but there was already one African American (AA) male enrolled in the program and the organization couldn't have two AA males in one AMA class, I was told. Made it pass that hurdle and commissioned in 1975 with the 2nd BN, DET 1, C Co, 39th IBCT. Six months after commissioning, I was transferred to 5th Battalion with a peer from AMA and he and the Battalion Commander assisted with securing me a full-time federal technician job. In this position, myself nor my peer were allowed to speak in staff meeting due to our ranks, the higher leaders stated we didn't know enough to speak. If there was anything to be said during the staff meetings, it would be written down and staffed by the Operations Officer (S3) before being presented for discussion. After about three years of this treatment, myself and the S3 became very good friends.

After being commissioned Infantry in May 1975 I transferred to the Field Artillery Battalion in West Memphis, AR and early in January 1976 I attended the Field Artillery Officer Basic Course (FAOBC) at Fort Sill, OK. However, after being hired as a Technician

(Training Officer) in May of that year the Adjutant General called me into his office to explain to me that as the first African American (AA) to be hired as such I needed to understand that some whites might not accept as their supervisor. The General explained, "that I would be the first black officer supervising white Soldiers and if some of the Soldiers didn't respect me, don't get upset because this was new concept and this would be a learning curve for the environment." I was completely shocked to hear these words from the General, however, there was another LTC (would later become a General Officer) with different standards and spoke differently against the other General and made it very clear that I would be respected.

Much later in my tenure as I was progressing in rank (CPT) several different members of the Command Group approached me (1982 - 83 timeframe) about coming to Camp Robinson and I shared with them my reluctance as it related to me coming as a General's Aide or to an EEO position. Basically, I would come only if there was a legitimate position that offered advancement potential! Consequently, it was mid 1986 before I accepted a position as the Assistant State Maintenance Manager (GS-12), and you wouldn't believe the entire time I'm in this position I never laid eyes on the Colonel serving as the State Maintenance Officer. January 1987, I'm promoted to Major and assigned as the STARC CDR (JFHQ) and around the same time, I'm promoted to the State Maintenance Officer (SMO) position, this position was a Directorate level position (initially a GM-13). I should add, as the SMO one of my first assignment was to write a proposal to establish a Combined State Maintenance Shop (CSMS) at Fort Chaffee and later a proposal for the State to take over total Operations of Fort Chaffee (very challenging and rewarding).

I remained the SMO for eight years and as new command groups came in new ideas came in as to how to deal with me and later manage me/control me. At various times I was confronted with statements such as "Being the only Black on Staff, people treat with kid gloves; you're a touch me not, people are afraid of you and won't tell you NO!" At times when I expressed concerns to the Chief of Staff or AG, I would be told that it was definitely not racism they were expressing; it was my youth and/or the fact that I was just a MAJ and later a LTC.

Finally, on the day of my pinning as Colonel I was confronted by another staff officer was told that I was definitely on the fast track because at 45 years of age, I was the youngest Colonel in the Guard. By this time, I had endured enough so I asked him what had he done that I hadn't done? By this time I was a College graduate, had completed the Non-Commissioned Officer Academy, Field Artillery Officer Basic and Advances Courses, Communications Security Training, Operations, Training & Readiness Training, Administrative Officer School, Military Intelligence Officer Advance Course, Signal Officer Advance Course, Ordnance Officer Advance Course, Garrison Commander's Course, Senior Officer Logistics Advance Course, Command and General Staff Course, ½ of the Army War College at Carlisle Barracks and was named the Class Leader and had completed a whole host of Professional Leadership Development Courses – on the TDA side I had been a Detachment Commander, Battery Commander, STARC Commander, Battalion Commander and Commander of the Regional Maneuver Training Center and just what the hell ELSE did he want from me or wanted me to do?

Shortly after being promoted, I learn through a friend that I was the only Black 06 in the then 5th Army Area which was comprised of seven States (Arkansas, Kansas, Missouri, New Mexico, Texas, Louisiana, Oklahoma). Around that same time National Guard Bureau (NGB) had mandated that each State must assign at least one minority 06 to any official Officer promotion Board. For over five years I travelled to each of those State to chair or co-chair their Board annually. Then, I got a call saying I had been assigned to the National Promotion Board in St. Louis, MO for each Major to

Lieutenant Colonel Board there. This was an amazing and rewarding assigned at least month a year for almost 10-years.

Q2. I researched that in 1982, the year SSG Taylor won her discrimination lawsuit the court ordered the Arkansas National Guard to hire one black for every two whites, until the blacks comprised 16% of the work force.

From your perspective, was there a diverse military during your tenure and did the AR ARNG adhere to this court order?

The organization wasn't diverse at all back in the 70s when I joined! I recall being assigned to a committee while serving in the 39th Brigade (BDE) and on numerous occasions I would recommend hiring strategies to the Brigade Commander (BDE CDR) on how to adhere to the court order. Blacks predominately live in Northeastern Arkansas along the Mississippi river and Delta with Pulaski County and Fort Smith being the exceptions. The State would announce Black Hire Only positions in those areas to adhere to the court order (one Black for three Whites) only after getting quotas of whites. Most Units only had three full-time positions. The leadership would verbally secure the first two positions with Caucasian Soldiers and scream that they didn't have any qualified blacks to fill the third position. Then the staff would complain about the vacancies and being short staff when in essence the leadership was hurting themselves because they didn't want to hire any blacks. On several occasions, I would recommend to the BDE CDR, to announce minority hire ONLY positions in the areas identified first to develop a pool of qualified Blacks that could go to those area less populated by Blacks. However, I was told that was pre-selection and not a good idea. I would try and explain to the BDE CMDR that in certain areas you really needed to hire Blacks as Unit Administrators to show the Community you respected the Community well to put a Black in charge (well respected member of the Community/A Center of Influence). That idea was rejected because "he would probably fill the Unit up with Blacks." I actually contacted different State

Agencies to get data to show how Blacks only made up less than 13% of the overall population and there was nothing to be fearful about. Did the BDE CDR accept my recommendations, *NO!* Leadership would select all whites for the Unit Administrator and Supply Sergeant Positions and hire minorities in the Armor Position if the leadership felt like it. I made suggestions such as hire people with a Career Progression Plan in place so they could see opportunities for them to train for better positions, how to get College credits and even possibly attend AMA and become Commissioned Officers – I was told those types of ideas was setting the Guard up for potential lawsuits when those plans weren't successful. One of the things I grasped from that experience was that in certain folk minds, when you actually help a minority become successful, you're actually taking something away from someone else. And if people refused to see things in a Win-Win-Win perspective it would take too long to change years of negative indoctrinations.

Q3. As I researched this case, respect was a key element that was missing. Respect alone is very important, personally, and equally important in the workplace. SSG Taylor endured a great deal of hardships and a tremendous amount of pressure during the years as she awaited the closure of her case.

Did you feel respected as a male and minority officer?

As a male and minority officer, I was determined to conduct and carry myself in a manner to be recognized because earlier the leadership attempted to ignore me. If you tried to talk to the Caucasian Leadership, they would not acknowledge you and walk away. Even in a staff meeting, I could make a suggestion with never a comment, and then the second or third person would speak and would say the exact same thing I had said earlier, and it would be greatest idea since sliced bread. I remember specifically getting another staff officer to brief a proposal I had written. The Command Group completely endorsed it and implemented it and several months later the Chief of Staff commented on how well it was working and whoever that Junior Officer was that actually wrote the plan should be brought in and be publicly recognized. The Senior Staff officer pointed out that I was the author.... Nothing else was ever said. As a minority you always had to work harder to prove yourself in all environments. I had been on staff at least three years before another staff officer would dare to say, "I agree with MAJ McGee or that MAJ McGee has a good idea. For the most part I didn't exist! I remember asking the Chief of Staff about attending a New Manager Seminar put on by the Office of Personnel Management. Because I was only a Major, he was reluctant because a Lieutenant Colonel had been sent earlier and he had a very difficult time completing the Course. When I returned as the Honor Graduate of the Course, it took almost three months (June – when most Units and Staff were at Summer Camps) to be publicly presented the plaque. My wife and I always made it a point to participate in all of the social events to show we could function in the workplace and socially. One of my goals was to get as many minorities involved in order to be seen and recognized but overall, my goal was to improve the overall posture of Army National Guard both in the State and Nationally.

Later, there was another Black officer assigned as the JAG and he I would laugh about on some drill weekend if he wanted to have an extended lunch I would go up on the hill and just walk about with my back mostly to people and we would laugh because they never missed him even to receptions at the Pike House and only one of would attend and people would swear they saw both of us. By the way, we looked nothing alike! I knew the Guard was better than what was being portrayed by many of the staff. There were excellent men and women out there in field units who deserved better and expected better. When I enrolled in the Arkansas Military Academy (AMA) there were 75 officers that I trained with, and I made it a point to know everyone in the class in order for us to progress together. I also made myself reputable by becoming qualified in several branches and becoming very proficient in each field, making myself very marketable which led to my overall success within the organization. One of my most embarrassing experiences was at a hotel downtown right after I had been promoted to Field Grade (Mess Dress Whites Uniform) during State National Guard Officer Association Conference. I had pulled under the canopy, walked around to open the door for my wife when this letter came up and grabbed my hand to hand me her keys and said, "get mine next, boy." That only hurt for a minute, but among my so-called peers.... And I don't mean this harshly, but I've never depended upon someone else to define me or even really needed their approval – I've always known who I was, what I was about! To be underestimated, marginalized, and undervalued only makes me stronger ever today!

Q4. SSG Taylor fought six long years; she filed her discrimination lawsuit in 1976. Approximately a year after she filed the complaint she was discharged from the AR ARNG in June of 1977. In 1982 she won her case and was reinstated within the R&R Section as a Computer Technician. In 1987, SSG Taylor received an Honorable Discharge and numerous awards. Five years after SSG Taylor's discharge, she passed away in 1992.

How did her case help you and do you feel you made an impact during your tenure?

More times than not, I felt that I made great impact during my tenure. SSG Taylor opened the door for many and one of my top three goals was to have the ability to recruit and bring onboard the best qualified, black and white Soldiers in the military, to include full-time opportunities. The decision to push through my critical times, changed the dynamics of people's lives for the better.

I remember working on the development of the Yearly Training Plan (YTP) for the organization, and I recommended that we needed to add Affirmative Action Goals and Lines of Efforts and make expectations known across the organizations. The response from one of the Caucasian staff members was, "McGee we heard you the first three times and we're not adding anything in the YTP about Affirmative Action Goals."

For the first 25 years of my career, all of the things that were bad within the Command Group, I thought stemmed from a lack of accurate information, knowledge and/or they were not informed on the decisions being made within the organization on the various levels. I was clearly making excuses for leadership! My last 10 years serving in the AR ARNG, I realized there was no lack thereof, the racial disparities and unjust behaviors where all intentional. Many leaders in the key leadership positions weren't capable of living up to the position, where the proof was in the pudding. The leadership intentionally held information from minorities about PME because this was an avenue for minorities to expand their horizons to gain experience and exposure for progression. Over the years, I was the first black to hold key leadership positions. For some reason, I thought that my knowledge base, work ethic, and dedication would open the door for other minority opportunities. Black officers only got command positions by the skin of their teeth; it was hard! Sad truth is.... this is how the leadership wanted the organization to operate. I was one of the first Battalion Commanders and at one time there were at least five of us in Command at the same time. At least four of those five made Colonel. Around the time I made Colonel there were at least eight Lieutenant Colonels and about ten Majors with a whole host of Captains. Since that time there has been one Colonel promoted to Brigadier General, none to Major General. But what is worse, there might be two Colonels, maybe three Lieutenant Colonels and maybe two Majors. Remember, it took 25-years to grow me from E-1 to Colonel! How does the Guard future look, not just for minority officers but its existence, where is the vision?

The Taylor vs. Jones case was a knock down drag out for the organization, but also necessary in order to bring critical issues to light for resolution. Her case definitely shaped the organization!

Q5. Overall, based on your experience, how did the organization

shape you into the person you are today? How were you overall affected by the organization?

Working for the AR ARNG ultimately made me a stronger person. When the leadership said that I couldn't, I worked harder and pushed myself to prove that I could. The AR ARNG didn't shape me, I would like to believe that I shaped the organization in many ways. When the leadership realized they couldn't run over me, the leadership made a wise decision to accept me.

Appendix II

Date: March 17, 2018
Name: COL(R) Anita E. Deason (Maiden name was Herron – Previous married name was Long)
Joined: 1979
Status: State Employee, Active Guard Reserve (AGR)
Service Time: State (1 year, 7 months); AGR (28 years); M-Day (5 years)
Key Positions Held:
Highest Command Position: 871st Troop Command Battalion Commander
Highest Staff Position: Director of Human Resources, Arkansas Army & Air National Guard
Retirement Date: March 2013
Interviewer: CPT Krystle F. Browning
Interviewee: COL(R) Anita Deason

Ma'am, you joined the Army in 1979, six years after SSG Corenna Taylor enlisted in the Arkansas Army National Guard. I've researched her story, tell me your story!

Q1. What were some of the challenges that you encountered being a member of the Arkansas Army National Guard? What was it like to be a female in the Arkansas Army National Guard?

“Lots of things were a challenge!” I started working for the Arkansas Army National Guard, as a state employee, two months after graduating from high school. I was 17 years old, full of dreams, and very naïve. I thought my small hometown was behind the times, but I found the environment at Camp Robinson to be even less progressive. There were many friendly and helpful people, but the overall feeling seemed to be about “knowing your place or staying in your place”.

After working around members of the Guard for over a year, I found that I enjoyed hearing about their drill weekends, schools, training, etc. and, I liked their camaraderie, their much larger paychecks, and they were working on their careers, and I was not. When I first began considering joining the Guard, I turned to a Chief Warrant Officer 4, who worked in the office. He was one the older people in the office and sort of like a father figure. He was hardworking, extremely knowledgeable, and was well respected. I asked him what he thought about me joining the Guard, and he replied, “If you were my daughter, I would not only tell you No, but I’d also tell you Hell No!” He also proceeded to tell me the only “types” of women that get in the military…. I was stunned and incredibly disappointed at his response. I had thought he would be excited for me and possibly provide some guidance. That experience was a very rude awakening.

Q2. I researched that in 1982, the year SSG Taylor won her discrimination lawsuit the court ordered the Arkansas National Guard to hire one black for every two whites, until the blacks comprised 16% of the work force.

From your perspective, was there a diverse military during your tenure and did the AR ARNG adhere to this court order?

At the office and in the first couple of units I served in, there was a mix of men and women, but not much racial diversity at all. I worked for the Director of Personnel and Administration (DPA), now known as Deputy Chief of Staff for Personnel (DCSPER). The Recruiting Office was also within DPA. One day, I overheard a phone conversation, a couple of desks away from mine. It was one of the key leaders in recruiting speaking to a field recruiter. The conversation went something like, "If *they* want to get in, you tell them you've met your quota." I couldn't believe what I was hearing and disappointed to find out that was a practice of deterring minorities from joining the Guard.

Later, I worked at the Technician Personnel Office, now known as the Human Resources Office. The Arkansas National Guard's effort to comply with the court order was to advertise every third job opening as Black Hire Only. Since these positions did not allow for the consideration of any other race applying for the positions, many felt that Black Hire Only was reverse discrimination.

It is my understanding the Guard continued the Black Hire Only practice for full-time positions, until reaching parity with the percentage of African Americans that were members of the Arkansas National Guard. To maintain parity, the Guard had to develop and execute an Affirmative Action Plan.

Q3. As I researched this case, respect was a key element that was missing. Respect alone is very important, personally, and equally important in the workplace. SSG Taylor endured a great deal of hardships and a tremendous amount of pressure during the years as she awaited the closure of her case.

Did you feel respected as a minority officer and female?

Overall, yes; however, being the first female or one of the first females in any job, can be challenging for all concerned. I felt like I had to work harder, give 110%, compared to my male counterparts. I think many females feel (or felt) that way. But from 1978, when I first arrived at Camp Robinson, to 2013 when I retired, there was definitely a positive transformation.

I have had female Service Members to tell me that I was hard on them, and looking back, I probably was, especially when they were not meeting the standards. But it was intended to be tough love for them and not against them. I am so thankful to the female Service Members that served before me and cut a path for me to follow.

Q4. SSG Taylor fought six long years, she filed her discrimination lawsuit in 1976. Approximately a year after she filed the complaint she was discharged from the AR ARNG in June of 1977. In 1982 she won her case and was reinstated within the R&R Section as a Computer Technician. In 1987, SSG Taylor received an Honorable Discharged and numerous awards. Five years after SSG Taylor's discharge, she passed away in 1992.

How did her case help you and do you feel you made an impact during your tenure?

I think her case helped create opportunities for minorities and females, long before it would have taken place otherwise. Equality will (or should) continue to be part of the development and shaping of the workforce.

Yes, I feel I made an impact during my tenure. Time and effort were given into mentoring and developing others; improving policies and procedures; and making improvements in the facilities/motor pools, etc., at locations I was assigned. I had to realize that some of the impact wouldn't come to fruition for many years to come.

Although I progressed in my career and made positive strides for the organization; at times, I hurt myself along the way by trying too hard or being too passionate for change. I occasionally went against the status quo; I spoke up when expected to remain silent, and I didn't fit into any cliques, so there were times, it was quite lonely. For those individuals that have taken much greater action to create significant and long-lasting change, I can only imagine the loneliness or stress they felt in their efforts.

Q5. Overall, based on your experience, how did the organization shape you into the person you are today? How were you overall affected by the organization?

With any organization and during any career, there are going to be challenging times. Overall, I am blessed to have worked with giants! These people signed a contract, took an oath, and made great sacrifices in support of their state and nation. They have the heart of a servant! These are the people and the experiences that have shaped me.

Without a doubt, I miss the people….and the mission. Everything we do in the military is bigger than us. When you think about it, most everything we do is in support of others; whether it is developing our Service Members when conducting training; responding to a natural disaster; or answering the call of our nation. Being in the Guard, means being a part of something greater than yourself.

Appendix III

Date: March 23, 2018
Name: CW5(R) Pamela Huff
Joined: October 1975
Status: M-Day; Federal Technician
Service Time: M-Day (8 years); Federal Technician (34 years); Total Years (42 years)
Key Positions Held:
    Military: Human Resource Personnel Technician
    Federal Technician: Supervisory Auditor Internal Review
Retirement Date: June 2017
Interviewer: CPT Krystle F. Browning

Interviewee: CW5 (R) Pamela Huff

Ma'am, you joined the Army in 1975, two years after SSG Corenna Taylor enlisted in the Arkansas Army National Guard. I've researched her story, tell me your story!

Q1. What were some of the challenges that you encountered being a member of the Arkansas Army National Guard? What was it like to be a female in the Arkansas Army National Guard?

When I first joined the military, I came in the 204th Dental Detachment. I didn't have any challenges in the 204th Det. However, I was introduced to discrimination in the Guard when I transitioned outside of the 204th for progression to the 39th IBCT. I experienced some challenges within the 39th IBCT but, some of the challenges weren't per say the unit, it was me adjusting to the IBCT field environment. I didn't encounter any discrimination issues personally; however, I saw several discrimination issues during my tenure in the 39th. In 1983, I began my full-time federal employment at Camp Joseph T. Robinson (CJTR) due to a class action lawsuit. The job announcement for the position that I was hired into was a black hire only position located at the Combined Support Maintenance Services (CSMS) on CJTR. The job position was a Clerk Typist, GS-4 and although this was a very low paying job, I was overjoyed by the opportunity of having a full-time job with the military. You wouldn't believe that I was the only female at CSMS, which at that time a male environment with only one bathroom. I must say, my counterparts at CSMS treated me with respect. When I think about the things I did encounter during my military career, I still wonder was it my ethnicity, my rank, my authority, or all of the above that people had an issue with. I had no issues progressing through the ranks on the military side. However, as I progressed in rank and became a CW5, I was advised to apply for the State Command Chief Warrant Officer position, which is a full-time position for the AR ARNG. Ironically, after competing three times for the State Command Chief position and being qualified, I was yet again not selected and was told that I was not a good fit. During the final time I applied for this position, an unprecedented situation occurred. I was interviewed not once, but three times for the same position with three different panels. The two GOs remained the same throughout the interview cycles, but additional staff were added. WOW!

Q2. I researched that in 1982, the year SSG Taylor won her discrimination lawsuit the court ordered the Arkansas National Guard to hire one black for every two whites, until the blacks comprised 16% of the work force.

From your perspective, was there a diverse military during your tenure and did the AR ARNG adhere to this court order?

Yes and no, the court order stated that the AR ARNG was to hire one black for every two whites and they did just that! The order was too vague, it should have specified upward progression throughout the organization at all levels, but it was not specific. The leadership hired blacks, but in the absolute lowest positions. The positions had no upward mobility and there was no diversity in key leadership positions.

Q3. As I researched this case, respect was a key element that was missing. Respect alone is very important, personally, and equally important in the workplace. SSG Taylor endured a great deal of hardships and a tremendous amount of pressure during the years as she awaited the closure of her case.

Did you feel respected as a minority officer and female?

Yes and No. I was the first black female NCO Instructor, and I was the first black female GS-11. I earned my respect by effectively performing my job duties at all levels. As I stated before, I was employed by the military at CJTR due to a discrimination lawsuit, so I didn't blatantly experience any personal disrespect.

Q4. SSG Taylor fought six long years; she filed her discrimination lawsuit in 1976. Approximately a year after she filed the complaint she was discharged from the AR ARNG in June of 1977. In 1982 she won her case and was reinstated within the R&R Section as a Computer Technician. In 1987, SSG Taylor received an Honorable Discharge and numerous awards. Five years after SSG Taylor's discharge, she passed away in 1992.

How did her case help you and do you feel you made an impact during your tenure?

SSG Taylor's case opened my eyes to the fact that we live in a white male culture and changes must take place. Positive change must start from the top leadership, the command, and directorates. Then the second order of affect should be ensuring that positive change permeates down to the lowest level. The change must also include a diverse culture with inclusion of all ethnicities and gender. A culture shift must take place in order for the dynamics to change. It is pointless to have a diversity committee/council if the committee is not diverse and effective. In addition, the diversity committee should be accountable to management, and management should be accountable for ensuring the action and change takes place within the organization.

The Taylor vs. Jones case was a knock down drag out for the organization, but also necessary in order to bring critical issues to light for resolution. Her case definitely shaped the organization!

Q5. Overall, based on your experience, how did the organization shape you into the person you are today? How were you overall affected by the organization?

I'm a resilient person, blessed and highly favored and because of this I have no regrets from my experiences within the AR ARNG. However, I would have preferred to witness a more diverse and progressive military environment. As I neared my retirement, it's unfortunate that I began to see a backwards shift and a decline in minority and leadership positions. In 2017, there were less than 10 AGR minorities in leadership. In 2017, there were less than 10 Technician minorities in leadership. Of course, I retired as the first black female CW5. Sadly stated, if there is no change in the current leadership culture this will remain the status quo.

Appendix IV

Date: March 20, 2018
Name: CW4 Celquetta D. Pride
Joined: 1979 (Active); 1982 (Arkansas National Guard)
Status: Active Duty, Federal Technician, Active Guard Reserve
Service Time: Active (3 years); Federal Technician (20 years); Active Guard Reserve (20 years)
Key Positions Held:

> **Highest Federal Technician:** Tools and Parts Attendance Supervisor
> **Highest Active Guard Reserve:** Property Book Officer (PBO) (First African American AGR and PBO for the AR ARNG)

Retirement Date: May 2019
Interviewer: CPT Krystle F. Browning
Interviewee: CW4 Celquetta D. Pride

Ma'am you, joined the Army in 1982, nine years after SSG Corenna Taylor enlisted in the Arkansas Army National Guard. I've researched her story, tell me your story!

Q1. What were some of the challenges that you encountered being a member of the Arkansas Army National Guard? What was it like to be a female in the Arkansas Army National Guard?

Times were very difficult for African Americans (AA), specifically of the female gender. I was 23 years young when I transitioned to the AR ARNG and trying to operate in an older, male dominant environment was a challenge in itself. I personally experienced racial tension, biased opinions from Caucasian and a small demographic of Black men. The environment was very chauvinistic. As a young female Soldier, I received very little support from my chain of command; they were very undermining and very intimidating. As I progressed in rank and position, expectations and goals as a supervisor were difficult attain. As an AA supervisor, the Caucasian supervisors displayed superiority, they would attempt to tell me who to hire when positions became available in my section. However, I would hire the best-qualified person for the position, not the color of their skin. Transitioning from the Active Duty (AD) environment was very challenging; on AD your main focus was doing your job to the best of your abilities. The AR ARNG had different systems in place which made it a very difficult to be an effective person or Soldier. On numerous occasions due to short staff, I would arrive to work at 0300 to catch up and stay afloat of daily task. I must say, the challenges I faced only forced me to stand firm and work harder; my dedication and work ethic led me through those very difficult times.

Q2. I researched that in 1982, the year SSG Taylor won her discrimination lawsuit the court ordered the Arkansas National Guard to hire one black for every two whites, until the blacks comprised 16% of the work force.

From your perspective, was there a diverse military during your tenure and did the AR ARNG adhere to this court order?

In my opinion, *NO* there was not a diverse military! The Military, Federal Technician nor AGR population was diverse. I transitioned from AD in 1982 and began my career as a GS-4. My technician position was not advertised as a Black Hire Only position, there was very little competition to attain a GS-4 position at that time. As I started my new career, I was very apprehensive, but the two Colonels who hired me were very great supervisors. Their actions displayed fairness, respect, and support. I genuinely feel they hired me based on being the best qualified and not my ethnicity or race.

Yes, the organization adhered to the court order by bringing African Americans onboard in the lowest positions with minimal progression to attain key leadership positions.

Bottom Line Up Front (BLUF)! The Taylor vs. Jones case was the baseline necessary change. We must remember, everyone that has come before us, has made a sacrifice. There is no such thing as a small, medium, or large sacrifice. The sacrifice that SSG Taylor made to stand, endure, and fight through a six-year long lawsuit was for the Soldiers and Americans coming after her and the *fight* is *not over*.

Q3. As I researched this case, respect was a key element that was missing. Respect alone is very important, personally, and equally important in the workplace. SSG Taylor endured a great deal of hardships and a tremendous amount of pressure during the years as she awaited the closure of her case.

Did you feel respected as a female and minority officer?

Yes, however, being young and the first minority to hold various position gaining respect was a challenge. I became a Warrant Officer is 2002, over the years progression has been made but very little. The favoritism, chauvinistic behavior, the racial disparities are still present in our organization only camouflaged differently. I had to work very hard, harder than many others to gain respect over the years. That's why mentorship is very important, not only is it important but the type of leader/Soldier mentoring you is equally important. When mentors groom mentees, that person is shaping that mentee by their standards and beliefs. That has been the issue for our organization over the years, the cycle hasn't been broken. I truly believe leaders within our organization don't consider the organization first when they're making decisions. Until we figure out Soldier care is imperative, we will continue to operate in a reactive state.

Q4. SSG Taylor fought six long years, she filed her discrimination lawsuit in 1976. Approximately a year after she filed the complaint she was discharged from the AR ARNG in June of 1977. In 1982 she won her case and was reinstated within the R&R Section as a Computer Technician. In 1987, SSG Taylor received an Honorable Discharge and numerous awards. Five years after SSG Taylor's discharge, she passed away in 1992.

How did her case help you and do you feel you made an impact during your tenure?

Within my circle of influence, impact has been made over the years. As a 920A-Property Accounting Warrant Officer, I've had the opportunity to meet numerous people who aided in my growth. The Taylor vs. Jones case helped me to understand and accept the environment we operate in, then and now. It all goes back to our leaders, the people we have in the positions are the people who shape the organization. I pride myself on being a solid leader who mentored many, at one point I was mentoring over 20 Soldiers, black and white. I had a very simple process, right after formation, I would ask five questions, 1) How are you; 2) How is your family; 3) Do you have a job; 4) Status on education; 5) What can I do to assist. Mentorship is key and it has extended beyond your circle and throughout the organization. In due course, these are the Soldiers you're taking to the battlefield!

The Taylor vs. Jones case was a knock down drag out for the organization, but also necessary in order to bring critical issues to light for resolution. Her case definitely shaped the

organization!

Q5. Overall, based on your experience, how did the organization shape you into the person you are today? How were you overall affected by the organization?

Overall, my experiences over my career were eye-openers for me. When I started, I wasn't aware there was a color barrier. I joined under the impression that I was a Soldier joining a team, I never thought that I would feel like a Soldier of one. After leaving Active Duty, reality set in and I realized that I wasn't identified as a Soldier, but truly identified as a black, female then a Soldier. I had to accept reality that I wasn't the same as everyone and I was treated differently, and sometimes being treated less than a Soldier. I was struggling to survive in a world that I didn't belong in, so I heard. My struggle was real, but by the grace of God and my mentors I was able to successfully push through 40 years of service, a great life, two degrees, and two retirements.

Nevertheless, if I had to do it all over again, I would! I've been exposed to a lot, good and bad. The organization shaped me in a way that forced me to accept who I was and that I didn't have to conform to who people wanted me to be. No one ever broke my spirit, the struggle leveraged growth. Have I endured some weak moments? Yes. Have I been pushed to the limits? Yes. But the key is embracing every moment, being proficient in your craft, exceeding the standards, being responsible, working hard, being fair, setting clear policies, holding everyone accountable and being the voice for the voiceless.

Appendix V

Date: March 22, 2018
Name: CSM(R) Ira Blueford
Joined: August 1975

Status: Technician, Active Duty (AD)
Service Time: Total Technician (41 years 4 months) (39 Technician; AD 2 years)
Key Positions Held:
Federal Technician: WS11 Aircraft Mechanic Supervisor
Military: Command Sergeant Major
Retirement Date: November 2014
Interviewer: CPT Krystle F. Browning
Interviewee: CSM (R) Ira Blueford

CSM, you joined the Army in 1975, two years after SSG Corenna Taylor enlisted in the Arkansas Army National Guard. I've researched her story, tell me your story!

Q1. What are some of the challenges that you encountered being a member of the Arkansas Army National Guard? What was it like to be an African American male in the Arkansas Army National Guard?

I joined the AR ARNG in 1975 and I was assigned to a unit in Warren, AR. The first thing I remember is the EO Representative trying to conduct EO Training, and all of the whites would immediately walk out of the room without receiving the EO Training. In Warren, I worked in the maintenance shop, I worked with the Shop Foreman he was a MSG, a really good guy, and his experience was profound. This specific MSG was again a really good person, and he even hired the very first black Soldier to work in the maintenance shop. I was allowed to display my experience gained from Active Duty (AD) throughout my daily operations. My knowledge base gained from AD combined with my M-Day experience, opened the door for greater opportunity. Shortly thereafter, my MSG articulated that a job was coming open at the new Aviation Company and I should consider applying. I will never forget when the job announcement was advertised; my MSG with the assistance from a Chief Warrant Officer 2 assisted, recommended me for the position and mailed the packet to the appropriate channels for consideration. Two weeks later, I received a phone call for an interview. I was interviewed by a Chief Warrant Officer 2, and he hired me as the Aircraft Refueler. The Chief Warrant Officer 2 asked me during the interview panel, "What are your goals?" I stated, "My goal is to sit in your seat and hold your job one day!" The Chief Warrant Officer 2 asked me one last question, "SPC Blueford, will you get a haircut?" I stated, "Yes!" I was hired on full-time, Feb 8, 1976, in a 76W-Petroleum Specialist position and placed in a 67N-Aircraft Service Supervisory slot. This 67N slot was an E6 slot which, managed the Petroleum, Oil and Lubricants Section, an all-white section. Of course, there was friction and Soldiers didn't want to take orders from me. So, I would have frequent "come to Jesus talks" with my section until we understood rank structure, duties, and responsibilities. Fast-forwarding, I'm now a qualified 67N and promoted to the rank of Sergeant/E5. When the time came for me to compete and board for Staff Sergeant/E6, this marks the beginning of my challenging times within the organization. After asking my Readiness NCO (RNCO) on numerous occasions when the Staff Sergeant/E6 board would be held, he stated to me the board would convene in November of that year. To my disbelief, I opened my 201 File and the board had convened in May and I had missed the opportunity to compete. I was furious when I found out the RNCO lied to me, and I immediately requested to meet with the Company Commander (CO CDR). The CDR agreed to meet with me immediately to address my concern. The meeting began and I state to him, "ever since I came onboard, I've done everything you all have asked of me. Why is it, when something is due to me, I'm being lied to?" The CDR immediately states, "I have a Sergeant/E5 Crew Chief position, let me show you how much money you can make in this position." I stated, I don't want the Crew Chief position and the following week I was promoted to Staff Sergeant/E6. Years later the challenges continue, the unit has now gained four Sergeant First Class/E7 slots. I'm once again overlooked as the number four Soldier on Order of Merit List (OML) and the unit attempts to promote the number five Soldier on the OML. I had to make contact with Personnel Office after the OML was published to ensure there were no discrepancies with the order. The Personnel Officer validated the OML was accurate and as the number four person on the OML the promotion would go to me. The Personnel Officer stated I would have to sign a

4100 turning down the promotion in order for the number five Soldier to receive the promotion. After weeks of back and forth, I'm now promoted to Sergeant First Class/E7. Years later the challenges continue, I'm now number one on the Master Sergeant/E8 list. Every other Master Sergeant/E8 was assigned to a First Sergeant/1SG position but, SFC Blueford. Another call was made to the Personnel Officer, which resulted in me being moved into a First Sergeant/1SG position. I now hold a 1SG position and it's time for me to complete my next level of Primary Military Education (PME), Sergeant Majors Academy (SMA). Due to the lack of respect for minorities at that time, the Battalion Sergeant Major and Battalion Operations Sergeant received new guidance in regard to SMA but failed to inform myself and another minority 1SG. We literally had two days to generate documents for the SMA in order to overnight the packets to NGB in order to be considered for the SMA. I explained this story in detail in order for you to picture the challenges we encountered. I had to fight for every position I attained, and I experienced the same challenges progressing on the technician side. African American's (AA) had to react to everything going on during these times due to the lack of information being held away from to the AA population.

Q2. I researched that in 1982, the year SSG Taylor won her discrimination lawsuit the court ordered the Arkansas National Guard to hire one black for every two whites, until the blacks comprised 16% of the work force.

From your perspective, was there a diverse military during your tenure and did the AR ARNG adhere to this court order?

The organization adhered to the order to a certain degree. The positions were filled with blacks but filled at the lowest level. The order didn't state where to place the 16% so there were no blacks in supervisory positions. By this time the small African American population were so determined to attain full-time employment, even if we were away at schools, we would complete the applications before we left leaving the position number blank. We would have a battle buddy fill in the position number and turn in the pre-filled packet to ensure we at least applied for positions. In Aviation specifically, there was no diversity in the Pilot Program, and they had no desire to recruit minorities. Civilians coming off of active duty and students from college were showing interest in becoming a pilot, and they too were getting the run around and never made it to Aviation Battalion or Brigade.

Q3. As I researched this case, respect was a key element that was missing. Respect alone is very important, personally, and equally important in the workplace. SSG Taylor endured a great deal of hardships and a tremendous amount of pressure during the years as she awaited the closure of her case.

Did you feel respected as a male minority Senior NCO?

Yes. I was respected. However, I had to earn and demand respect after the fact, after the one-on-one conversations. Once they realize that you're not a push over, you were respected and all news travels fast! As a Senior NCO and Leader, on numerous occasions I would have to continue working up my chain of command to receive resolve on numerous issues. As a male and a minority Senior NCO, one thing I had on my side was having the ability to get along with Soldiers, NCOs, Leaders, and Officers. My job history, work ethic, and respect for Soldiers followed me throughout my military career.

Q4. SSG Taylor fought six long years, she filed her discrimination lawsuit in 1976. Approximately a year after she filed the complaint she was discharged from the AR ARNG in June of 1977. In 1982 she won her case and was reinstated within the R&R Section as a Computer Technician. In 1987, SSG Taylor received an Honorable Discharge and numerous awards. Five years after SSG Taylor's discharge, she passed away in 1992.

How did her case help you and do you feel you made an impact during your tenure?

Yes, I feel I made tremendous impact during my tenure and mentorship was paramount! I mentored many, up and down the chain and across the organization as a whole. I wanted smart people around me so, I provided Soldiers with the tools needed for success. It's a win-win situation when everyone is progressing. Soldier care is how you earn the respect of Soldiers. I also served on numerous boards which allowed me to learn and pay the information forward to my peers and Soldiers. But most importantly serving on boards allowed me the opportunity to ensure the criteria was adhered to and processes were completed correctly and fair for all within the organization.

The Taylor vs. Jones case was a knock down drag out for the organization, but also necessary in order to bring critical issues to light for resolution. Her case definitely shaped the organization!

Q5. Overall, based on your experience, how did the organization shape you into the person you are today? How were you overall affected by the organization?

Overall, I had a great career, blessed to have served in positions as the 1SG and CSM; having CDRs who allowed me to do my job. I only had one CDR as CSM throughout my career that didn't understand the role of a CSM. After a having a conversation with the SEL, this issue was immediately addressed. I had to earn and demand my respect; everyone knew I had the trust of the Soldiers. I learned how to stand up for myself, mentored Soldiers and I never thought twice about the color of their skin. Why? Because we were in the "US" Army, the United States Army together and everything we were to accomplish would be accomplished easier together as a team. It didn't matter if I liked the Soldier, it was about establishing and adhering to fair rules and regulation and taking care of Soldiers. As the CSM, I was charged with writing and dictating polices, enforcing regulations and the keeper of the uniform, that's a CSM's job and I enjoyed being a Senior NCO every day. I honestly defined my career at SFC, but when I made SFC so fast, I knew that I could go further. I promised God that if I progressed, I would serve the uniform and rank in the correct manner. I learned early in my career that God was in control of my career, not the human hand. God always set me up for success and every job that the military asked of me was the job that was just right for me. I had to work hard to keep my rank and I wasn't going to let anyone take it away from me.

Appendix VI - References

Arkansas National Guard (2018, April 01). *Arkansas National Guard.* Retrieved from Arkansas National Guard Public Affairs Office: http://www.arguard.org/PublicAffairs/index.asp

Arkansas National Guard Black Heritage Committee. (1992). *A Look at History's Missing Pages.* Arkansas National Guard Black Heritage Committee.

Arnold, R.S. (1980). *Order.* U.S District Court, Eastern District Arkansas.

Blueford, I. (2018, March 22). Racial Equality in the Arkansas Army National Guard. (K. F. Browning, Interviewer)

Bonilla-Silva, E. (2017). *Racism Without Racists: Color-blind Racism and the Persistence of Racial Inequality in the United States.* Rowman & Littlefield.

Deason, A. (2018, March 23). Racial Equality in the Arkansas Army National Guard. (K. F. Browning, Interviewer)

Dillahunty, W.H., Chavis, A.D, Loewenburg, P.B, & De Mets, A.R. (2018). *Motion by the United States to reconsider, to amend, and to stay the order of February 22, 1980, in Taylor v. Jones.* U.S District Court, Eastern District Arkansas Civil Action no LR-C76-90.

Edelman, B., Luca, M., & Svirsky, D. (2017). Racial discrimination in the sharing economy: Evidence from a field experiment. *American Economic Journal: Applied Economics,* *9*(2), 1-22.

Johnson, J. P. (1992-1993). A Look at History's Missing Pages. *In*

Memory of Correna Taylor 1945-1992, 4.

Justia U.S. Law (1980). *Justia U.S. Law.* Retrieved from *Taylor v. Jones*, 495 F. Supp. 1285 (E.D. Ark. 1980): https://law.justia.com/cases/federal/district-courts/FSupp/495/1285/2007315/

Justia U.S. Law (1981). *Justia U.S. Law.* Retrieved from 28 Fair Empl.prac.cas. 1024,26 Empl. Prac. Dec. P 31,923 Correna Taylor, Appellee, v. General Jimmie "Red" Jones, Appellant. United States of America, Intervenor. Correna Taylor, Appellee, v. General Jimmie "Red" Jones, United States of America, Appellant, 65: https://law.justia.com/cases/federal/appellate-courts/F2/653/1193/313231/

McGee, N. (2018, March 28). Racial Equality in the Arkansas Army National Guard. (K. F. Browning, Interviewer)

Open Jurist (1980, November 11). *Open Jurist.* Retrieved from 653 F. 2d 1193 - *Taylor v. Jones* Taylor: https://openjurist.org/653/f2d/1193/taylor-v-jones-taylor

Pride, C. (2018, March 20). Racial Equality in the Arkansas Army National Guard. (K. F. Browning, Interviewer)

Wikipedia. (2018, April 26). *Wikipedia, The Free Encyclopedia.* Retrieved from The Little Rock Nine: https://en.wikipedia.org/wiki/Little_Rock_Nine

Williams, D.L. (1980). *Motion to shorten time for filling response and to expedite consideration.* U.S District Court, Eastern District Arkansas.

Conclusion

The Arkansas National Guard is a microcosm of the state it represents, and much like the state it has struggled with issues like racism, corrosive polices, unequal treatment, and unfair labor practices. The immense cultural pressures of the time(s) fostered disparate treatment for African American servicemembers, which created hostile work environments, and the prejudicial hiring practices resulted in a disparate impact, which would be felt by the organization for years to come. Yet, African American Servicemembers, then and now, have continued to rise to the occasion and achieve unprecedented levels of success that has largely gone publicly unnoticed.

African American servicemembers have always served with distinction when answering the call to service whether it's to the state or country. African American's service can be traced back to the Civil War and other wars up to 1890 as members of the Arkansas State Militia. During the end of the Civil War then President Lincoln credited these "men of color" with helping turn the tide of the war, calling them "the sable arm" (Warren, 2022). "In 1964, the first African American was enlisted into the Arkansas National Guard and the first employed was in 1971, even though the population of African Americans in Arkansas was 23%." African American Soldier's struggles were many and changes to the National Guard's culture would be slow, but the organization has changed by court ordered decisions, through rulings of Judge Richard S. Arnold, changes in leadership and by the bravery of a few individuals like Corena Taylor. The population of African American

Servicemembers represent 17% of the population, we still have work to do.

Brigadier General Leland T. Shepherd quoted at his promotion and change of command ceremony that "if you can see it, you can be it" and we hope that this book will inspire, motivate, and genuinely give you a great sense of pride, to anyone, as you read the articles, biography's, interviews and follow the timeline. Let the stories of their struggles of inequality instill in you the drive and dedication to succeed and let us celebrate their triumphs of success together, which will make each one of us stronger.

Warren, S. L. (2022, July 7). *Black Union troops*. Encyclopedia of Arkansas. Retrieved January 16, 2023, from https://encyclopediaofarkansas.net/entries/black-union-troops-5135/

Price, Polly (2009. April 21st). Judge Richard S. Arnold: A Legacy of Justice on the Federal Bench.